University
tio Services

THE PROFESSIONAL PRACTICE SERIES

The Professional Practice Series is sponsored by the Society for Industrial and Organizational Psychology (SIOP). The series was launched in 1988 to provide industrial/organizational psychologists, organizational scientists and practitioners, human resource professionals, managers, executives, and those interested in organizational behavior and performance with volumes that are insightful, current, informative, and relevant to organizational practice. The volumes in the Professional Practice Series are guided by five tenets designed to enhance future organizational practice:

1. Focus on practice, but grounded in science
2. Translate organizational science into practice by generating guidelines, principles, and lessons learned that can shape and guide practice
3. Showcase the application of industrial/organizational psychology to solve problems
4. Document and demonstrate best industrial and organizational-based practices
5. Stimulate research needed to guide future organizational practice

The volumes seek to inform those interested in practice with guidance, insights, and advice on how to apply the concepts, findings, methods, and tools derived from industrial/organizational psychology to solve human-related organizational problems.

Previous Professional Practice Series volumes include:

Published by Jossey-Bass

Improving Learning Transfer in Organizations
Elwood F. Holton III, Timothy T. Baldwin, Editors

Resizing the Organization
Kenneth P. De Meuse, Mitchell Lee Marks, Editors

Implementing Organizational Interventions
Jerry W. Hedge, Elaine D. Pulakos, Editors

Organization Development
Janine Waclawski, Allan H. Church, Editors

Creating, Implementing, and Managing Effective Training and Development
Kurt Kraiger, Editor

The 21st Century Executive
Rob Silzer, Editor

Managing Selection in Changing Organizations
Jerard F. Kehoe, Editor

Evolving Practices in Human Resource Management
Allen I. Kraut, Abraham K. Korman, Editors

Individual Psychological Assessment
Richard Jeanneret, Rob Silzer, Editors

Performance Appraisal
James W. Smither, Editor

Organizational Surveys
Allen I. Kraut, Editor

Employees, Careers, and Job Creation
Manuel London, Editor

Published by Guilford Press

Diagnosis for Organizational Change
Ann Howard and Associates

Human Dilemmas in Work Organizations
Abraham K. Korman and Associates

Diversity in the Workplace
Susan E. Jackson and Associates

Working with Organizations and Their People
Douglas W. Bray and Associates

The Brave New World of eHR

The Brave New World of eHR

Human Resources Management in the Digital Age

Hal G. Gueutal, Dianna L. Stone

Editors

Foreword by Eduardo Salas

JOSSEY-BASS
A Wiley Imprint
www.josseybass.com

Published by Jossey-Bass
A Wiley Imprint
989 Market Street, San Francisco, CA 94103-1741 www.josseybass.com

Jossey-Bass books and products are available through most bookstores. To contact
Jossey-Bass directly call our Customer Care Department within the U.S. at 800-956-7739,
outside the U.S. at 317-572-3986 or fax 317-572-4002.

Jossey-Bass also publishes its books in a variety of electronic formats. Some content that
appears in print may not be available in electronic books.

Library of Congress Cataloging-in-Publication Data

The brave new world of eHR : human resources management in the digital age
/ Hal G. Gueutal and Dianna L. Stone, editors.
      p. cm.
Includes bibliographical references and index.
ISBN 0-7879-7338-6 (alk. paper)
1. Personnel management—Data processing. 2. Personnel
management—Technological innovations. 3. Information storage and
retrieval systems—Personnel management. 4. Management information
systems. I. Gueutal, Hal G. II. Stone, Dianna L.
HF5549.5.D37B73 2005
658.3'00285—dc22

                                                         2004020702

Printed in the United States of America
FIRST EDITION
HB Printing   10 9 8 7 6 5 4 3 2

Contents

Foreword

Technology is everywhere in our world. We see it every day in activities such as banking, shopping, flying, entertainment, or communicating. We live with technology and we are surrounded by it. We cannot escape its influence and how it shapes our lives. But work organizations are also as dependent on technology as we all are for our daily activities. Organizations use technology for manufacturing, sales, production, marketing and, yes, for human resources actions and interventions.

So this is the focus of this volume—electronic HR (eHR), a new world order for managing human resources in organizations. A world where scientists and practitioners in the industrial/organizational psychology field have much to say and much to offer in order to promote the effectiveness and optimization of eHR technologies and services. And so the motivation behind this volume—to provide practical advice to those who compose, manage, and develop human resources in work organizations.

Hal G. Gueutal and Dianna L. Stone have succeeded in assembling a diverse and powerful group of scholars, practitioners, and providers, all much involved in promoting the optimal use of eHR technology to achieve organizational effectiveness. The authors of the chapters herein focus on providing practical guidance and insights to those who are applying (or currently are using), designing, or delivering HR technologies. Hal and Dianna have done our field a tremendous service by editing this unique volume. The documented practical thoughts, the applied research discussed, the highlighted lessons learned, and the documented guidelines embedded in the chapters will provide an invaluable and rich resource for managers, executives, or those involved in optimizing human resources. And for that, on behalf of SIOP's Professional Practice Book Series Editorial Board and our membership, we thank you both. We hope this volume stimulates, influences, and promotes eHR to the benefit of people and organizations.

September 2004   Eduardo Salas
                                           University of Central Florida
                                           Series Editor

Preface

Welcome to the new world of eHR. Things will look a bit different here. No longer will you deal with an HR professional to handle your HR needs. The HR portal will take care of you. Need to change your address? How about some online training? Want to check on your latest performance review? The portal is here to help. You can try calling the HR staff, but remember they have been reduced by a third since we went online. Oh, and by the way, most of the HR staff has been outsourced, but our vendor in Bombay assures us that the new staff is well-versed in our practices and in U.S. law.

The foregoing is not fiction, but rather describes HR practice in many organizations today. Our field is changing, rapidly and profoundly. Those of us in HR once wished that we could eliminate all the routine paperwork and concentrate on "strategy" and being a "business partner." Well, be careful what you wish for . . . . Today technology has finally begun to deliver on the promises of the 1990s. We are providing more and better service to all our stakeholders. We have finally made HR data accessible to those who need it. We are no longer the bottleneck in HR information flow. We talk about portal strategy, employee self-service, and data ownership. We have the analytic tools to allow us to be more strategic and become true strategic business partners.

However, all change comes at some cost. Skill sets and skill priorities are changing. Our personal knowledge base may now be vested to an information system, and we may feel isolated from our customers (employees and managers). There may be fewer of us. Our budget may go for different priorities such as online recruiting systems and "analytic modules" rather than training and on-campus recruiting programs. We welcome you to this brave new world, and this book will serve as your introduction.

Contents of the Book

It should be clear from our description that the field of HR is undergoing some dramatic changes, and technology is propelling it in some entirely new directions, labeled electronic human resources management (eHR). Given these changes, this book is designed to provide HR professionals and industrial and organizational psychologists with some insights about the major technological trends in the field. In addition, we take a look into the future of HR and provide a preview of the nature of HR practice in the next decade. Our authors represent a cross section of highly knowledgeable experts in the area of eHR. They range from senior executives at the two leading global systems vendors (PeopleSoft and SAP), to HR professionals with great depth in eHR applications, and researchers with specialized expertise in eHR.

The book is divided into nine chapters. We begin with a very interesting chapter by Patricia A. K. Fletcher, a senior executive at SAP. In Chapter 1, Ms. Fletcher describes the history of eHR and reviews the transformation of HR from manual processes to completely automated systems. In particular, she focuses on three phases of the evolution of eHR, including: (a) the efficiency and control phase, (b) the enabling insight or partnership phase, and (c) the creating value or player phase. The next five chapters concentrate on the effects of technology on several key HR functions, including recruitment, selection, training, performance management, and compensation. For example, in Chapter 2, Dianna L. Stone, Kimberly M. Lukaszewski, and Linda C. Isenhour discuss e-recruiting and consider the effectiveness of online strategies for attracting talent. In addition, they review the existing research literature on e-recruiting and offer some suggestions for HR professionals based on the results of that research. They also discuss some of the unintended consequences of using e-recruiting systems, including adverse impact and privacy issues.

The next chapter, by Jerard F. Kehoe, David N. Dickter, Daniel P. Russell, and Joshua M. Sacco, provides a thought-provoking review of the issues associated with using e-selection systems in organizations. Furthermore, they offer valuable guidelines that should help organizations design, deliver, implement, and sustain these systems. For instance, in their chapter they consider preparation for testing, test administration, strategies for managing applicant flow, and issues in managing vendor partnerships. In Chapter 4, "Research-Based Guidelines for Designing Distance Learning: What We Know So Far," Eduardo Salas, Renee E. DeRouin, and Lisa N. Littrell present an exceptionally useful review of the recent research on the effectiveness of distance learning in educational and organizational settings. These authors also offer guidelines based on research that can help HR professionals with the design and delivery of e-learning systems in organizations. Given that eHR systems are new in organizations, there is relatively little research on the topic; however, this chapter should be particularly beneficial to HR professionals.

In the next chapter, Robert L. Cardy and Janice S. Miller address "eHR and Performance Management: A Consideration of Positive Potential and the Dark Side." The authors examine the potential advantages and disadvantages of using eHR to manage employee performance in organizations. In particular, they argue that the use of technology for performance management has the potential to increase productivity and enhance organizational effectiveness. Furthermore, they suggest that technology often facilitates several important processes, including performance measurement, performance evaluation, and feedback. However, they also contend that technology may have some unintended consequences and cause organizations to focus on narrow performance criteria or arbitrary top-down controls. In addition, it may increase the distance between supervisors and subordinates, which can decrease trust and negatively affect leader-member relationships. They also offer some very helpful suggestions for HR professionals concerned with implementing electronic performance management systems.

In the next chapter, "e-Compensation: The Potential to Transform Practice?", James H. Dulebohn and Janet H. Marler consider how technology supports the administration of compensation systems in organizations. In particular, the authors highlight how technology can facilitate decision making about compensation, enable round-the-clock access to salary and benefits information, streamline processes, and increase the effectiveness of strategic decision making. Furthermore, they argue that these systems should help organizations enhance internal equity, external equity, and the overall administration of compensation systems. Apart from these issues, they point out some of the challenges that HR professionals will need to recognize when they implement these systems.

In Chapter 7, Hal G. Gueutal and Cecilia M. Falbe review the recent trends in delivering HR products and services. In particular, they describe and discuss the issues associated with managing several new delivery systems, including HR portals, employee self-service systems (ESS), managerial self-service systems (MSS), and knowledge bases. In addition, they present a business case for using these systems, including their cost effectiveness, user-satisfaction levels, and potential for return on investment. Furthermore, they highlight a number of best practices that can be used to implement these systems and share common errors that organizations should avoid when using them.

In "The Effects of eHR System Characteristics and Culture on System Acceptance and Effectiveness," Eugene F. Stone-Romero reviews the functional and dysfunctional consequences of using eHR to attract, select, and manage the performance of employees in organizations. He also provides an intriguing review of the cross-cultural differences in the acceptance and effectiveness of these systems. The premise of the chapter is that many eHR systems are developed in Western cultures (for example, the United States and Germany) and, consequently, the HR processes inherent in these systems are rooted in Western cultural values (meritocracy, individualism). As a result, eHR systems may be less effective when implemented in nations with different cultures (Asia, South America, the Middle East, Africa). Thus, various aspects of the systems may have to be modified to make them compatible with values of other cultures. Given that eHR systems are being implemented worldwide, this chapter should be of tremendous help to HR professionals in international or multinational corporations.

In the final chapter of the book, "The Next Decade of HR: Trends, Technologies, and Recommendations," Row Henson presents a fascinating and futuristic look at HR and technology in the decades to come. In particular, she highlights the needs of organizations in the future and considers prospective changes in workforce demographics, workforce balance, and the increased competition for a diminished set of workers. She also suggests that technology will continue to transform organizations and help them become smarter, easier to manage, and more adaptable. She describes some remarkable technological changes that may be available in tomorrow's organizations, including the use of intelligent self-service systems, interchangeable devices, cognitive software, nanotechnology, and the convergence of the Internet, digital TV, and wireless communication into a "vibrant network." In addition, she offers some valuable suggestions for the HR professional of the future.

In view of the fact that eHR is having a profound effect on the fields of human resource management and industrial and organizational psychology, we hope that you will find the chapters in this book to be interesting and informative. They should provide suggestions for enhancing the practice of HR management, and we hope they will also foster additional research on eHR issues.

In closing, we want to express our gratitude to each of the authors who contributed to this volume. Without their hard work and dedication, this book would not have been possible. In addition, we want to thank Eduardo Salas, editor of the SIOP Professional Practice Series, for serving as the creative force and champion behind this book. We would also like to convey our gratitude to Margaret C. Nelson for her help and support with editing the book. Finally, we want to express our appreciation to Eugene F. Stone-Romero, our mentor and advisor. Gene taught us to chase knowledge throughout our careers, and without his professional guidance and support we would not be where we are today.

November 2004

Hal G. Gueutal
Albany, New York

Dianna L. Stone
Winter Springs, Florida

HGG: To Meg

DLS: To Gene, Mavis, Joey, Patricia, Sharon, JoAnna, and J.S.Q.B.S.S.

The Authors

Hal G. Gueutal, Ph.D., is a nationally known consultant and scholar in the area of human resource management and is the director of an MBA program in HRIS at the University at Albany, State University of New York. Over the past decade, he has worked with a variety of organizations to redesign, enhance, and improve their human resource practices. He has published more than twenty scholarly articles and books and has made over fifty presentations at professional conferences. His work has also been cited in publications such as *USA Today* and *The Wall Street Journal.* He has frequently served as an invited speaker for organizations and professional groups. In 2001, he was named one of just two faculty "thought leaders" by the Board of Directors of the Society for Human Resource Management Foundation.

Dr. Gueutal has extensive experience in helping domestic and international organizations, ranging from small businesses to Fortune 500 companies. For example, he developed national skill standards for manufacturing workers and educational professionals. This national initiative on manufacturing work led to the creation of job standards, training programs, and certification standards for manufacturers across the United States. In addition, he has assisted a variety of organizations with HR issues, including HMOs, business start-ups, financial institutions, banks, and firms in Eastern Europe. He has also taught courses in human resource management in graduate business programs in Zurich, Switzerland; Shanghai, the People's Republic of China; Saabrucken, Germany; and Budapest, Hungary.

Dianna L. Stone, Ph.D., received her doctorate from Purdue University and is currently a professor of management and psychology at the University of Central Florida. Her research focuses on employees' reactions to electronic human resource systems; information privacy; and diversity in organizations, including issues of race, culture, and disability. Results of her research have been published in the *Journal of Applied Psychology, Personnel Psychology, the Academy of Management Review, Organizational Behavior and Human Decision Processes, the Journal of Management, Applied Psychology: An International Review,* and *Research in Personnel/Human Resources Management.* She is a Fellow of the American Psychological Association and the Society for Industrial and Organizational Psychology. She has also served as the chair of the Human Resources Division of the Academy of Management and as financial officer for the Society for Industrial and Organizational Psychology. In 2003, she edited *Advances in Human Performance and Cognitive Engineering Research* on the topic of eHR.

Robert L. Cardy, Ph.D., is a full professor of management in the W. P. Carey School of business at Arizona State University. He received his Ph.D. in industrial/organizational psychology from Virginia Tech. His master's and undergraduate degrees are from Central Michigan University. Dr. Cardy has consulted with a variety of organizations, particularly in the areas of performance appraisal and competency model development and implementation. His recent work has focused on identifying key competencies and developing and linking performance standards to those competencies. His consulting work has provided organizations with concrete models of employee success that can be used to drive performance management, employee selection, and self-improvement/management. Dr. Cardy's consulting work has included automobile manufacturers, organizations in the automotive field, as well as consulting firms and tool manufacturers.

Dr. Cardy has served multiple terms as a member of the executive committee of the Human Resources Management Division of the Academy of Management. He has regularly written columns for the *HR Division Newsletter* on new and innovative issues since 1991. Dr. Cardy was the co-founder and editor of the former *Journal of Quality Management.* He has been a member of the editorial review boards for the *Journal of Applied Psychology* and the *Journal of Organizational Behavior* and serves as a reviewer for several publications. He has published articles in a variety of journals, including *Journal of Applied Psychology, Organizational Behavior and Human*

Decision Processes, Journal of Management, Management Communication Quarterly, and *HR Magazine.* In addition, he has authored or edited several books on human resource management and performance management. He has twice received a "best paper" award from the Human Resources Management Division of the Academy of Management and received a "University Mentor Award" for his work with doctoral students at Arizona State University.

Renee E. DeRouin is a doctoral student in the industrial and organizational psychology program at the University of Central Florida. She is the recipient of the Society for Industrial and Organizational Psychology's Robert J. Wherry Award for 2004. Her research interests include training, distance learning, learner control, and stereotype threat, and her work will soon appear in the *Journal of Management, Human Resource Management Journal, Research in Personnel and Human Resource Management, Advances in Human Performance and Cognitive Engineering Research,* and the *Handbook of Human Factors and Ergonomics Methods.*

David N. Dickter, Ph.D., is an industrial-organizational psychologist with Psychological Service, Inc. Previous positions include personnel selection management positions at AT&T and Aon Human Capital Services. In those positions he was responsible for AT&T's employment selection program for customer service jobs and sales jobs, and for AT&T's computerized employment testing system. Dr. Dickter is co-author of several articles, book chapters, and conference presentations on various topics. He is a member of the American Psychological Association, the Society for Industrial and Organizational Psychology, the Society for Human Resource Management, and the Personnel Testing Council of Southern California. He earned his Ph.D. in industrial-organizational psychology from the Ohio State University.

James H. Dulebohn, Ph.D., is an associate professor of human resource management and organizational behavior at Michigan State University. He earned his Ph.D. from the University of Illinois at Urbana-Champaign. His research focuses on human resource information systems, employee compensation and benefit programs, and decision making in organizations, and it has appeared in the

Academy of Management Journal, Personnel Psychology, Journal of Management, Journal of Risk and Insurance, Journal of Organizational Behavior, and others. Dr. Dulebohn has also written chapters that have appeared in *Advances in Human Performance and Cognitive Engineering Research, Research in Personnel and Human Resources Management, Research in Sociology of Organizations,* and *The Handbook of Human Resources Management.* Prior to graduate school, Dr. Dulebohn was employed in the area of information and database management for various organizations, including IBM. He has conducted research and consulting in compensation and benefits for organizations including Monsanto, Dow Chemical, TIAA-CREF, State of Texas, State of Illinois, and Marriott.

Cecilia M. Falbe, Ph.D., is chair of the Management Department at the School of Business and a member of the organizational studies doctoral faculty at the University at Albany. Professor Falbe's research includes work on the development of entrepreneurial strategies, the role of government intervention to promote entrepreneurship in the telecommunications industry, technology implementation, the impact of vision on financial performance, and an examination of alliances between high-tech start-up firms and their large-firm partners. These works are published in *Administrative Science Quarterly, Academy of Management Journal, Journal of Business Venturing, Journal of Small Business Management, Journal of Applied Psychology, Journal of Organizational Behavior, International Small Business Journal, International Journal of Management, International Journal of Psychology, Group and Management Studies,* and in a number of book chapters. She also co-edited two books on business and society. Professor Falbe holds a Ph.D. from Columbia University.

Patricia A. K. Fletcher, MBA, is responsible for mySAP ERP strategy and business development at SAP. In this role, she is responsible for contributing to the direction and strategy and positioning and messaging of the mySAP ERP solutions, including mySAP ERP Human Capital Management, mySAP ERP Financials, mySAP ERP Operations, and mySAP ERP Corporate Services. Ms. Fletcher has held a variety of sales, strategy, and management HCM positions at SAP, including pre-sales, solution engineer, business development director, and product marketing strategy director. Prior to joining

SAP, she was a business transformation consultant in Europe and Asia. She has an MBA from the Richmond School of Business in London, England, and a bachelor of science degree in business administration from the University of Phoenix.

Row Henson is a PeopleSoft fellow and has been involved in HR and HR management systems for the past thirty years. For eight years she held the role of vice president of HRMS global product strategy at PeopleSoft, Inc., where she was instrumental in setting the direction of PeopleSoft's flagship human resources product line. Before PeopleSoft, she spent fifteen years in the computer software industry with Dunn & Bradstreet (previously MSA) and Cullinet Software, primarily focused on marketing, sales, support, and development of HR systems. Voted one of the Top Ten Women in Technology by *Computer Currents,* Ms. Henson is the recipient of IHRIM's coveted Summit Award for lifetime achievement in her field. In 2002, Ms. Henson was named the first Visionary of HR Technology at the Annual HR Technology Conference. She is a frequent speaker and has been published in numerous personnel and software periodicals, including *Personnel Journal, CFO Magazine, Software Magazine, IHRIM Journal,* and *Benefits & Compensation Solutions Magazine.*

Linda C. Isenhour, M.S., is a doctoral candidate and is completing her dissertation on the relationship between applicant culture and recruitment outcomes at the University of Central Florida. As a Sloan Fellow, Ms. Isenhour earned her M.S. in management from the Massachusetts Institute of Technology and has extensive industry experience in human resource management. She has presented papers at the meetings of the Academy of Management, the Society for Industrial and Organizational Psychology, and the Southern Management Association. She has published chapters on human resources in virtual organizations, and the impact of human resource information systems and of the Internet on organizations. Her research interests include recruitment, compensation, human resource information systems, and strategic management.

Jerard F. Kehoe, Ph.D., received his doctorate in quantitative psychology in 1975 from the University of Southern California. After serving on Virginia Tech's psychology faculty in the Applied Behavioral Sciences Program, he joined AT&T in 1982. At AT&T, he was responsible in various positions for the design, implementation, validation, and maintenance of selection programs for manufacturing, customer service, sales, technical, management, and leadership jobs. In 1997, he assumed overall leadership and direction for AT&T's selection program. He founded Selection & Assessment Consulting in 2003 and serves as its president. Dr. Kehoe has been active professionally, with publications and conference presentations on employment selection topics including computerized testing, fairness, and test validity. In 2000, he edited the Society of Industrial/Organization Psychology's (SIOP) Professional Practice Series volume, *Managing Selection in Changing Organizations: Human Resource Strategies*. In 2002, he began serving as an associate editor of the *Journal of Applied Psychology*. He also has served on numerous professional committees, including the SIOP subcommittee that revised that Society's *Principles for the Validation and Use of Employment Selection Procedures* in 2003. In 2002, SIOP awarded him with the Fellow membership status for contributions to this profession.

Lisa N. Littrell is a doctoral student in the industrial and organizational psychology program at the University of Central Florida. Her research interests include cross-cultural training, team adaptability, team leadership, expatriate employment, and distance learning. She has presented her research on cross-cultural training at the conference of the Society for Industrial and Organizational Psychology.

Kimberly M. Lukaszewski, Ph.D., is an assistant professor of management at the State University of New York at New Paltz. She received her MBA in HRIS and her doctorate in organizational studies from the University at Albany, State University of New York. Her research focuses on human resource information systems, information privacy, and race and disability issues in organizations. She has presented numerous papers at national and regional conferences and has published articles on eHR in *Advances in Human Performance and Cognitive Engineering Research* and the *International Human Resource Information Management Journal.*

Janet H. Marler, Ph.D., is an assistant professor of management at the University at Albany, State University of New York, School of Business. She earned her Ph.D. in industrial and labor relations from Cornell University. Prior to earning her doctorate, she was a CPA and held executive and professional positions in the financial services industry. Her research centers on the strategic use of human resource information systems, employee and managerial self-service, compensation and benefits strategy, and alternative employment arrangements. Her research has been published in the *Journal of Organizational Behavior, Journal of Quality Management, Academy of Management Proceedings,* and *IHRIM Journal.* She teaches full-time, part-time, and executive MBA programs in HRIS, HR, and compensation strategy.

Janice S. Miller, Ph.D., is an associate professor of organizations and strategic management at the University of Wisconsin-Milwaukee, where she also serves as associate dean for academic affairs. She received her Ph.D. from Arizona State University, with a concentration in human resource management. Dr. Miller has conducted research in a variety of HR functional areas. One of her primary interests is performance appraisal, particularly in the context of multi-rater or 360-degree settings. Her recent work focuses on employee satisfaction with performance appraisal. In addition, she has done research in executive compensation, both from a theoretical and an applied perspective, and has also investigated technology's impact on human resource management and job attitudes among part-time and seasonal workers. Since joining the University of Wisconsin-Milwaukee, Dr. Miller has consulted for a number of nonprofit organizations in the Milwaukee area, focusing on multi-rater appraisal practices and their link to appraisal satisfaction. She presently serves on the University of Wisconsin-Milwaukee Information Technology Advisory Board.

Dr. Miller is a member of the Academy of Management, the Society for Industrial and Organizational Psychology, the American Psychological Society, and the Decision Sciences Institute. She is a recipient of the Business Advisory Council Teaching Award and was a Wisconsin Teaching Fellow in 2002. Her research has appeared in *Academy of Management Journal, Journal of Organizational Behavior, Journal of Labor Research, Group and Organization Management, Human*

Resource Management, Human Resource Management Review, and *Journal of Management Education.*

Daniel P. Russell, M.S., joined Aon Consulting in 1998. He is a member of Aon's Product Solutions Resource Group. His work with the group includes research and development activities with Aon's web-based applicant tracking and assessment products. In addition to research and development activities, Mr. Russell has consulted on and managed a number of projects to develop, validate, and implement selection systems in several different industries for various occupations. His projects have included clients in the public and private sectors, manufacturing, telecommunications and technology, service and retail, healthcare, entertainment, and protective services. This work has led to several innovative high-tech (and low-tech) solutions to organizations' various HR challenges in the areas of recruiting, selection, performance management, talent management, and job classification. Mr. Russell's previous professional experience includes work at the American Institutes for Research, QI International, the U.S. Department of the Army AMEDD Board, and the Oak Ridge Institute for Science and Education. He received his M.S. from and is currently a doctoral candidate in industrial/organizational psychology at Virginia Tech.

Joshua M. Sacco, Ph.D., joined Aon Consulting in 1999 and is a member of Aon's Product Solutions Resource Group. He is currently the product manager for Aon's *Performance Pathfinder* platform of performance management, talent management, and employee selection applications. His consulting work mainly focuses on performance management, talent management, employee development, large-scale employee selection system design and validation, and research examining the return on investment for selection systems. Much of his consulting work involves implementing technology solutions in these practice areas. He has worked with clients in a variety of industries, including automotive, healthcare, insurance, manufacturing, protective services, retail, and food services. He has presented and published a number of papers on topics such as personnel selection, psychological measurement, and diversity. He received his Ph.D. from Michigan State University in industrial/organizational psychology. At MSU, he held a National Science Foundation Graduate Research Fellowship and a Michigan State University Distinguished Fellowship. His doctoral dissertation on racial diversity and organizational financial performance won the Society for Industrial/Organizational Psychology's S. Wallace Rains Dissertation Award, and the Michigan Association of Industrial/Organizational Psychologists' Best Student Paper Award.

Eduardo Salas, Ph.D., is professor of psychology at the University of Central Florida and program director of the human systems integration department at the Institute for Simulation and Training (IST). He has authored over 250 journal articles and book chapters and co-edited eleven books. He is editor of *Human Factors* and is on the editorial boards of *Journal of Applied Psychology, Personnel Psychology, Military Psychology, Group Dynamics,* and *Journal of Organizational Behavior.* He is a Fellow of the Society for Industrial and Organizational Psychology, and his research interests include team training, distributed training, learning principles, and training evaluation. In addition, he served as editor for the SIOP Professional Practice series that sponsored this book.

Eugene F. Stone-Romero, Ph.D. (University of California-Irvine), is a professor of psychology and management at the University of Central Florida. He is a Fellow of the Society for Industrial and Organizational Psychology, the American Psychological Society, and the American Psychological Association. He is also a member of the Academy of Management and the Society of Indian (Native American) Psychologists. He previously served as the associate editor of the *Journal of Applied Psychology* and on the editorial boards for it, the *Academy of Management Journal,* and the *Journal of Management.* He is now on the editorial boards of *Personnel Psychology, Organizational Research Methods,* and the *Asian Journal of Business and Information Systems.* Dr. Stone-Romero's research interests include unfair discrimination in employment, personality-based biases in selection, cross-cultural issues in organizations, organizational justice, job design, reactions to feedback, work-related values, job satisfaction, moderator variable detection strategies, performance ratings, privacy in work organizations, job involvement, and work quality. The results of his research have been published in such journals as the *Journal of Applied Psychology, Organizational Behavior and Human Performance, Personnel Psychology, Journal of Vocational Behavior, Academy of Management Journal, Journal of Management, Educational and Psychological Measurement, Applied Psychology: An International Review, Journal of Applied Social Psychology,* and the *Journal of Educational Psychology.* His work has also appeared in the *International Review of Industrial and Organizational Psychology* and *Research in Personnel and Human Resources Management.* He is also the author of numerous book chapters and several books, including *Research Methods in Organizational Behavior* and *Job Satisfaction: How People Feel About Their Jobs and How It Affects Their Performance.*

The Brave New World of eHR

CHAPTER 1

From Personnel Administration to Business-Driven Human Capital Management

The Transformation of the Role of HR in the Digital Age

Patricia A. K. Fletcher

What an exciting time to be in HR! Over the past thirty-plus years, we have seen the emergence of the personnel department and have participated in the transformation of this role from that of an administrator to, more recently, a critical component in the competitive success of the business. When HR (the Personnel Department) first began to surface as a function in business, executives and other decision makers were focused on tangible goods and financial resources. HR's role was to support back-office functions, mainly legislation requirements, payroll, and personnel data maintenance. Fast forward to today—now, every CEO speaks of the people behind the corporation's success. In fact, many corporations brand their workforce as part of their marketing campaigns to attract not only the right talent, but also to attract business and consumer buyers.

Savvy executives understand that, in a tighter, tougher, less predictable economic climate, they have to take maximum advantage of the skills and expertise available in the existing employee pool.

During these past few years, corporations have begun to embrace a "human capital approach," one that considers the money spent on fostering innovation in the workforce as an investment. As with any asset, by nurturing, protecting, and growing this investment, organizations that align workforce strategies with business goals and objectives will benefit from capturing and focusing the attention of the workforce.

Just as HR's role continues to change, technology has continued to evolve. If HR's role has always been to deliver the workforce support and management based on the needs of the business, then technology's role has been that of an enabler. Over the past years, HR processes and procedures have been supported by everything from complicated file-folder systems to automation, going from usage of multiple systems and databases to a single version of the truth with comprehensive HRMS. Now companies are not only leveraging technology to support the function of the HR department, but they are also leveraging human capital technologies for use by everyone in the business. Human resources as a function has evolved into human capital management (HCM). Where HR was the responsibility of a centralized, or sometimes decentralized, department, HCM is the job of everyone in the business, from employees to executives.

Using the Transformation of HR to HCM in Business graph (Figure 1.1) as a guide, in this chapter I review the transformation of HR from the emergence of the personnel department to the current HR and talent organizations as they stand today. This chapter also provides a review of the evolution of HR processes from manual to complete automation. The transformation of HR is broken down into three main categories that talk not just to the focus of the HR department, but more important, to the value of HR total company value.

Efficiency and Control: Polite and Police Phase

Key Business Issues

For the many who lived through them, the 1970s were turbulent times at best. The collapse of the gold standard and the oil crisis were just a few factors of the struggling economy. With a mostly

Figure 1.1. Transformation of HR to HCM in Business.

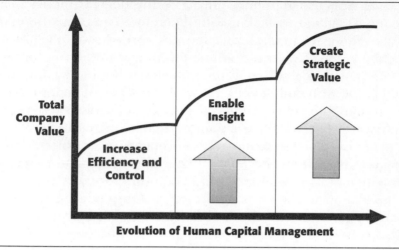

opposed and controversial war that resulted in dramatic social change and disillusionment with government, the United States, as a nation, was in a state of chaos. As America struggled internally with conflict and distrust, businesses surged forward with the emergence of new industrial nations, while new legislature promised to ensure employment equality and worker safety. With mostly manual processes in place to support compliance, the worry from the corporate world was not necessarily the legislation itself, but the increased and new burden of paperwork and processes and no internal group to support these new requirements. For many companies, this is when the personnel department was born and employee rights and relations began to take a more focused role in business and the press.

Despite new legislation to protect them, the 1970s and 1980s also marked the beginning of a new feeling for employees: the lack of job security. With the promise of cheaper labor in developing countries, manufacturers began to close down factories in the United States in favor of cheaper facilities and labor in developing countries. This resulted in the same products for less money to consumers, but a loss of jobs for Americans. At the same time, lower-cost items from foreign companies, particularly Japanese car manufacturers, made a huge impact on the U.S. GDP.

As Detroit was struggling with the unforeseen competition of smaller, more economic cars, Americans worried about the impact of closing down factories combined with the increase in foreign goods consumption. Economic forecasters began to assure the public that, with millions of service jobs being created during this decade and into the next, the economy would not suffer as long as there was a shift in skills and training among the workforce.

The continued shake-up in the corporate world added to budding workforce fears beyond the 1970s. Leveraged buy-outs, mergers and acquisitions, and hostile takeovers resulted in market consolidation and, at times, confused business models. The effects of market consolidation on business efficiency, insight, and effectiveness became even more critical as much of Eastern Europe opened up when the Cold War ended and the Berlin Wall came down, giving new opportunities for globalization. Western companies knew that they needed to act fast on the emerging market opportunities and often did so, with little understanding of the impact on the existing business. With so many changes to business dynamics, combined with a fluctuating economy and increasing customer demands for better goods at lower prices, executives struggled to maintain control and competitiveness in operational efficiency with little insight into business operations and efficiency. The first step for these executives to compete in the rapidly changing business environment was clear: efficiency in and control of business operations.

HR Transformation in the Digital Age

In the early part of the 20th century, tax and wage legislation was introduced to businesses, and by 1943 federal tax was mandated. To comply with these new requirements, a new function/profession was created—the payroll professional. This was a huge responsibility, with significant consequences for miscalculation and noncompliance. Payroll clerks struggled manually through hundreds and, at larger firms, thousands of payroll records, often with human error, making auditing, efficiency, and control a virtual impossibility. For some companies, technology could not come soon enough. Those who could afford it, like GE, pioneered the automation of the complicated and cumbersome payroll process. GE implemented the first homegrown mainframe payroll solution; they also had the first automated payroll system to process the tens of thousands of employees across the United States.

At the end of the 20th century, social legislation such as Affirmative Action, Equal Employment Opportunity, the Occupational Safety and Health Act, and the Employee Retirement Income Securities Act created a demand for companies to collect, store, manage, and report more personnel data than ever before. It had become very difficult to keep up with legislation and to put it into a practice that did not cost significant time and money. At the same time, employees were becoming more and more aware of their rights, evidenced by the emergence of lawsuits and challenges to corporate policies. What had previously been accepted was now under scrutiny. The consequences for noncompliance or discriminatory practices were significant fines and monetary rewards for victims of wrongdoing.

Due to legislated corporate responsibility for compliance of workforce practices and worker safety, a new function was created—the personnel department. Combined with the payroll department in many businesses, the personnel department was primarily responsible for managing personnel information, data, and processes, and ensuring that the business was compliant with employment legislation. The HR function served as a police officer of sorts to ensure that employment practices were adhered to throughout the business. But HR was also the polite group in the business—often responsible for coordinating company picnics and other outings, sending birthday notes to employees, and carefully treading in a business where little value was placed on the business impact of HR.

As the century progressed, so did technology. As mentioned above, some companies, like GE, forced the issue by creating their own technology before one was available on the market. Payroll vendors began to emerge, offering not only technology, but in some cases, also services to outsource this function.

With the onslaught of legislation, companies began to look seriously at technology to gain control over workforce information without significantly increasing costs to the business. With other companies, sophisticated, and often complicated color-coded filing systems were used to store employee data, but reporting remained an issue. Vendors began to promote ERP solutions that combined personnel data and payroll applications. Some vendors also integrated financial controlling systems with the HR systems, so that companies could not only make more efficient financial decisions, but also increase control over where corporate dollars were spent. Companies could leverage the HR systems to generate reports that demonstrated compliance with legislation, thereby protecting against costly fines, lawsuits, and bad publicity. With technology, businesses were beginning to automate processes that, although important and critical to achieve, did not contribute value. The payoff of technology was not just compliance, operational efficiency, and control; it also helped to focus resources on other activities beyond keeping manual records.

As the 1980s came to a close, academics discussed the changing role of HR. They speculated that many HR organizations would transform from a police and polite administrator role into a more strategic role in the business. Many thought leaders were beginning to suggest practices through which employees were actual resources, who, if taken care of, could improve their contribution to the company. This, of course, required that the HR function move closer to the business. This was also a time for legitimizing the HR function. Professional organizations such as the International Association for Human Resource Information Management (IHRIM) were founded as a place for HR professionals to meet, learn about, and share new practices and technologies to help their businesses be more efficient.

Enable Insight: Partner Phase

Key Business Issues

As the 1990s approached, the pace of competition continued to quicken as customers became more sophisticated in their demands and Internet technologies began to emerge and tear down the barriers to entry for competition. Manufacturing and services organizations alike began to decentralize functions, while trying to maintain centralized control through standardized processes and information. Many manufacturing organizations, which had long embraced such quality improvements as Total Quality Management (TQM), began to rely more heavily on offshore facilities and companies that were spun off into separate businesses to bring products and services to market. While TQM and other similar business methodologies may have remained, manufacturers struggled with the human side of decentralized business, including basic insight into the demographics of the extended global workforce. For example, until a few years ago, Dow Corning maintained a decentralized organizational structure with a fragmented IT architecture. Employees reported in to a region, a country, or a division, resulting in a lack of insight, coordination, and best practices and processes. In addition to perceived enhancements of operational excellence, Dow Corning wanted a change to the decentralized structure in order to improve workforce performance. Dow Corning found both tangible benefits as well as intangible gains from streamlining HR and other business processes through a global installation of an HRMS. The benefits that Dow Corning realized included a reduction in global organization barriers, a decrease in redundant activities, and a reduction in cycle time for key processes.[1]

In other markets that rely heavily on "knowledge workers," such as services and high-tech industries, companies were beginning to embrace telecommuting or virtual work as part of everyday operations. With a much more diversified workforce in terms of location, gender, race, talent/skills, career aspirations, and culture, companies not only required better, more dynamic insight into personal data, but also tools through which employees could feel "empowered" and connected to the corporation.

From the mid- to late 1990s, for the United States and many other Western countries, the dot-com era was alive and well. Venture capital was being plugged into companies, promising new technologies that would change the way we live and the way we do business. Many of these companies were promoting fairy dust, with little or no technology having been developed, compounded by the fact that many of these start-ups lacked solid business plans or business models that clearly defined how the new products or services would or could make money. This was a time when technology was being dreamed up and, in some cases, created for technology's sake, rather than for an actual market need. With sites like e-Bay and Amazon.com, online commerce broke down competitive barriers and opened new opportunities for budding businesses and a new breed of entrepreneurs. Established businesses such as bookstores, particularly in the west, were feeling the pressure of the Internet push by consumers, business partners, and even employees.

As the century came to a close, companies were not only focused on the Internet, but the entire market was scrambling, waiting with bated breath to see what would happen when the new year began. Consumers with the same fears of data loss were withdrawing savings from banks with the worry that all of their savings would be lost if the bank systems failed when the clock turned at midnight on New Year's Eve 1999. The Y2K scare enabled many software vendors to sell solutions at record rates with the promise of protection against data loss. Businesses needed to ensure that valuable customer, employee, financial, inventory, and supply-chain information would not be lost due to a feared glitch in many software solutions that would not recognize "000" when the new decade began. For many, this meant a migration of core data from old, legacy systems to new enterprise solutions that promised foolproof protection against the potential hazards of Y2K data loss. Additionally, businesses were looking at vendors who could not only promise data protection against loss during Y2K, but also data protection in the form of privacy, particularly with the new Internet technologies and information exchange. In particular, companies that operated in the European Union during this time were beginning to feel the heat from privacy protection acts created by the EU to protect employees from information exchange about them.

But what companies required most was control and insight into business operations. As globalization continued, so did the rapid pace of competition. Continued downsizing and offshoring meant there was a need for businesses to operate at much lower costs in order to be competitive. Service organizations and pharmaceutical companies, who competed mostly based on the talent of their people, required insight into the current skills and gap in talent. With the war for talent a critical issue on many CEOs' minds and a shortage of real talent available in the market, more and more businesses began to focus on branding as a form of recruiting smart MBAs and other key talent. Understanding where the talent was needed and how to quickly close the talent gap was a core concern for every CEO, which resulted in a push for more strategic technology and human resources practices that were linked to business strategies, which were starting to be coined "human capital management." In an ROI study conducted by Gartner Consulting in 2003 of SAB Limited, the brewing giant from South Africa, researchers found that HR and managers were once forced to make decisions about attracting and retraining talent based on disparate information consolidated across multiple regions over the course of time, often making decisions based on outdated information. Faced with the strategic focus of innovation and efficiency and through the use of an HRMS, HR and managers alike now make recruiting and workforce development decisions based on current needs, such as skills gaps and up-skill requirements. Now at SAB Miller Limited, the data is real-time, so the right decisions are made at the right time.[2]

HR Transformation in the Digital Age

In the 1980s and into the 1990s, the role of the personnel department continued to transform. In fact, most of these had re-branded themselves as "human resources" in an effort to better align the new needs of the business. And as quickly as the economy began to turn around, the pace of competition also began to quicken. The HR department, which was viewed by most in the business as an expense, was feeling pressure from executives across the business to provide better data on even the most core information, such as total headcount. The running joke among many CEOs and CFOs was that if they asked for a headcount report from five different people, they would get five different numbers. As a result, HR knew that if it was going to change its role in the business, it simply had to adopt a more suitable IT landscape, like what had been implemented across the rest of the business. The hope was that, with better information, HR would be able to deliver better insight into the workforce so that, together, executives and HR could make better, more informed, workforce decisions.

At the same time, confidence in the HR department continued to go down. In most companies, HR remained separate from the rest of the business, with no links to executives, their decisions, or the workforce or managers. And those HR organizations that wanted to integrate with the business struggled with how to do it.

Executives were used to making decisions based on tangible assets such as revenue and supply chain. HR and its value of employee relations and development were not tangible and hard for executives to understand—and even harder for HR to articulate in real, tangible business terms. As a result, HR was very rarely consulted or included in business decisions, both at the board level and day-to-day. Executives and managers alike rarely turned to HR for help with strategies, programs, or people decisions beyond headcount reductions. Employees also held little trust for HR. HR was no longer seen as the group that paid their employees and set up holiday parties, but instead as an agent for executives.

Managers, like employees, had little interaction with HR. Hiring contingent or permanent staff was not a seamless process. Managers wanted the right people to help them deliver and had little confidence that HR understood the needs of the business in order to hire the right people. When HR was involved, managers found the process too lengthy and often missed the opportunity to hire the right candidate. As a result, managers often took matters into their own hands and recruited on their own, bringing HR into the process during the search or hire phase, instead of during the planning phase. This may have shortened the cycle time from recruit to hire, but many times, it drove up the cost to hire.

The employee experience with HR was not that much better. Even the simplest transactions, such as an address change, were often at least partially manual or required help from HR. This resulted in processes that took multiple steps and lead times, which further resulted in errors that aggravated the employee and created extra steps for both the employee and HR and cost the business money, perhaps in the form of paycheck errors.

With such deep dissatisfaction by its stakeholders and a strong desire to be seen as a key member of the business, HR knew it had to change its role in the business and it needed the right tools and systems in order to do so. HR would have to prove its place in the business, and that meant talking in a language the decision makers would understand—with as much tangible information as possible. Using data from such companies as Saratoga, HR departments began to collect employee metrics to compare themselves to others in their industry on such measures as cost per hire, time to hire, and HR headcount per FTE (full-time-equivalent). Many of these measurements were used as justification of the purchase and implementation of HRIS to automate the more non-value-added transactions for which HR was responsible.

The hope for HR was that with the non-value-added processes automated, the HR workforce could concentrate on providing key services to executives, managers, and employees. At companies such as TransAlta Corporation, a major North American utilities player, reducing the amount of time on transactional tasks meant the ability to focus on activities that would positively impact its business. As shown in the ROI study conducted by Gartner Consulting of TransAlta's human resources system implementation, Shandra Russell, a director of HR at TransAlta, sees the benefits of a new focus: "This cycle-time reduction allows for HR to spend less time completing administrative tasks and more time focusing on strategic activities that are core at TransAlta's business."[3]

Because employee empowerment was such a critical concern for the workforce and because the war for talent included the need to retain staff, HR knew that it had to deliver better services to the workforce. Many HR executives began to understand that the best way to be seen as a valued member of the management team was to partner with key business executives and managers. Depending on the business, this included line-of-business heads and sales managers, among others, to deliver the right tools to the right users, enabling better access to information and better decision making. HR was transforming its role from just a payroll and benefits provider into a key business partner who could enable insight and deliver strategies on the business's most important and critical resource: its workforce. As the war for talent raged on in both white-collar and blue-collar jobs, the timing was perfect.

By the mid-1990s, the Internet, or the Worldwide Web, was a common topic of both social and business discussions. Many businesses had branded corporate intranets that provided information for their employees, virtual bulletin boards for information ranging from internal job postings to a calendar of events, even allowing employees to post "for sale" notices of private property. More and more, companies were providing workers with home access to corporate systems via an intranet. Companies were able to offer employees a way to manage their personal and personnel information, working toward work/life balance, while employers were able to keep employees connected to their own information, enabling a better, more accurate depiction. In a time when the buzzword for employees was "empowerment," corporations began to focus on deploying applications that could give employees all the tools and information they needed to perform their jobs and make better decisions.

In many businesses, HR positioned itself as a partner to the business. Forward-thinking HR departments began to reorganize themselves to match the rest of the business. HR associates were assigned to business groups and became part of the "team," often joining meetings and working with the management team to make the best workforce decisions on such topics as succession and career planning, recruiting, development programs, compensation, and education. As the HR team members became more visible and value-added programs began to be employed, employees in many businesses began to have a better relationship with HR, often seeking them out for career advice. Despite the turnaround in many businesses, there still were many other companies where HR struggled to be seen as valuable.

In order to gain insight into even the most seemingly basic information about the workforce in the 1990s, more and more companies were beginning to embrace a more comprehensive approach to HR automation through which disparate systems and broken processes would be replaced with a "Human Resources Information System" (HRIS). In fact, most large businesses embraced an HRIS strategy that enabled them to replace antiquated, time-consuming personnel processes with streamlined automation. With re-engineering being the technology-to-business buzzword of these times, along with automation came painstaking reviews of antiquated systems and procedures. Academics, business leaders, and vendors alike agreed that simply placing applications on top of antiquated processes and systems would not result in enhanced efficiency, let alone increase insight into business operations. Instead, with re-engineered processes, the promise was that companies would replace most non-value-generating, highly labor-intensive and expensive processes, such as payroll, benefits administration, and employee data capture, with streamlined back-office solutions requiring little human interaction.

A critical component to HR's success would be its ability to capture the right and most accurate information while increasing its service level to executives and the workforce. As we moved further into the decade, corporations expanded the automation of payroll and personnel data and began to capture time worked, as well as intangible information that helped plan careers and successions to key roles in the business. HR began to evaluate self-service applications to help streamline business processes, capture better data, and—most importantly—put information into the hands of those who most wanted and needed it: managers and employees. Additionally, in order to keep control over the integrity of the data and how the systems were used, many processes leveraged workflow to create "checks and balances." With workflow, the corporation maintained control over data, but the processes were streamlined, therefore minimizing the amount of time to completion.

With better data, of course, came better information; and with better information came better and more informed decisions. Businesses were beginning to rely on data warehousing and analytic tools to gain valuable insight into the workforce through dynamic information gathered from across the business. Not only were HRIS applications enabling operational efficiency, cost reductions, and control, no matter where or how the company did business, but they were also starting to enable the type of insight required for key business decisions. With technology enabling the use and deployment of workforce information, human capital management systems began to be pushed into the market and across the business.

Just as HR was at this stage, the business tools and services designed for employees, managers, and executives to both maintain and leverage workforce and personal career information were also being pushed into the market. These tools were designed to enable employees to input personal data such as address changes or direct deposit bank information, as well as to give direct access to corporate information. However, what began to happen—and still continues to be a problem with many systems in use today—with the advent of the "information age" came info-glut. Thus, many vendors began to market "portal" solutions to enable the user to have a window into information he or she would need to perform on the job, manage career decisions, as well as manage personal business more proficiently. Users across the business would gain access to the information needed to make better, more informed decisions on anything from career mobility and job performance to better training options and work/life decisions. As this phase continues, human capital management has become the job of everyone in the business, putting HR in the position of not only helping the business run better, but partnering with key players to make the right business-focused workforce decisions at the right time.

Create Strategic Value: Player Phase

Key Business Issues

From 2000 to the present, the world has seen tremendous change in a very short span of time. Continued globalization, rising customer and shareholder expectations, a volatile social and economic climate plagued by the fear of terrorism, corporate scandal and the resulting rise of corporate governance issues, downsizing, off-shoring, and a "job-less economic recovery" in the Western world have combined to create tremendous pressure on executives to create highly flexible and innovative strategies to outperform the competition and increase profits and market share while decreasing the cost of doing business.

Executives not only have to ensure that they are delivering shareholder value; they have to be able to prove it. With Sarbanes Oxley, Basel II, and International Accounting Standards, governments across the world are now holding executives personally accountable for what they say about their business's performance, with stricter guidelines and legislation than ever. No longer will executives be able to hide behind the corporate curtain; if found and convicted of any wrongdoing, executives will not only face penalties, but potentially also face prison. Originally intended for public companies, these laws are now becoming business practices for privately held and nonprofit organizations, especially those seeking additional funding. Investors and lenders want to ensure honest dealings and clear insight into business operations and financials.

Not only are they looking for insight to prove and protect corporate statements about earnings and performance, but executives must look for innovative ways to deliver value to customers while outperforming the competition. The economy is slowly turning around, and executives must be ready to take advantage of new opportunities as they arise.

More and more companies have realized that, in order to achieve business objectives, as many resources as possible have to be focused on value-added activities, as well as on leveraging existing assets into new market opportunities. Many corporations are beginning to outsource the standardized back-office functions in order to focus resources on competitive activities.

With fewer people, less money, and the increasingly rapid rate of competition, CEOs cite organizational innovation and the efficient and effective management of the workforce as key competitive advantages, enhancing the importance of human capital management. The problem becomes how to manage and measure the contribution of the business's talent. Employees are unlike other points of leverage, such as financial capital, patents, products, and state-of-the art facilities and machinery. This makes the management of the workforce assets the most challenging for the business.

Executives struggle with what to measure and how to clearly tie employee metrics to business performance. With 30 to 60 percent of a company's revenue spent on human capital management, executives want a way to understand how this money is being spent and what the payback is in terms of impact on business performance and shareholder value. Adding to the pressure to better understand human capital strategies is the increasing number of financial analysts whose valuations consist partly of measuring such intangible assets as the ability of the corporate leadership's team to execute on strategy or the ability of the business to attract and retain skilled talent. Mostly, when it comes to people, executives are not sure what to report to analysts to prove that their workforce delivers better and creates more value than that of the competition. Most financial analysts hear revenue per employee as a gauge on how successful the workforce is. Although an important measure, this metric does not tell the story. Indeed, financial analysts struggle with the form through which they can receive data on the results from investments in people and other intangible corporate assets.

With such a strong focus on finding ways to accurately report the results from human capital, business executives, market researchers, and financial analysts alike continue to spend a lot of time trying to identify standardized measurements that can be used. They need to take this information one step further—to make critical strategic decisions on the right human capital approach that will achieve business goals and objectives. This has resulted in the need for new human capital technology that focuses on creating value for the business, but it also has created the need for continued transformation of the HR department and its role in the business.

HR Transformation in the Digital Age

For most HR departments, the struggle to gain and maintain partnerships across the business continues. Like any other line of business, HR has to prove itself and its value time and time again. What has changed is how businesses are managing people. Unlike the traditional HR approaches of the past, the practice of human capital management views employee and collective workforce success as a responsibility of everyone in the business. No longer are corporate "people issues" the exclusive province of the HR team—a group that was, and many times still is, distant from strategic decision making and whose contribution to the bottom line often goes unrecognized.

The organization that heartily embraces HCM understands that maximizing the workforce is the job of CEOs, board members, business unit executives, departmental managers, and every employee who wants the company to succeed. Every stakeholder has a role to play in the process of maximizing the value and contribution of the company's human capital. It is HR's job to help drive and steer the HCM strategies to align with corporate goals and objectives and to find a way to measure the success of programs against these objectives. To be a player in this new corporate world, HR must be a proven successful partner who understands the needs of the business and can leverage this understanding to attract and retain a robust, competitive, engaged, and impassioned customer-focused and competitively driven workforce. HR must also possess a technology acumen like never before. They must recommend and provide the right tools that not only give access to personal information, but also aid in workforce productivity and value creation.

With this type of value creation, HR can no longer be viewed as a mere cost of doing business. In today's knowledge-based economy, how well a company leverages its human capital determines its ability to develop or sustain competitive advantage. For some, this may mean a shakeup in the HR department. Some believe that a new business unit that focuses solely on talent acquisition and the value creation of this talent should be formed. In some businesses where talent truly is the only competitive advantage, Chief Talent Officers (CTOs) have been named and focus on attracting, growing, and retaining the right talent to meet current and future business requirements.

As a player in this new business age, HR or the organization focusing on talent must be able to translate business opportunity into strategies that will clearly impact the bottom line. In order to be taken seriously as a player, this function, like any at the decision table, must be able to clearly measure its impact. This requires not only the insight capabilities from data mining and analytics tools created in the 1990s in and into today, but also the new ability to interpret and use this information to make value-creating human capital decisions about investments and divestitures.

In order to meet the needs of the new HR department, many companies have begun to seek out executives from the business to head HR or the "talent" organization. It is believed that these executives, many of whom have led a line of business and have had P&L responsibility, understand what it means to be accountable for delivering business results. Additionally, these are the very executives who have either ignored HR in the past or have seen HR as an inhibitor, or in some cases an enabler, for success in sales, development, or other line of business. It is this experience and business acumen that the new HR requires.

For existing HR executives who remain in the game, many are turning to MBAs and other trained businesspeople to help reshape HR. No one really believes that HR will ever be a profit center, but it is believed that HR should ultimately be accountable for the performance of the workforce, enabling the most profitable, engaged, loyal, and innovative workforce in the market. That is how an HR player in the business can create value.

A key element for HR to create value at the decision-making level is for them to deploy the right people to the appropriate strategic initiatives throughout the business. Executives must quickly respond to changes in business by making workforce-related decisions based on real-time information—decisions that align corporate strategies with team and individual goals, supporting employees in all phases of the employee lifecycle.

A successful human capital strategy enables success because employees are truly engaged, which means that their focus (this includes contractors, temporary staff, and full-time equivalents or FTEs, as well as part-time workers) is aligned with the goals and objectives of the business. It also means that workers are actively contributing to achieving individual and team goals that in turn contribute to the success of the business. Engaged employees work productively and are dedicated to achieving optimum business performance because they feel a sense of ownership in the success of the business.

If HR can deliver tools and services that focus employees on activities that increase their contribution to the bottom line, then HR is creating tremendous value to the business. By minimizing administrative tasks, HR can focus on what is important to the company's bottom line. At TransAlta, for example, HR has achieved the ability to create value by automating approximately two thousand employee data transactions yearly, thereby enabling the HR department to refocus. Shandra Russell, director of human resources at TransAlta, stated in the company's business value assessment white paper: "This cycle time reduction [from implementing an HRMS] allows for HR to spend less time completing administrative tasks and more time focusing on strategic activities that are core to TransAlta's business."

As HR's role transforms into a partner and player in the business, the focus has broadened and now includes, in some cases, workforce productivity. Now when HR looks to technology to enable business functions, it no longer looks to solutions to solely automate back-office functions, both transactional and strategic; they also want solutions that enable a more productive and focused workforce. As a result, many corporations have adopted a portal strategy that leverages not only internal production systems, but also enables collaboration across and outside of the business.

Considering that it is impossible for the competition to copy the talent of the workforce or the relationships among the workforce, a new portal strategy with a strong focus on collaboration is critical to competitive success. Now employees can collaborate with partners, customers, and other employees, leveraging private and secure virtual chat rooms and private knowledge management warehouses to share data across teams of internal and external players. These warehouses also ensure that all IP (intellectual property), such as trade secrets or R&D (research and development) works in progress, is kept with the business and does not leave when an employee does. With a growing number of the workforce, particularly those in high-tech and services industries, being virtually based, this type of collaboration enables better, more efficient teamwork than ever before.

As the market is slowly turning around, many businesses are looking at and implementing e-recruiting solutions to not only attract outside talent, but to manage talent internally. New e-recruiting solutions enable employers to maintain a talent pool, with CRM-like capabilities to maintain relationships with viable internal and external applicants, alumni, and partners, even if employment is not offered immediately.

As the market struggles to recover, corporations continue to look for ways to maintain an educated workforce that can meet customer demands and help bring products to market faster without driving up the cost of doing business. Many companies have cut training costs, but still need to get out new information in order to maintain competitiveness. HR and training organizations alike are increasingly turning to e-learning solutions, many of which provide simulated training so that employees are better prepared to perform their jobs. e-Learning solutions that are integrated with performance management and development programs provide automatic links to suggested training for employees, based on performance requirements, career aspirations, and so forth. Online scoring enables employees and managers to identify areas of strength and where more work is required. In many applications, e-learning is also integrated with knowledge management so that employees can access training documents and other related materials.

From an individual perspective, many HR organizations are turning to an automated balanced scorecard approach to link employee and team goals to corporate objectives. Balanced score-cards provide a series of predefined indicators built around metrics that measure the effectiveness of the HR department, as well as ensuring that employee and department goals are consistent with company strategies. With performance management solutions, employees can view how individual performance impacts corporate success. Managers can monitor progress in terms of employee-level and team-level objectives, so that opportunities or challenges can be managed before problems occur.

As companies implement more value-added, strategic HCM applications, insight into learning and talent strengths and gaps means better decisions around customer service, product go-to-market, and so on. Executives can make better decisions on whom to ramp up and leverage the workforce, regardless of economic conditions. As metrics and methodologies that help to define how the investments in human capital programs and their impact in shareholder value become available and automated as part of analytical decision support, executives and HR will be able to move forward and make forward-thinking decisions with known impacts to business performance.

Conclusion

Today, every HR department is in the midst of a seemingly endless transformation, one that not only encompasses the function of the HR department, but also its role within the business, the relationships it maintains, and the technology it uses and is responsible for deploying. It is clear that transformation of HR is inevitable. More and more, businesses are realizing that people are the only true differentiating factor in long-term competitive success. For so long, workforce strategies have not been aligned with business objectives. HR technology was focused only on automating back-office functions and was not necessarily leveraged throughout the business to give employees, managers, and executives the tools they needed to make better personal decisions, let alone better people management decisions.

Now that human capital management permeates the business, companies are committed to deploying the right collaborative tools to employees so that they can not only make better decisions about such personal options as healthcare or 401(k) investments, but also leverage collaborative tools that enable better teamwork across and outside of the business. With this teamwork comes innovation, access to better and more relevant information, and so forth. HR can now contribute to the many capabilities that impact key performance drivers and ultimate business performance, workforce productivity, and leadership developments. With a more strategic role that extends beyond ensuring efficiency in back-office functions, HR is primed to help businesses change the way they leverage their people to compete and deliver unmatched customer satisfaction. HR will continue to create strategic value for the business.

Notes
1. mySAP HCM at Dow Corning. This study was conducted by Gartner Consulting in 2003.
2. mysSAP ERP HCM: ROI Analysis—SAB Limited. This study was conducted by Gartner Consulting in 2003.
3. A Business Value Assessment: mySAP ERP HCM at TransAlta. This study was conducted by Gartner Consulting in 2003.

CHAPTER 2

e-Recruiting
Online Strategies for Attracting Talent

Dianna L. Stone
Kimberly M. Lukaszewski
Linda C. Isenhour

Organizations have long been concerned with attracting and retaining highly talented employees. The primary reason for this is that they depend on the skills and talents of their workforce to compete in an ever-changing global environment. In order to facilitate the recruitment process, organizations are increasingly using electronic human resources (eHR) systems, including web-based job sites, portals, and kiosks to attract job applicants (Stone, Stone-Romero, & Lukaszewski, 2003). For example, the most common practices used for online recruitment involve (a) adding recruitment pages to existing organizational websites, (b) using specialized recruitment websites (for example, job portals, online job boards), (c) developing interactive tools for processing applications (for example, online applications, email auto responding), and (d) using online screening techniques (for example, keyword systems, online interviews, or personality assessment) (Galanaki, 2002). Hereafter we refer to these practices as e-recruiting or online recruiting. Although estimates vary, surveys show that between 70 and 90 percent of large firms now use e-recruiting systems, and it is anticipated that over 95 percent of organizations plan to use them in the near future (Cappelli, 2001; Cedar, 2003). Similarly, reports indicate that many large firms now use intranet systems to post job openings, which provides current employees with greater advancement opportunities and may enhance their satisfaction and commitment levels (Cedar, 2002; Stone, Stone-Romero, & Lukaszewski, 2003).

Interestingly, some high-technology firms (Cisco Systems, for example) recruit employees only through the Internet; and estimates indicate that 20 percent of all hires now come from online systems (cf. Cascio, 1998). Furthermore, firms such as Walt Disney World and Cisco are using e-recruiting websites or web-based portals to help establish "brand identities" that distinguish them from their competitors (Stone, Stone-Romero, & Lukaszewski, 2003; Ulrich, 2001). For example, the Disney World brand identity involves high levels of customer satisfaction and a quality entertainment experience for all. This identity is fostered in the organizational culture, becomes part of a company's website, and plays a pivotal role in attracting new employees to the firm. Thus, applicants can review unique information about the firm's "brand identity" on the company's website to determine whether their personal goals and values fit with the organization's culture. Then they can apply for jobs when they perceive there is an overlap between the company's goals and their own value systems.

In addition to the communication of brand identity, surveys show that 38 percent of organizations are now using online systems to increase employee retention levels by identifying and resolving employee salary inequities before employees search for other jobs (Cedar, 2003). It is clear that these firms are aware that it may be much easier to retain and develop existing talent than to acquire new or unproven talent (Cedar, 2003). Furthermore, it is evident that eHR systems have become important means of helping organizations establish a brand identity, attract talented workers, and retain valuable employees.

Apart from the reasons for using online recruiting noted above, these systems may also increase the effectiveness of the recruitment process by (a) reaching large numbers of qualified applicants, including those in international labor markets (Cappelli, 2001; Galanaki, 2002), (b) reducing recruitment costs (Cappelli, 2001), (c) decreasing cycle time (Cardy & Miller, 2003; Cober, Brown,

Levy, Keeping, & Cober, 2003), (d) streamlining burdensome administrative processes (Stone, Stone-Romero, & Lukaszewski, 2003), and (e) enabling the organization to evaluate the success of its recruitment strategy (Stone, Stone-Romero, & Lukaszewski, 2003). For instance, online systems helped Cisco Systems attract more than 500,000 individuals in one month and enabled them to hire 1,200 people in three months' time (Cober, Brown, Blumental, Doverspike, & Levy, 2000). In addition, some reports indicate that online recruiting costs 95 percent less than traditional recruiting. For example, some estimates indicate that the cost of online recruitment is $900 as compared to $8,000 to $10,000 for traditional systems (Cober, Brown, Blumental, Doverspike, & Levy, 2000). In the same way, research shows that firms can reduce hiring cycle times by 25 percent when using online recruitment (Cober, Brown, Blumental, Doverspike, & Levy, 2000), and can use these systems to provide easy and inexpensive realistic "virtual" previews to job applicants (Stone, Stone-Romero, & Lukaszewski, 2003). Finally, these systems enable organizations to evaluate the effectiveness of the recruitment process and examine the validity of assessment techniques (Mohamed, Orife, & Wibowo, 2002; Stone, Stone-Romero, & Lukaszewski, 2003).

Although there are certainly numerous benefits of using online recruitment systems in organizations, some analysts have argued that there may also be a number of dysfunctional or unintended consequences of using such systems (cf. Bloom, 2001; Stone, Stone-Romero, & Lukaszewski, 2003). For example, replacing traditional recruiters with computerized systems may make the recruitment process much more impersonal and inflexible and, therefore, have a negative impact on applicants' attraction and retention rates (Bloom, 2001; Stone, Stone-Romero, & Lukaszewski, 2003). Likewise, the use of online recruitment may have an adverse impact on members of some minority groups because these individuals may not have access to computerized systems or possess the skills needed to use them (Hogler, Henle, & Bemus, 2001). In addition, applicants may perceive that online systems are more likely to invade personal privacy than other recruitment sources. As a result, applicants may be less willing to use e-recruiting systems than traditional systems to apply for jobs (Harris, Van Hoye, & Lievens, 2003; Stone, Stone-Romero, & Lukaszewski, 2003).

Purpose of the Chapter

Despite the widespread use of online recruiting, relatively little research has been done to examine the effectiveness of these systems or consider their impact on job applicants. We believe this is problematic because technology has dramatically changed recruitment practices, and organizations have invested substantial resources in these new systems without the benefit of research. Thus, organizations may be able to use the knowledge gained from research to increase the acceptance and enhance the effectiveness of these new recruiting systems. Therefore, the primary purposes of this chapter are to (a) consider the effects of e-recruiting practices on applicants' attraction to organizations, (b) review the findings of recent research on the topic, and (c) offer guidelines for human resources (HR) professionals concerned with developing and implementing e-recruiting systems. In order to accomplish these goals, we first provide a framework for understanding the recruitment process (Rynes, 1991) and consider the degree to which online systems facilitate each element in this process.

Model of the Recruitment Process

One of the key goals of this chapter is to consider the effects of online recruitment practices on individuals' attraction to an organization and motivation to apply for a job. In order to understand this process, we first provide a framework for understanding the antecedents and outcomes of recruitment. In particular, we consider the model of recruitment presented by Rynes in 1991.

Quite simply, Rynes's (1991) model of recruitment suggests that applicants gather information about organizations to assess the types of rewards offered by the organization and to determine whether or not they meet the requirements of the job. In addition, they attend to signals that cue them about the culture and climate of the organization (for example, poor administrative practices may signal that the organization is inefficient or not well managed). Furthermore, this model suggests that four key factors affect applicants' attraction to organizations, including (a) recruiter characteristics, (b) source characteristics, (c) administrative policies and practices, and (d) vacancy characteristics. Finally, the model indicates that when applicants are attracted to organizations they are more likely to apply for jobs, accept job offers, and remain with the organization over time. Given that recruiters are not often part of online recruiting systems, we do not consider recruiter characteristics in our review. However, we do discuss online recruitment as a source of applicants, as an administrative practice, and as a means of communicating vacancy characteristics in sections below. In addition, we consider the effectiveness of an e-recruiting strategy as a means of supporting an organization's mission and goals.

Online Recruitment as a Source of Applicants

Online recruitment can be viewed as just one of the many sources used by organizations to attract job applicants. Other alternatives include direct applications, employee referrals, newspaper advertising, employment agencies, and executive search firms. Given that firms often use a variety of recruitment sources to attract applicants, we believe that HR professionals may want to know how e-recruiting compares to other sources in terms of its acceptance and effectiveness. Thus, we review the results of research on e-recruiting as a source of applicants.

Applicant Preferences for Online Recruitment

It is clear that many job applicants are now using online systems to search for jobs and gather information about employment opportunities in organizations. Furthermore, organizations often use online systems to attract passive job seekers who are currently employed, but secretly searching for new or better employment opportunities. Although e-recruiting is widely used, there is still a great deal of uncertainty about its acceptance among job applicants (Galanaki, 2002; Zusman & Landis, 2002). For example, research shows most applicants continue to prefer newspaper advertisements to e-recruiting; and surveys consistently indicate that the Internet is not the number one source of jobs for most candidates (Galanaki, 2002; Zusman & Landis, 2002). In addition, many applicants still rate employee referrals and personal recruitment more favorably than the Internet because they can gather realistic information about the company from current employees

(McManus & Ferguson, 2003). However, studies show that *students* often view online recruitment more favorably than other recruitment sources. One potential reason for this is that they have grown up with computers and are accustomed to seeking a wide array of information on the Internet (Zusman & Landis, 2002). Furthermore, surveys indicate that e-recruiting may be particularly effective when firms are searching for applicants in information technology or when companies have a prominent reputation in the marketplace (Galanaki, 2002).

Yield Rates from Online Recruitment

Organizations often adopt online systems because they believe e-recruiting is more likely than traditional recruitment sources to uncover individuals with unique talents and skills. The logic here is that e-recruiting systems permit firms to cast a wide net across a broad labor market and, therefore, may be more likely to reach high-quality applicants than other sources. Although this argument seems quite plausible, research does not provide support for it. In fact, research shows that companies *do not* attract higher-quality candidates, but *do* attract greater numbers of candidates with e-recruiting than traditional sources (Chapman & Webster, 2003; Galanaki, 2002). One explanation for the increased volume of applicants is that individuals often spend more time searching for jobs online because the process is much simpler and faster than traditional systems (Chapman & Webster, 2003). However, increasing the volume of applicants may also increase the administrative burden in an organization and increase overall transaction costs over time.

Furthermore, some analysts have argued that online systems allow employers to tailor their recruitment to specific labor markets (for example, black engineers or bilingual applicants) through the use of specialized websites or job boards that target applicants with distinctive skills and backgrounds (for example, Asian-net.com. or nsbe.com for black engineers). However, research on the use of these specialized job boards indicates they do not always produce higher-quality candidates, but do yield candidates with higher levels of education than general job boards (Jattuso & Sinar, 2003). Furthermore, research shows that general job boards do produce candidates with more work experience than other sources do (Jattuso & Sinar, 2003).

Types of Candidates Attracted by Online Recruitment

Although online systems generate a large number of job applicants, it is also clear that some candidates may be more receptive to e-recruiting and more likely to use these systems than others. One explanation for this is that online recruiting requires that candidates have access to computers and have the skills needed to use this technology. As a result, e-recruiting systems are likely to attract individuals who are well educated, have the ability to navigate the Internet, and are searching for relatively high-level jobs. Not surprisingly, research supports these arguments and has indicated that online systems attract candidates with higher achievement, drive, and persistence levels than traditional recruitment sources (McManus & Ferguson, 2003). However, results of this research also revealed that candidates recruited through online systems have a less favorable background than those recruited by personal sources and may be more likely to be job hoppers than those recruited from other sources (McManus & Ferguson, 2003). For instance, 35 percent of those recruited by the Internet had three or more jobs in a five-year period (McManus & Ferguson, 2003). Furthermore, McManus and Ferguson (2003) found that online recruiting was less likely to attract members of diverse groups than impersonal recruitment sources (such as newspaper ads), suggesting that e-recruiting may not help firms increase the diversity of their workforces. Given that some types of candidates may be more likely to use e-recruiting than others, the use of these systems may affect the characteristics of new hires in organizations and influence the overall composition of the workforce. These issues will be discussed in more detail in the section below on strategic issues.

In summary, it appears that, despite the widespread use of online recruiting, many candidates still prefer traditional sources such as newspaper ads and employee referrals to online sources. Furthermore, online recruitment may not always increase the quality of job candidates, but is likely to increase the number of candidates who apply for jobs. In addition, applicants who use e-recruiting systems may be likely to have higher achievement and persistence levels, but may also have less favorable backgrounds or switch jobs more frequently than those recruited from more traditional sources. Furthermore, online recruiting may be less likely to attract candidates from diverse backgrounds and affect the overall composition of the workforce. In light of these research findings, the following guidelines are suggested for HR professionals:

Guideline 1: Organizations that are well-known or have prominent reputations may benefit more from online recruiting than those that are not well-known.

Guideline 2: Organizations should use e-recruiting as one source of applicants, but should not use it as the only source for recruiting applicants.

Guideline 3: Organizations should capitalize on the strengths of e-recruiting and use it when large numbers of candidates are needed or when they are searching for individuals in high-level jobs requiring fairly high education levels. In addition, they should use e-recruiting to target candidates in specific labor markets, including those in high-technology jobs and students who are searching for part-time employment or full-time jobs right out of college.

Guideline 4: Organizations should recognize that e-recruiting may not be the preferred source for most job applicants and may not always reach the types of applicants that can help the organization meet its goals. Thus, organizations should be aware that e-recruiting may not attract the most qualified job applicants, may not be particularly effective for reaching minority candidates, and may actually be more attractive to individuals with unfavorable rather than favorable backgrounds (those who switch jobs frequently).

Administrative Issues Associated with Online Recruitment

Organizations have long recognized that their administrative practices influence applicants' attraction to an organization because these practices provide candidates with cues about (a) the nature of the company (for example, efficiency, ability to pay, co-workers, how well they are managed) and (b) their chances of receiving job offers (cf. Rynes, 1991). For example, some evidence suggests that applicant perceptions of the timeliness of firm responses to recruitment inquiries, company reimbursement policies, and realistic recruitment messages influence their attraction to organizations (Rynes, 1991). Therefore, we consider some of the administrative issues associated with the use of online recruitment in the sections below, including (a) the attributes of the website (that is, attractiveness, ease of use, and orientation), (b) the reliability and validity of screening systems, and (c) the use of these systems for providing realistic job previews.

Attributes of the Website

Organizations often invest considerable resources in website development because they believe that the attractiveness, quality, and ease of use of the website will influence applicants' attraction to the organization (Zusman & Landis, 2002). However, research suggests that although some attributes of the website may affect applicants' motivation to apply for jobs, others do not (Zusman & Landis, 2002). For example, research has examined the degree to which the attractiveness of the website influences job seekers; however, the findings of this research have been quite mixed. In particular, research has found that individuals prefer companies with high-quality websites (Zusman & Landis, 2002) and that website designs influence applicants' impressions of the organization (Scheu, Ryan, & Nona, 1999). However, other research has indicated that the attractiveness of the website has little or no influence on applicant attraction to organizations (Cober, Brown, Levy, Keeping, & Cober, 2003). As a result, these researchers argue that vacancy characteristics (for example, pay, benefits, or advancement opportunities) are much more important determinants of applicants' attraction to organizations than the attractiveness of the website.

Although research does not show that the attractiveness of the website influences job applicants, research does suggest that the speed with which websites can be navigated and ease-of-use of the website affect applicants' attitudes toward the organization

(Cober, Brown, Levy, Keeping, & Cober, 2003). In fact, studies have consistently shown that applicants are more likely to apply for jobs when the website is easy to navigate than when it is not (Sinar, Paquet, & Reynolds, 2003; Williamson, Lepak, & King, 2003). Furthermore, this research indicates that candidates react more positively to online selection systems when they feel the website is efficient and user-friendly than when it is difficult to use (Sinar, Paquet, & Reynolds, 2003). It merits noting, however, that research also shows that inexperienced job candidates are more likely to be influenced by the attributes of the website than applicants with job experience (Sinar, Paquet, & Reynolds, 2003).

Another attribute that may affect applicants' reactions to online recruiting is the orientation of the website. Even though most websites are designed with a recruiting orientation, many new websites are designed to include online screening and assessment systems (Jones & Dages, 2003). As a result, it is important for organizations to determine whether the orientation of the website influences its acceptance and effectiveness. Not surprisingly, research has indicated that individuals are more likely to be attracted to organizations that use a recruiting-oriented website than a screening-oriented website (Williamson, Lepak, & King, 2003). One potential explanation for this is that organizational screening systems may be more likely to increase applicants' evaluation apprehension than simple recruiting systems and, therefore, decrease their willingness to apply for jobs. In addition, this research revealed that applicants who preferred e-recruiting systems were more likely to use the website as a cue about the organization's quality than those who did not prefer these systems (Williamson, Lepak, & King, 2003). As a result, these findings support the arguments noted above that suggested some individuals are more likely to be influenced by the attributes of the website than others.

In summary, it appears that the orientation of the website and its ease of use are likely to influence applicants' attraction to organizations, but the attractiveness of the website may have little or no effect on their willingness to apply for jobs. Furthermore, candidates with little job experience and those who favor online recruiting may pay more attention to website characteristics than others. Thus, we offer the following guideline for HR practitioners:

Guideline 5: Organizations should ensure that their websites are designed to be easy to use, simple to navigate, and focus on attracting candidates rather than screening them for jobs.

Effectiveness of Online Assessment Techniques

Organizations use online recruiting systems for multiple purposes, including attracting candidates, communicating benefits about the organization, and assessing applicants' knowledge, skills, abilities, and other requirements (such as personalities). For example, some firms now use software (for example, Resumix) to scan applicant résumés for key words and provide them with immediate feedback about whether they are qualified for jobs. Other organizations use online aptitude tests, personality inventories, or simulations to assess candidates' critical thinking and decision-making skills (for example, Price Waterhouse Coopers, JPMorgan Chase) (Cappelli, 2001). Still other firms conduct online interviews or allow candidates to submit video clips as part of the application process (Cappelli, 2001). Interestingly, a recent survey indicated that 12 percent of organizations now use e-recruiting systems to test or assess applicants' knowledge, skills, and abilities because these systems allow a large number of applicants to be screened quickly and efficiently (Recruitsoft/iLogos, cited in Cappelli, 2001).

Given the growing use of online screening systems, analysts have argued that there are a number of advantages and some potentially dysfunctional consequences of using these systems. For example, Stone, Stone-Romero, and Lukaszewski (2003) contend that online assessment techniques may be much more objective and, therefore, less biased by non-job-related factors (race, gender, or age, for example) than more subjective selection techniques (for example, interviews). In the same way, the use of key word systems to screen résumés may quickly distinguish whether applicants meet the job requirements, and often provide applicants immediate feedback about the status of their application (Stone, Stone-Romero, & Lukaszewski, 2003). As a result, members of some protected groups (racial minorities, people with disabilities) may perceive they have a better chance of being selected for jobs when online screening systems are used rather than traditional selection systems (Stone, Stone-Romero, & Lukaszewski, 2003). Interestingly, some recent research by McManus and Ferguson (2003) supports this argument and found that many African American applicants preferred online application systems to traditional systems. Also, some research suggests that people with disabilities may be more receptive to online screening systems than to traditional systems because they can be easily modified to fit their special needs (for example, use of larger font sizes) (Stone & Williams, 1997).

In spite of the advantages of using online systems to screen applicants, other researchers have noted a number of potential dysfunctional consequences of using e-recruiting systems (Stone, Stone-Romero, & Lukaszewski, 2003). In particular, Mohamed, Orife, and Wibowo (2002) have questioned whether these systems actually help organizations make accurate predictions about the performance of job applicants. Other researchers have expressed concern that online systems have the potential to result in a large number of misclassification errors, which means that the organization may eliminate qualified candidates in favor of those who are not qualified (Stone, Stone-Romero, & Lukaszewski, 2003). Moreover, researchers have argued that online screening systems may not always produce reliable or valid results (Jones & Dages, 2003; Mohamed, Orife, & Wibowo, 2002). In particular, Mohamed, Orife, and Wibowo (2002) maintained that the criteria used in key word systems may not always be based on job analyses and, therefore, may not be job related. In addition, these authors contend that an applicant's résumé writing skills or choice of words may bias the screening process so that applicants who use words listed in the job posting often have a better chance of getting the job than those who do not. As a result, organizations may select candidates who use the right words, rather than the ones most qualified for jobs.

Similarly, we believe, as do others, that online ability tests and personality assessments may be less reliable and valid than traditional systems because applicants complete the tests without being monitored (Chapman & Webster, 2003). Thus, there is often no way of ensuring that applicants completed the tests honestly or without assistance from others. There is also no way to be certain that applicants do not copy tests online, research the answers, and share them with others (Chapman & Webster, 2003). In an effort to resolve these problems, some organizations are using very creative means of screening job applicants, including computer adaptive testing, which varies the test items and length of the test based on the examinee's responses (Jones & Dages, 2003). Despite the use of these methods, there is still a great deal of uncertainty about the effectiveness of online screening systems, and organizations must ensure that these systems produce reliable and valid results before using them to select applicants.

Realistic Previews

One of the potential advantages of online recruiting systems is that organizations can provide applicants with unique information about their company and give them a more realistic preview of what it is like to work for the organization. For example, some companies allow applicants to observe the firm's activities through virtual systems, and others use highly creative means of providing applicants with realistic job previews. Cisco Systems offers online applicants a chance to "Make a Friend at Cisco," helping them establish a relationship with someone inside Cisco who can describe what it is like to work for the organization (Cascio, 1998). It is clear that organizations believe using online systems to provide realistic previews will enhance applicants' subsequent satisfaction levels and retention rates (Rynes, 1991).

Interestingly, some research supports these arguments and has consistently found that online systems may be a useful means for providing realistic previews to job applicants (Rozelle & Landis, 2002). In particular, this research indicated that applicants felt they had more of a chance of collecting realistic information from websites than from traditional sources because websites allowed some flexibility in gathering data that were relevant to them. Thus, the use of online recruiting may be a particularly useful means of conveying the unique characteristics of the organization and/or providing realistic previews to applicants.

Apart from the realistic information provided by online recruiting, HR professionals know that applicants choose jobs and organizations that fit with their personal values, beliefs, and attitudes. As a result, many organizations emphasize information about their strategic goals and culture on their websites so that applicants can make informed decisions about whether they will be satisfied with the organization. This phenomenon has been labeled person-organization fit; and research has suggested that communicating information about an organization's culture does affect employees' retention rates. In particular, Sheridan (1992) found that firms emphasizing interpersonal-relationship value systems had a higher employee retention rate than organizations that emphasized work-task values. Furthermore, Dineen, Ash, and Noe (2002) indicated that feedback about applicants' fit with an organization's culture influenced their attraction to organizations. Thus, organizations might be able to increase employee satisfaction and retention rates by conveying information about the organization's culture on the website and by providing applicants with immediate feedback about the degree to which their values and goals fit with the organization's culture. It merits noting, however, that the use of this strategy alone may not always be effective because highly talented applicants who do not feel they fit with the organization's culture may self-select themselves out of the application process. Thus, we believe, as do others (Cascio, 1998), that organizations may want to use websites to promote values that are attractive to most new employees rather than just select candidates who fit with the traditional value system in the organization. Given these research results, we offer the following guidelines for HR professionals:

Guideline 6: Organizations should develop online screening systems based on job analyses and ensure that the inferences made from these systems are reliable and valid.

Guideline 7: Organizations should develop e-recruiting systems that provide applicants with information about the unique characteristics of the organization and ensure they are given a realistic preview of the firm.

Guideline 8: Organizations should use websites to promote values that will be attractive to most new employees rather than just select those that fit with the traditional culture.

Communication of Vacancy Characteristics

Another potential benefit of online recruitment systems is that websites can easily be used to communicate vacancy characteristics (for example, pay, benefits, perquisites, and advantages of working for the organization) and enhance applicants' attraction to the organization (Rynes, 1991). Furthermore, online systems can highlight unique aspects of the corporate culture and provide important signals about the nature and benefits of working for the organization (Cober, Brown, Blumental, Doverspike, & Levy, 2000). For example, the Shell Oil Company website provides information about the types of knowledge, skills, and attitudes they are looking for in potential employees; and many other firms convey the benefits of working for their organizations on their websites (McCourt-Mooney, 2000). Not surprisingly, some research has shown that using a website to convey vacancy characteristics may be a particularly effective means of attracting job candidates. For instance, research by Cober, Brown, Levy, Keeping, and Cober (2003) found that communicating information about pay levels and developmental opportunities on a job site had a positive effect on applicants' attraction to organizations. Other research has shown that displaying job descriptions and salary levels may also be effective strategies for attracting potential job candidates (Mohamed, Orife, & Wibowo, 2002).

In view of these arguments, we conducted a simple review of the types of data posted on the websites of the Fortune 100 companies between July 15 and August 15, 2004. The results of our review revealed that 66 of the Fortune 100 companies highlighted the advantages of working for the organization on their websites. Some notable exceptions included Wal-Mart, General Motors, Exxon, Ford Motor Company, Citigroup, Home Depot, and Bank of America. Given that many of these organizations have established reputations, they may not perceive the need to promote the benefits of working for the organization on their websites. In addition, most of the companies did post job descriptions on their websites, and only Exxon-Mobil, Altria Group, Bank of America, Berkshire Hathaway, Sears, and Costco Wholesale did not provide this information. Furthermore, most of the Fortune 100 websites did provide information on employee benefits (e.g., medical insurance, retirement benefits) or allowed applicants to create a benefits profile on their websites. However, only a few companies included salary levels on their websites, including Sprint, Prudential Financial, Cigna, Aetna, Verizon Communications, and MetLife. Some other companies (UPS and American International Group) provided salary levels for only part-time positions.

Thus, it appears that most large firms communicate vacancy characteristics on their web pages and use that information to attract applicants, including passive job seekers who are currently employed and not actively looking for jobs. Interestingly, however, firms may not post salary information because they do not want to share salary data that might create internal inequities or deter potential candidates from applying for jobs.

Although it is clear that organizations use online systems to convey information about the benefits of working for their companies, employers also use websites to communicate a particular image to potential job candidates (Galanaki, 2002). In fact, Galanaki contends that companies often adopt online recruitment systems because they fear falling behind in the labor market, and "jump on the e-recruiting bandwagon" in order to keep up with other organizations. Others, however, suggest that some types of organizations use online recruiting to project their image or create a specific brand identity in the labor market (Chapman & Webster, 2003; Ulrich, 2001). In support of this argument, research by Chapman and Webster (2003) found that organizations wanting to project a people-oriented image were less likely to invest in e-recruiting systems than those wanting to project an aggressive or innovative image. Similarly, analysts have suggested that online recruiting systems may serve as a symbol that the company is up-to-date, innovative, and flexible (Galanaki, 2002).

Despite these arguments, others contend that online systems may not always project a positive image for the firm and may signal that the organization is rigid, inflexible, or impersonal in its management style (Gutek, 1995; Stone, Stone-Romero, & Lukaszewski, 2003). In particular, Stone and her co-authors maintain that online systems may be viewed as rigid because they are often incapable of dealing with the inevitable exceptions that arise when applicants submit data online. For example, online applications may not allow candidates to enter a complete description of their background or abilities because the data entry fields may be too narrow or small. Thus, applicants may perceive that the use of online applications will decrease their chances of being selected for jobs. Similarly, research on customer satisfaction suggests that the use of online recruitment may negatively affect applicants' satisfaction levels because these systems lead to impersonal encounters with machines and eliminate personal relationships with recruiters (Gutek, 1995). As a result, some applicants may feel that e-recruiting systems are unfair because these systems do not allow them to fully convey their qualifications for the job and may not permit them to display their interpersonal or communication skills. In view of these arguments, we offer the following guideline for HR professionals:

Guideline 9: Employers should ensure that e-recruiting systems are not adopted as a fad, but are used to enhance applicants' attraction to organizations or increase the number of successful placements made.

The Alignment of e-Recruiting Systems with an Organization's Strategic Goals

It is clear from our review that online recruiting systems are often adopted to increase the efficiency of the recruitment process and decrease the overall costs of recruiting. Although these reasons are laudable, we believe that the principal goal of recruitment should be to attract talented individuals who can help the firm meet its strategic goals. However, despite this important goal there is still a great deal of uncertainty about whether e-recruiting always helps a firm enhance applicants' attraction to organizations. For example, given that online recruiting requires that applicants have technical skills in order to use the systems, some individuals may be more likely to use e-recruiting than others. As a result, if organizations use e-recruiting systems as their primary source for staffing, then these systems will certainly influence the types of individuals who are attracted to and join organizations. Furthermore, these systems will indirectly influence the overall composition of the company's workforce and may decrease the level of diversity.

Therefore, it is essential that HR professionals determine whether online recruiting systems support their overall staffing goals and enable them to hire individuals who can help them meet their firms' strategic objectives. For example, if a firm has an innovation strategy that focuses on developing new information technologies, then e-recruiting systems are likely to identify individuals who have the skills that can help them meet these goals. The logic here is that applicants with highly technical skills may be more likely to use online recruiting than other recruitment sources because computer technology is a key element of their jobs. However, if an organization has adopted a quality enhancement strategy and requires a diverse workforce to help them meet the needs of a diverse customer base, e-recruiting may not always allow them to achieve these goals. One reason for this is that minority applicants or those with diverse backgrounds may be less likely to use online recruiting systems than traditional systems, and, therefore, these systems may not uncover applicants with the characteristics organizations need to be successful. In addition, quality enhancement strategies often require that employees have good interpersonal skills and can work effectively in teams. However, online screening systems (key word systems) may not be capable of assessing these characteristics and, therefore, may not help support the organization's strategic goals. Thus, in order for e-recruiting to be effective it must be accepted and used by applicants who have the types of skills and abilities the organization needs to meet its objectives. In view of these arguments, we briefly review the results of research on the types of individuals who are most likely to accept and use online recruitment systems to search for jobs.

Age, Gender, and Ethnic Differences in Use of Online Recruitment

It has often been argued that there are age, gender, and ethnic differences in reactions to and usage of online recruitment sources (Galanaki, 2002; McManus & Ferguson, 2003; Zusman & Landis, 2002). In particular, research shows that online recruitment is likely to attract young, computer literate, and well-educated individuals (Galanaki, 2002). Furthermore, research has found that employed men are more likely to search for jobs on the Internet than employed women (Kuhn & Skuterud, 2000). Similarly, surveys show that white candidates are more likely to use online recruitment than minority candidates (McManus & Ferguson, 2003). For example, a review of usage rates revealed that only 7 percent of Hispanics use online recruitment, compared to 9 percent of blacks and 16 percent of whites (Kuhn & Skuterud, 2000). Furthermore, some research shows that candidates who are 55 years of age and older are less likely to use the Internet as a source for jobs than younger candidates (McManus & Ferguson, 2003). As a result, research suggests that online systems are more likely to attract young, white male applicants than those who are older, female, or members of ethnic minority groups. Thus, the use of online recruitment may limit the types of applicants who apply for jobs and ultimately affect the heterogeneity of the organization's workforce. Accordingly, online recruitment may not be aligned with all types of business strategies and may be far less useful for firms that focus more on quality enhancement or diversity strategies than other types of firms. Therefore, HR professionals must consider whether online recruitment systems enable them to attract the types of candidates they need to meet their strategic goals.

Interestingly, although we argued above that ethnic minorities may be less likely to use online systems than traditional systems, some recent studies show that African American candidates may be more likely to use e-recruiting than personal recruitment sources (McManus & Ferguson, 2003). In addition, other research shows that racial minorities often react quite favorably to online recruiting and use it to self-select themselves out of the application process (Sinar & Reynolds, 2001). One possible explanation for this is that African Americans may perceive that online recruiting is less likely to be discriminatory than other recruitment sources; however, it may also be the case that online systems signal minorities that they are less likely to be comfortable in the organization. Thus, online recruitment may signal applicants that the organization has a potentially chilly climate because there are few minorities or women employed by the organization. For example, many high-tech firms are dominated by white males, and researchers argue that women and minorities are less likely to pursue jobs in these organizations because they may not feel welcome (Johnson, Stone, Phillips, & Stone-Romero, 2004).

Although research shows that in some cases African Americans are more likely to use online systems than other recruitment sources, research consistently shows that Hispanic Americans are less likely than members of other ethnic groups to use e-recruiting systems. The reasons for the low usage rates among Hispanics are not clear, but some researchers suggest that poverty and lack of access to computers are key sources of the problem (Kuhn & Skuterud, 2000). However, other researchers suggest that the low usage rate among Hispanics may be much more complex and argue that cultural values or low computer self-efficacy levels may affect Hispanics' acceptance of these systems (Johnson, Stone, Phillips, & Stone-Romero, 2004). In support of this argument, some recent research revealed that individuals from other cultures (for example, the Chinese) are often less satisfied with web portals developed in the United States and find them harder to use than do individuals from the American culture (Fang & Pei-Luen, 2003). This research indicated that individuals from China often have different cognitive styles and thought processes, and websites developed in the United States may not fit the Chinese style or be useful for individuals from that culture. Given these arguments, we offer the following guidelines for HR professionals:

Guideline 10: Organizations should ensure that e-recruiting systems are aligned with the strategic goals of the firm and allow them to attract the types of individuals who can help them meet their strategic objectives.

Guideline 11: Organizations should regularly collect feedback from job applicants about the types of implicit or explicit messages that are conveyed about the climate of the organization on the company's website.

Guideline 12: Organizations should develop e-recruiting systems that are culturally sensitive and include special features (for example, use of multiple languages, alternative system designs) for attracting applicants from diverse cultural backgrounds.

Educational, Skill Level, and Personality Differences in Use of Online Recruiting

Apart from age, gender, and ethnic differences in the use of online recruitment, applicants' educational background and personality characteristics may also affect their use of these systems. For instance, research by McManus & Ferguson (2003) revealed that the Internet is more likely to attract candidates with high levels of computer skills and four-year degrees than traditional recruitment sources. Furthermore, research shows that individuals with high levels of computer anxiety or low levels of computer self-efficacy may be less likely to use computers than others (Marakas, Yi, & Johnson, 1998). However, some other research shows that applicants who are not especially computer savvy may still be able to find jobs on the Internet (Van Rooy, Alonso, & Fairchild, 2003).

In summary, we have argued that in order for online recruitment to be effective, it should be aligned with the goals of the organization and attract individuals with the requisite characteristics needed by the organization to meet its strategic objectives. Despite these arguments, it appears that online recruiting may not reach all job applicants, especially those who are older, women, ethnic minorities, and individuals who have low levels of education or computer self-efficacy. As a consequence, the use of e-recruiting may affect the overall composition and heterogeneity of the workforce. Therefore, we offer the following guideline for HR professionals concerned with developing and implementing e-recruiting systems:

Guideline 13: Organizations should develop simple e-recruiting systems that can easily be used by individuals with all educational levels and that are sensitive to those who have high levels of computer anxiety or low levels of computer self-efficacy.

Some Potentially Dysfunctional Consequences

Although we have highlighted a number of benefits of using e-recruiting throughout this chapter, we believe that such systems may also produce some unintended or dysfunctional consequences for organizations and job applicants. Therefore, we consider two of these unintended consequences (potential for adverse impact and invasion of privacy) in the sections that follow.

Potential for Adverse Impact

Despite the fact that e-recruiting is thought to have a number of advantages for organizations, it has been argued that these systems may have an adverse impact on members of several ethnic minority groups (for example, African Americans, Hispanic Americans,

Native Americans) (Hogler, Henle, & Bemus, 2001; Stone, Stone-Romero, & Lukaszewski, 2003). The basis for this argument is that there is a "racial or digital divide" in access to and use of computers, and Anglo Americans are more likely to own and use computers than are African Americans or other ethnic minorities. For example, research shows that 33 percent of African American households in the United States own computers; and 24 percent have access to the Internet (U.S. Bureau of Census, 2001). In contrast, 56 percent of Anglo American households have computers and more than 46 percent have Internet access (U.S. Bureau of Census, 2001). As a result, African Americans may have fewer opportunities to gain access to jobs online than majority group members. In addition, some evidence shows that women are less likely to use computers than men (Johnson, Stone, Phillips, & Stone-Romero, 2004).

In addition, those applicants who come from low socioeconomic status backgrounds (that is, those in rural areas, inner cities, or on Native American reservations) often have less access to computers than those who are more economically advantaged (Stone, Stone-Romero, & Lukaszewski, 2003). Furthermore, some reports indicate that there are fewer computers in schools or libraries that serve a large percentage of ethnic minorities as compared to those in primarily white areas (Hogler, Henle, & Bemus, 2001). Also, some research shows that women have less experience with computers, have lower levels of computer self-efficacy, and are less likely to use computers than are men (Ogletree & Williams, 1990). As a result, the use of e-recruiting systems may place some individuals at a considerable disadvantage in the job market and may have an adverse impact on women and members of some protected groups. Thus, organizations that use *only* online recruiting may be subject to charges of unfair discrimination in the recruiting process. Consequently, organizations should ensure that online recruitment systems do not have a disproportionately negative impact on minority group members. Thus, we offer the following guideline for HR practitioners:

Guideline 14: Organizations should recognize that online recruitment systems may have an adverse impact on members of some protected groups and regularly assess the degree to which these systems are in compliance with civil rights laws.

Although the use of online recruiting may have the potential for adverse impact for members of some minority groups, analysts have argued that e-recruiting may actually increase the number of applications organizations receive from people with disabilities (Stone & Williams, 1997). One reason for this is that applicants with disabilities may find it much easier to apply for jobs online than in person. In addition, online systems may make it much easier for organizations to reach applicants with disabilities and help remove potential barriers that disabled individuals might experience in the application process (Employers' Forum on Disabilities, 2003). For example, employers can use technology to facilitate the application process by (a) making websites more accessible (for example, larger font sizes), (b) enhancing applicants' abilities to communicate with organizations, (c) conveying employment policies and procedures relevant to people with disabilities, and (d) modifying assessment methods to accommodate people with disabilities (Employers' Forum on Disabilities, 2003). In view of the potential advantages of using e-recruiting to attract candidates with disabilities, we offer the following guideline for employers:

Guideline 15: Organizations should design e-recruiting systems so that they attract and accommodate the needs of ethnic minorities and individuals with disabilities.

Potential to Invade Privacy

Another potentially dysfunctional consequence of using e-recruiting is that applicants may perceive that these systems have the potential to invade their personal privacy (Stone, Stone-Romero, & Lukaszewski, 2003). In fact, previous research has shown that there is growing concern among job applicants about using online application systems (Linowes, 1989; Pillar, 1993; Stone & Stone, 1990). One explanation for this is that data in computerized systems can easily be merged or networked with other systems, and individuals can be permanently stigmatized in the process. For example, when an applicant applies for a job online, the data from the résumé can be used to gather additional data about his or her credit, lifestyle, or medical history. As a result, an applicant who had a credit problem very early in life may have difficulty purging various computerized systems of the negative information. Thus, data that have no bearing on the person's current job performance may prevent the individual from being hired by organizations.

Furthermore, we believe that perceptions of invasion of privacy are important because they affect applicants' attraction to organizations and willingness to use online systems to apply for jobs (Harris, Van Hoye, & Lievens, 2003; Stone & Stone-Romero, 1998). In addition, applicants' perceptions of invasion of privacy may negatively affect their test performance and increase the likelihood they will take legal action against the organization (Harris, Van Hoye, & Lievens, 2003). Therefore, three key privacy issues are considered below: (a) unauthorized access to data, (b) unauthorized disclosure of data, and (c) lack of privacy protection policies.

Unauthorized Access to Data

Job applicants are often concerned about the use of e-recruiting systems because these systems permit others inside or outside of the organization to gain access to their personal information (for example, Social Security number, address, personality data, credit reports, medical data). For example, in 2002 a person posing as a recruiter downloaded 2,400 résumés from a job site used by biotechnical professionals and developed his own job board with the data (Brotherton, 2004). Not surprisingly, applicants were upset when they learned that their information had been stolen and used for unauthorized purposes. In response, the owners of the original job site took legal action against the thief. Similarly, reports indicate that over 80,000 individuals experience identity theft per year in the United States, and this number is expected to rise with the increased use of Internet-based business transactions (Dixon, 2003). As a result, many applicants fear that if their personal data or Social Security numbers are accessed by others, they are likely to experience a number of negative outcomes (such as denial of a job, loss of money or credit). Given these concerns, research shows that applicants in the United States are often reluctant to submit their applications online because they worry that their personal data will fall into the wrong hands (Harris, Van Hoye, & Lievens, 2003).

Unauthorized Disclosure of Data

Apart from unauthorized access to data, applicants are also concerned that personal data collected and stored in online systems can be released to others without their approval (Stone, Stone-Romero, & Lukaszewski, 2003). In fact, analysts have argued that applicant data often have a market value; and some firms sell these data to marketing firms or spammers (Dixon, 2003). For example, one report indicated that Hotresumes.com recently sold over 4,900 résumés and email addresses to other companies for 33 cents each (Dixon, 2003). Furthermore, previous research (Linowes, 1989) revealed that 70 percent of organizations regularly disclose employment data to creditors, 47 percent release it to landlords, and 19 percent disseminate it to charitable organizations. In addition, 60 percent of employers do not inform applicants or employees when their data are disclosed to others (Society for Human Resources Management and West Group, 2000). Thus, the use of online recruiting systems may allow organizations to disseminate or sell personal data without applicants' knowledge. At present, there are no legal restrictions in the United States that prevent the disclosure of these data, leaving some applicants reluctant to use online recruiting systems.

Lack of Privacy Policies

Despite the widespread use of online recruiting systems and growing concerns about privacy, many companies have not established policies that protect the privacy of job applicants or employees (Linowes, 1989). Indeed, only 10 percent have policies that conform to federal standards for fair information practices (Dixon, 2003). However, results of recent surveys revealed that most Americans (76 percent) are concerned about the use and dissemination of personal information via computerized networks and that 62 percent want increased legislation that protects their personal privacy (Pew Internet & American Life, 2001). Nevertheless, there are currently no federal restrictions on the collection, storage, or release of employment data by private-sector organizations.

Although there are no legal restrictions on privacy in the United States, the European Union passed legislation in 1998 that restricts the transmission and unauthorized disclosure of employment data. As a result, some recent research shows that applicants in European countries (Belgium, for example) may be much less reluctant to apply for jobs online than are U.S. applicants (Harris, Van Hoye, & Lievens, 2003). Thus, U.S. employers may want to develop privacy policies and practices that decrease applicants' concerns about privacy and reluctance to submit online applications.

Given the growing concerns about privacy and its potential impact on applicants' attraction to organizations and use of online recruiting systems, we offer the following guideline for HR professionals:

Guideline 16: Organizations should recognize that online recruitment systems have the potential to invade applicants' privacy, and therefore should develop privacy protection policies that (a) restrict access to data, (b) restrict disclosure of data, and (c) ensure that only job-relevant data are collected for decision-making purposes.

Conclusion

Given the increased use of e-recruiting systems in organizations, in this chapter we considered the impact of online recruiting systems on applicants' attraction to organizations and reviewed the existing research on the effectiveness of these systems. In addition, we offered a number of research-based guidelines that may help HR professionals enhance the acceptance of e-recruiting systems, ensure they are ethical, and increase the extent to which they support the firm's strategic goals. It merits noting we provide a summary of our guidelines in Exhibit 2.1. It is clear from our review that HR professionals should be actively involved in decisions regarding the purchase and development of e-recruiting systems so that these systems will meet their intended objectives.

Exhibit 2.1. Guidelines for
Developing e-Recruiting Systems.

Guideline 1: Organizations that are well-known or have prominent reputations may benefit more from online recruiting than those that are not well-known.

Guideline 2: Organizations should use e-recruiting as one source of applicants, but should not use it as the only source for recruiting applicants.

Guideline 3: Organizations should capitalize on the strengths of e-recruiting and use it when large numbers of candidates are needed or when they are searching for individuals in high-level jobs requiring fairly high-education levels. In addition, they should use e-recruiting to target candidates in specific labor markets, including those in high technology jobs and students who are searching for part-time employment or full-time jobs right out of college.

Guideline 4: Organizations should recognize that e-recruiting may not be the preferred source for most job applicants and may not always reach the types of applicants that can help them meet their strategic goals. Thus, organizations should be aware that e-recruiting may not attract the most qualified job applicants, may not be particularly effective for reaching minority candidates, and may actually be more attractive to individuals with unfavorable rather than favorable backgrounds (those who switch jobs frequently).

Guideline 5: Organizations should ensure that their websites are designed to be easy to use, simple to navigate, and focus on attracting candidates rather than screening them for jobs.

Guideline 6: Organizations should develop online screening systems based on job analyses and ensure that the inferences made from these systems are reliable and valid.

Guideline 7: Organizations should develop e-recruiting systems that provide applicants with information about the unique characteristics of the organization and ensure they are given a realistic preview of the firm.

Guideline 8: Organizations should use websites to promote values that will be attractive to most new employees rather than just select those that fit with the traditional culture.

Exhibit 2.1. Guidelines for
Developing e-Recruiting Systems, Cont'd.

Guideline 9: Employers should ensure that e-recruiting systems are not adopted as a fad, but are used to enhance applicants' attraction to organizations and increase the number of successful placements made.

Guideline 10: Organizations should ensure that e-recruiting systems are aligned with the strategic goals of the firm and allow them to attract the types of individuals who can help them meet their strategic objectives.

Guideline 11: Organizations should regularly collect feedback from job applicants about the types of implicit or explicit messages that are conveyed about the climate of the organization on the company's website.

Guideline 12: Organizations should develop e-recruiting systems that are culturally sensitive and include special features (for example, use of multiple languages, alternative system designs) for attracting applicants from diverse cultural backgrounds.

Guideline 13: Organizations should develop simple e-recruiting systems that can easily be used by individuals with all educational levels and that are sensitive to those who have high levels of computer anxiety or low levels of computer self-efficacy.

Guideline 14: Organizations should recognize that online recruitment systems may have an adverse impact on members of some protected groups and regularly assess the degree to which these systems are in compliance with civil rights legislation.

Guideline 15: Organizations should design e-recruiting systems so that they attract and accommodate the needs of ethnic minorities and individuals with disabilities (for example, larger font sizes, easier communication, firm disability and accommodation policies, assessment policies).

Guideline 16: Organizations should recognize that online recruitment systems have the potential to invade applicants' privacy, and therefore should develop privacy protection policies that (a) restrict access to data, (b) restrict disclosure of data, and (c) ensure that only job-relevant data are collected for decision-making purposes.

It is also evident from our review that the proliferation of e-recruiting systems is likely to accelerate as organizations face increasing pressures to attract and retain talented employees in a highly competitive marketplace. We hope that our chapter provided important information that can help HR professionals design and develop systems that meet the needs not only of the organization, but of job applicants as well. Furthermore, we hope that our chapter provides a step forward in nurturing the linkage between HR research and practice in the "Brave New World of eHR."

References

Bloom, N. (2001). In search of intelligent self-service. *International Human Resources Information Management Journal, 5,* 53–61.

Brotherton, P. (2004). Protect applicant privacy to be safe. Available at www.shrm.org/hrtx/library_published/nonIC/CMS_006617.asp. [Retrieved June 30, 2004]

Cappelli, P. (2001). Making the most of on-line recruiting. *Harvard Business Review, 79,* 139–146.

Cardy, R. L., & Miller, J. S. (2003) Technology: Implications for HRM. In D. L. Stone (Ed.), *Advances in human performance and cognitive engineering research* (pp. 99–118). Greenwich, CT: JAI Press.

Cascio, W. F. (1998). *Managing human resources: Productivity, quality of work life, & profits* (5th ed.) New York: Irwin, McGraw-Hill.

Cedar. (2002). *Cedar 2002 human resources self services/portal survey.* Available at www.cedar.com/800/index.asp?lang=usa. [Retrieved June 2002]

Cedar. (2003). *Cedar 2003 human resources self services/portal survey.* Available at www.cedar.com/800/index.asp?lang=usa. [Retrieved January 2004]

Chapman, D. S., & Webster, J. (2003). The use of technologies in the recruiting, screening, and selection processes for job candidates. *International Journal of Selection and Assessment, 11,* 113–120.

Cober, R. T., Brown, D. J., Blumental, A. J., Doverspike, D., & Levy, P. (2000). The quest for the qualified job surfer: It's time the public sector catches the wave. *Public Personnel Management, 29(4),* 479–494.

Cober, R. T., Brown, D. J., Levy, P. E., Keeping, L. M., & Cober, A. L. (2003). Organizational websites: Website content and style as determinants of organizational attraction. *International Journal of Selection and Assessment, 11,* 158–169.

Dineen, B. R., Ash, S. R., & Noe, R. A. (2002). A web of applicant attraction: Person-organization fit in the context of web-based recruitment. *Journal of Applied Psychology, 87,* 723–734.

Dixon, P. (2003) *Resume database nightmare: Job seeker privacy at risk.* Available at www.privacyroghts.org. [Retrieved June 30, 2004]

Employers' Forum on Disability (2003). *Making e-recruitment barrier-free for people with disabilities.* Available at www.employers-forum.co.uk/ www/csr/er/. [Retrieved June 30, 2004]

Fang, X., & Pei-Luen, P. R. (2003). Culture differences in design of portal sites. *Ergonomics, 46,* 242–254.

Galanaki, E. (2002). The decision to recruit online: A descriptive study. *Career Development International,* pp. 243–251.

Gutek, B. A. (1995). *The dynamics of service: Reflections on the changing nature of customer/provider interactions.* San Francisco: Jossey-Bass.

Harris, M. M., Van Hoye, G., & Lievens, F. (2003). Privacy and attitudes toward internet-based selection systems: A cross-cultural comparison. *International Journal of Selection and Assessment, 11,* 230–236.

Hogler, R., Henle, C., & Bemus, C. (2001). *Internet recruiting and employment discrimination: A legal perspective.* Available at www.biz.colostate.edu/ faculty/rayh/netantrev.html. [Retrieved February 25, 2001]

Jattuso, J. I., & Sinar, E. F. (2003). Source effect in internet-based screening procedures. *International Journal of Selection and Assessment, 11,* 137–140.

Johnson, R., Stone, D. L., Phillips, T. N., & Stone-Romero, E. F. (2004). *African-American and Anglo-Americans' beliefs, attitudes, and intentions to pursue careers in information technology.* Unpublished manuscript, University of Central Florida, Orlando.

Jones, J. W., & Dages, K. D. (2003). Technology trends in staffing and assessment: A practice note. *International Journal of Selection and Assessment, 11,* 247–52.

Kuhn, P., & Skuterud, M. (2000). Job search methods: Internet versus traditional. *Monthly Labor Review, 123,* 3–11.

Linowes, D. F. (1989). *Privacy in America: Is your private life in the public eye?* Urbana: University of Illinois Press.

Marakas, G., Yi, M., & Johnson, R. (1998). The multilevel and multifaced character of computer self-efficacy: Toward clarification of the construct and an integrative framework for research. *Information Systems Research, 9,* 126–163.

McCourt-Mooney, M. (2000). Internet briefing: Recruitment and selection—R&D using the Internet—Part III. *Journal of Managerial Psychology, 15,* 737–740.

McManus, M. A., & Ferguson, M. W. (2003). Biodata, personality, and demographic differences of recruits from threes sources. *International Journal of Selection and Assessment, 11,* 175–183.

Mohamed, A. A., Orife, J. N., & Wibowo, K. (2002). The legality of key word search as a personnel selection tool. *Employee Relations, 24,* 516–522.

Ogletree, S. M., & Williams, S. W. (1990). Sex and sex-typing effects on computer attitudes and aptitude. *Sex Roles, 23,* 703–712.

Pew Internet & American Life Project, (2001). *Fear on online crime.* Available at www.pewinternet.org/PPF/r/32/report_display.asp. [Retrieved June 1, 2004]

Pillar, C. (1993). Privacy in peril. *MacWorld, 10,* 124–130.

Rozelle, A. L., & Landis, R. S. (2002). An examination of the relationship between use of the internet as a recruitment source and student attitudes. *Computers in Human Behavior, 18,* 593–604.

Rynes, S. L. (1991). Recruitment, job choice, and post-hire consequences: A call for new research directions. In M. Dunnette & L. Hough (Eds.), *Handbook of industrial and organizational psychology* (2nd ed., pp. 399–444). Palo Alto, CA: Consulting Psychologists Press.

Scheu, C., Ryan, A. M., & Nona, F. (1999). *Company web-sites as a recruiting mechanism: What influences applicant impressions?* Paper presented at the 14th Annual Conference of the Society of Industrial and Organizational Psychology, Atlanta, Georgia.

Sheridan, J. E. (1992). Organizational culture and employee retention. *Academy of Management Journal, 35,* 1036–1056.

Sinar, E. F., Paquet, S. L., & Reynolds, D. H. (2003). Nothing but net? Corporate image and web-based testing. *International Journal of Selection and Assessment, 11,* 150–157.

Sinar, E. F., & Reynolds, D. H. (2001). *Candidate reactions to internet-based selection techniques.* In F. L. Oswald (Chair), *Computers = Good? How test-user and test-taker perceptions affect technology-based employment testing.* Symposium conducted at the annual meeting of the Society of Industrial and Organizational Psychology, San Diego, California.

Society for Human Resources Management (SHRM) and West Group (2000). *Workplace privacy survey.* Available at www.shrm.org/surveys. [Retrieved May 3, 2004]

Stone, D. L., & Stone-Romero, E. F. (1998). A multiple stakeholder model of privacy organizations. In M. Schminke (Ed.), *Managerial ethics: Morally managing people and processes* (pp. 35–59). Mahwah, NJ: Lawrence Erlbaum.

Stone, D. L., Stone-Romero, E. F., & Lukaszewski K. (2003). The functional and dysfunctional consequences of human resource information technology for organizations and their employees. In D. L. Stone (Ed.), *Advances in human performance and cognitive engineering research* (pp. 37–68). Greenwich, CT: JAI Press.

Stone, D. L., & Williams, K. J. (1997). The impact of ADA on the selection process: Applicant and organizational issues. *Human Resources Management Review, 7(2),* 203–231.

Stone, E. F., & Stone, D. L. (1990). Privacy in organizations: Theoretical issues, research findings, and protection mechanisms. In K. Rowland & G. R. Ferris (Eds.), *Research in personnel/human resources management* (pp. 349–471). Greenwich, CT: JAI Press.

Ulrich, D. (2001). From e-business to eHR. *International Human Resources Information Management Journal, 5,* 90–97.

U.S. Bureau of Census (2001). *Home computers and internet use in the United States.* Available at www.usbureauofcensus.gov. [Retrieved August 10, 2003]

Van Rooy, D. L., Alonso, A., & Fairchild, Z. (2003). In with the new, out with the old: Has the technological revolution eliminated the traditional job search process? *International Journal of Selection and Assessment, 11,* 170–174.

Williamson, I. O., Lepak, D. P., & King, J. (2003). The effect of company recruitment website orientation on individuals' perceptions of organizational attractiveness. *Journal of Vocational Behavior, 63,* 242–263.

Zusman, R. R., & Landis, R. S. (2002). Applicant preferences for web-based versus traditional job postings. *Computer in Human Behavior, 18,* 285–296.

CHAPTER 3

e-Selection

Jerard F. Kehoe
David N. Dickter
Daniel P. Russell
Joshua M. Sacco

The purpose of this chapter is to describe issues and guidelines that will help organizations design, implement, and sustain e-enabled employment selection processes and systems. e-Enabled employment selection is only part of the potential scope of e-enabled HR. Indeed, perhaps the greatest promise of eHR is the complete integration of all HR systems and processes based on common HR data and information and on interdependent tools and processes. For example, in the broadest sense, fully e-enabled HR could provide the data-gathering tools, analysis capabilities, and decision support resources for business managers to recruit, hire, pay, promote, terminate, assign, develop, appraise, and reward employees in ways that fully engage them in managing their own outcomes, maximize the contribution of each employee, and directly support the business strategy.

Organization Issues

The manner in which organizations will implement e-enabled selection programs will depend on whether these programs are being implemented as part of a broad e-enablement of HR processes and systems or are being implemented independent of other

HR processes and systems. Both are possible. Indeed, it is even possible that specific e-enabled assessment applications may be implemented independent of each other. For example, one large company e-enabled its employment testing processes at the same time that related processes such as internal staffing processes and employee competency management systems were also being e-enabled. Rather than fully integrate all of these processes, the testing processes for external and internal candidates were integrated into a single e-enabled testing process, but the competency assessment processes were not integrated into the e-enabled employment assessment processes largely because these processes were "owned" by different organizations and a full integration would have required a substantial redesign of either the employment or the competency assessment processes, which the organization was not ready to do.

In any case, the scope of the e-enablement will determine the key strategic issues and policy decisions that should be made along the way. The primary purpose of this section is to describe the key strategic and policy issues for organizations that are associated with e-enabled assessment applications. Of course, many of these strategic and policy issues relating to selection also apply more generally to other HR processes and systems.

The strategic issues relating to e-enabled selection relate to the purposes of the e-enablement and the guiding principles that will govern the way the e-enabled selection processes and systems are designed and used.

Purposes

Generally, the fundamental purposes for e-enabling selection processes are the same as for all other HR e-enablement: to minimize cost and to maximize the utilization of the organization's human capital. e-Enabled selection processes that do not reduce costs or do not improve utilization of the workforce are not likely to be implemented and, if implemented, are not likely to be sustained. In addition to these two fundamental purposes, a third purpose—sustainability—should also be acknowledged and managed.

Cost Reduction

In the design and planning of the e-enabled processes and systems, the organization should build into the applicable database and management tools the capability to measure costs at the transaction level. To manage costs, the organization should view tracking and management systems as part of the e-enabled process. For example, if an organization is implementing an e-enabled employment system that includes 800-number scheduling, web-based testing, and face-to-face interviewing and job offering, part of the effort to design that system should be to define those elements of the end-to-end process that will have identifiable costs associated with them and develop reporting capabilities to routinely aggregate those costs for monitoring purposes. In the case of employment systems, the major cost factors are shown in Exhibit 3.1.

Maximum Utilization of Human Capital

As with cost, managing the purpose of maximizing the utilization of human capital requires that measures be designed into the e-enabled selection system. This may not be easy. In general two types of measures are needed—one that measures the "capital" represented by each person who goes through the process and another that measures the extent to which the process results in decisions that maximize the utilization of that "capital." Consider the example of an e-enabled employment testing process. The

Exhibit 3.1. Cost Drivers for e-Enabled Selection.

- Costs of sourcing candidates into the employment process
- Costs of administering the individual screening events
- Loss rates between events in the whole process (Key loss factors include the percentage of candidates who decline job offers, the percentage of candidates who are screened out by test events, and the percentage of candidates who fail to show up for scheduled testing events)
- Administrative costs associated with elements of the process that may not be e-enabled, such as interviewing, offer negotiation, drug testing, background checking, and the like

measure of "capital" for each person going through the process includes the set of test scores, interview ratings, résumé quality indices, background check results, drug test results, and any other quantifiable evaluation of the skills, experiences, abilities, or other attributes the candidate brings to the organization. Metrics of the extent to which the "capital" is utilized may include a variety of measures, as described in Exhibit 3.2.

A frequent question in this matter of utilization measurement is whether outcome measures such as turnover rates and supervisor satisfaction with new hires should be included. On the one hand, such measures can be direct manifestations of the extent to which the e-enabled employment process is delivering employees who satisfy organization requirements. On the other hand, such measures are not under the direct control of the e-enabled employment process. Our experience has taught us that, first, such measures are valuable to collect because of their close link to organization needs, and, second, if such measures are collected then it is all the more important to collect the measures of "capital" described above so that the organization may analyze the link between the desired outcomes that the employment process does not control and the measures of "capital" that the employment process does control.

The experience of one company that e-enabled its employment selection process may be instructive. Prior to e-enablement,

---

Exhibit 3.2. Examples of Measures of Human Capital Utilization.

- Ratio or difference between average test scores for selected candidates to average test scores for all candidates
- Percentage of candidates who satisfy minimum requirements such as for drug tests or background checks
- Percentage of candidates who satisfy employment requirements as a function of recruiting source
- Retention rates, post-hire
- Percentage of candidates who exceed agreed-on standards of "high capability" even if that standard is higher than the minimum employment requirements
- New hire performance management results

employment process metrics such as time-to-fill and cost-per-hire measures were routinely gathered and reported to the client organizations as client-oriented measures of the employment transaction management process. In contrast, measures of applicant quality, that is, "capital," such as ability test scores, interview scores, and the like were not routinely reported to the clients. Rather, the industrial/organizational psychologists responsible for developing and validating the selection procedures regularly monitored applicants' skill and ability scores and incorporated them into validation documents as needed. In effect, the time and cost of employment testing was viewed as a process to be managed by attending to metrics, but the outcomes of the testing processes—the measures of applicant capital—were not viewed as a transaction process to be managed by attending to regular metrics. The introduction of vendor-provided e-enabled testing gradually began to change that mindset, in part to provide test outcome as one measure of the accuracy of the vendor's scoring and reporting processes.

Sustainability

Unlike cost reduction and human capital utilization, sustainability is not, itself, a valued business end. But because sustainability is necessary to ensure the ongoing business results, it is wise to consider sustainability a purpose of the e-enablement design and planning. Sustainability refers to the organization's willingness and ability not only to maintain the e-enabled system but to progressively evolve the system to satisfy changing requirements and capitalize on improvements in technology and the science of selection. Our experience has been that at least five major elements are important for the progressive sustainability of e-enabled assessment processes (see Exhibit 3.3).

Exhibit 3.3. Key Elements That Enable Sustainability.

- Clear ownership
- Funding strategy
- Business contribution
- User satisfaction
- Professional support

Of these five elements, ownership, funding, and contribution are requirements for the sustainability of virtually any business process. *Ownership* refers to the business owner of the e-enabled selection process. Typically, ownership is defined by budget and authority, although they do not necessarily reside in the same person or role. *Funding* strategy refers to the understood mechanism by which the budget is funded that pays for the process and system. Business *contribution* refers to the level of understanding among all business stakeholders of the value of the e-enabled selection strategy to the business. In addition to these three factors, user satisfaction and professional support are uniquely important to sustain e-enabled selection processes. e-Enabled selection generally has three categories of users: the people—external candidates and internal employees—who are assessed by the e-enabled system; the employees who use the system to make business decisions; and the HR specialists who use the system to execute their business function. While user satisfaction is determined in part by ease of use, accessibility, and the capacity to deliver the needed transaction, user satisfaction with selection processes is also frequently a function of the decision outcome for the user, for example, whether the applicant passed the employment screening or not. One implication of this reality is that organizations that are building user satisfaction measures into the e-enabled system should look for opportunities to request user satisfaction feedback before the users are faced with the ultimate outcome of the decisions resulting from their use of the system. In addition, assessment systems can be designed to incorporate features known to influence user satisfaction such as clear feedback that is relevant to the user's need, information about how the system works, and the ability to practice or train on the system.

The importance of professional support derives from the fact that selection processes are the domain of professional expertise in human skills and abilities, psychometrics, job performance, and HR systems design and, in employment-affecting applications, are regulated by anti-discrimination legislation that depends on professional standards for a demonstration of job relevance and business necessity. It is this professional expertise that largely determines whether the assessment system will accomplish the second purpose of human capital maximization and whether legal requirements will be satisfied.

Guiding Principles

The organization's purpose for e-enabled assessment addresses the question of *why* the organization chooses to support such an HR practice. Guiding principles or policies, on the other hand, reflect *how* the organization wants to do business in this domain of HR processes. These guiding principles are largely determined by the organization's overall culture and HR strategy. Also, these guiding principles are much more specific to the selection application than are the purposes. These principles will inform not only the design of the e-enabled system and processes but will also inform the policies that will be established to govern the organization's behavior.

Each organization that implements e-enabled assessment systems and processes will need to develop guiding principles regarding several issues relating to the management of human resources based on assessment data. In most organizations, these issues include the following:

1. Risk management relating to employment discrimination;
2. Buy versus build and the roles of internal HR IT and third-party providers;
3. HR expertise versus automaticity in the e-enabled assessment process;
4. Whose functions the system will be designed to support;
5. Ownership;
6. The integration of e-enabled assessment with other HR systems and processes; and
7. "Free market" versus "regulated" processes.

Risk Management

The e-enablement of personnel selection processes is likely to have certain unique implications for managing the risk associated with employment discrimination laws. Prior to e-enablement, most manually delivered selection processes involve the intervention of functional HR specialists, such as employment office recruiters, interviewers and test administrators, and business unit HR staff who would typically have accountability for minimizing risk by monitoring indicators of risk such as group differences in selection or promotion rates and by administering assessment procedures according to prescribed rules and practices. To the extent that e-enablement of selection and employment allows employees and managers to provide these services for themselves and reduces the roles of HR specialists, the organization will need to determine how the design of the process will continue to minimize risk. Typically, the choice is between increased reliance on process rules and increased training and broader responsibility among users who may not be functional specialists. Increased reliance on process rules may take the form of specific automatic system triggers that are built into the process either to stop or to warn users when a risky situation is evident. For example, an e-enabled employment process could monitor the ratios of majority and minority candidates who are receiving job offers or who are satisfying skill requirements and trigger a warning to a process owner when the ratios indicate an undesirable discrepancy between groups. Similarly, system rules could prevent job offers from being processed until a vacancy had been posted for a minimum amount of time. In contrast, following a "tools, not rules" guiding principle, an organization could design systems that attempt to maximize the discretion and capability of managers to gather and use assessment information with as few rules as possible. In this case, the system could be designed to provide users with risk levels for various possible decisions. For example, an employment system could be designed to provide skill and group membership information about the available group of candidates to inform the manager as much as possible about the sources of risk for any particular hiring decision. Our experience has been that the most effective method for minimizing risk in large complex organizations with highly diffused accountability across units is to build rules and process boundaries into the system and capitalize on automatic rule checking as much as possible. In smaller organizations with strong cultures of individual accountability, such automatic checks may not be necessary if users are adequately trained in managing the risk factors in employment.

An additional concern for e-employment systems is the organization's legal accountability for electronically sourced résumés. The question is whether persons who merely submit résumés that are "seen" by an employer must be regarded as applicants in a regulatory sense. If yes, then an employer may have an obligation to make a good faith effort to gather and document race, ethnicity, and gender information for potentially tens of thousands of such applicants. This is not a new obligation, but the potential of e-employment to greatly increase the number of applicants may add a considerable administrative burden and may also substantially increase potential class sizes in possible class action lawsuits relating to employment discrimination. As of this chapter's publication date, there is no firm answer to the question. However, a federal interagency task force consisting of the Department of Justice, the Department of Labor's Office of Federal Contract Compliance Programs (OFCCP), the Equal Employment Opportunity Commission (EEOC), and the Office of Personnel Management issued on March 4, 2004, proposed new guidance in the *Federal Register* (69 Fed. Reg. 10152). Essentially, the proposal was that individuals sourced via Internet-based processes should be considered "applicants" if three criteria are met. First, "the employer has acted to fill a particular position"; second, "the individual has followed the employer's standard procedures for submitting applications"; and, third, "the individual has indicated an interest in the position." While these proposed criteria provide some clarification, they leave unaddressed the issue of whether the individual must also possess the basic qualifications for the position in order to be considered an applicant. For example, must an employer treat an individual with no technical training or experience as an applicant for a technical position if the three suggested criteria are satisfied? Shortly after this task force issued its proposed guidance, the OFCCP, in the *Federal Register* on March 29, 2004, proposed conforming regulations that are similar but also added the criterion that the individual possess the "advertised, basic qualifications" for the position in question. After these agencies gather comments about their proposed guidance and regulations, they may choose to make modifications. The outcome will significantly impact the design of e-enabled employment processes to ensure compliance with the new guidance and regulations.

Currently, it is our experience that some organizations (using the EEOC's previous guidance that an applicant is one who expresses an interest in working for the employer) and individuals whose résumés the organization has received are inviting voluntary submission of race/ethnicity and gender information. In the cases we are aware of, the invitation is made either by postcard or email.

Other organizations are operating based on more restrictive applicant definitions that in some cases include the requirements that the job seeker possess the basic qualifications for the job and that the organization is acting to fill vacancies for which the job seeker has expressed an interest. This latter approach typically defines "basically qualified" as surviving some form of résumé-sorting process designed to identify those candidates who have the training, education, work experience, degrees, licenses, certificates, or other documented achievements required by the job. In sum, in early 2004 the jury is out, as it were, on this question.

Buy Versus Build

One of the most difficult strategic decisions an organization may have to make is whether to buy or build and, if buy, how to integrate the roles of the third-party provider(s) with the existing HR IT group. This may be a difficult decision if not primarily for the cost implications, for the role implications. In some ways, the decision to buy is becoming increasingly attractive as vendors are developing more specialized and flexible systems for e-enabled assessment applications as well as for broader e-enabled HR management. For common HR processes, internal HR IT groups are simply less and less able to compete with vendors who develop standardized, yet flexible, tools. As a result, the dynamics of this decision are becoming less about cost and more about roles. At the far end of the spectrum is the increasingly popular outsourcing approach in which the organization not only adopts a vendor's system but also moves functional specialists from the business to the vendor to provide the support for the business's use of that system. A hybrid approach is to adopt a vendor's systems, retain functional specialists in the business, and integrate the ongoing management of the vendor into the role of the specialist. At the other end of the spectrum, the business acquires the vendor's system, tailors it to its specific requirements, and absorbs management responsibility for the system.

In the case of e-enabled selection systems, given the growing range of specialized and flexible products now on the market, it is increasingly likely that organizations will choose to buy and to rely on an ongoing relationship with the vendor to support the organization's use of the system.

Expertise Versus Automaticity

Similar to the buy versus build issue, organizations are also likely to be faced with the fundamental question of how much HR expertise to build into the e-enabled system. In other words, does e-enablement provide an opportunity to reduce the number of people who provide HR expertise by, in effect, building that expertise into the system? This is likely to be a very relevant question for the e-enablement of assessment processes. Employment processes, in particular, tend to be staffed by HR functional specialists, at least in medium to large organizations. To e-enable an entire employment process or even just the selection assessment component raises the prospect of replacing HR specialists with systems. Further, this issue is not only about the replacement of HR specialists who support the delivery of employment transactions such as test administrators, but it is also about the possible replacement of HR generalists who guide employees and managers in deciding how and when to use an organization's employment process.

For example, if an organization sought to maximize employee self-service by the design of an e-enabled employment system, it is likely the organization would design into the system the information necessary for any employee to use the system to apply for a job, be assessed, post a job vacancy, review available candidates, choose and hire candidates, and initiate the on-boarding process—all with minimal HR expert support. The fundamental decision is what type and level of HR expertise is best exported into e-enabled processes.

From the standpoint of long-term success, the best answer is probably not to move as much expertise into the system as is technically possible. In professional disciplines such as HR, many specialists typically have both expertise and accountability and the decisions, advice, and counsel that represent accountability are necessarily rooted in the specialized expertise. Effective accountability requires expertise. Separating expertise from accountability by building expertise into the system is likely to weaken the ability of remaining HR staff to be effectively accountable. A principle that organizations might consider is that expertise that is not associated with significant accountability is a good candidate for systemization. (For example, in the case of employment selection,

HR staff who manually score employment tests frequently do not have significant accountability for the overall effectiveness of the employment process, aside from the correctness of the manually produced test scores.) Expertise that is associated with significant accountability may be a poor candidate for systemization.

Functions That Should Be e-Enabled

The design of any e-enabled assessment system requires that the users of the system be identified. For assessment systems, there are three categories of users, as mentioned above: (a) people, such as job candidates, who will be assessed by the system; (b) HR specialists, such as employment process managers, who will be accountable for the functions performed by the system; and (c) managers, such as hiring supervisors, who will use the system to make personnel decisions.

The interface of each group of users with the system must be specified in advance to define the appropriate system requirements. Generally, this is not simply a description of the interface of these users with the current system. Almost certainly, the e-enablement will change the roles of each user with respect to the system. So this process requires the redesign of user relationships and roles with the e-enabled system. The trend of e-enablement has generally increased the involvement and interaction of the people being assessed and, especially, of the managers who use the system to make decisions. This is the fundamental question of self-service. Whose role is migrated to the now self-serving employee and manager?

Organizations whose HR strategy is to increase the self-service capabilities of non-specialist employees will design systems to facilitate or enable a wider range of functions to be performed by those employees. Organizations whose HR strategy is to retain a significant role for HR specialists in the delivery of assessment processes will design such systems primarily to support lower cost, more efficient HR functionality.

Ownership

This issue of user roles is closely related to the issue of system ownership. To the extent that e-enabled selection systems are designed to facilitate HR-managed processes, the HR organization should be viewed as the owner of the system. In that case, the vendor supporting the system would be accountable to the HR organization for service level agreements negotiated with that HR organization. On the other hand, if organizations are using e-enablement to advance a strategy of employee self-service that reduces the role of HR staff, then alternative ownership and accountabilities should be considered.

In effect, self-service is a business management strategy that moves more of the cost of HR processes directly onto the operational budgets of business units. This happens because the responsibility for executing HR processes becomes a larger part of the work responsibilities of non-HR employees and managers. In this case, an increased role for operational business units in defining and owning service level agreements with both the vendor and the remaining HR organization would be consistent with the business unit's increased financial responsibility. Of course, even in this case, it remains true that HR expertise is the primary source for the design and operational oversight of the e-enabled process.

This more collective accountability might be operationalized in a variety of ways, including the creation of a joint council of HR and business representatives to periodically review service level metrics and to establish priorities for changes to the system.

Integration with Other Systems

e-Enabled employment selection may function independently of other HR systems and processes or may be integrated to some extent with those other systems. Even if the initial intent is for the selection system to be independently e-enabled, the organization would be wise to consider possible benefits of future integration and to provide for such possibilities in the design of the assessment system. Perhaps the narrowest application of e-enabled selection systems that we have seen has been solely for employment test administration only in specific locations.

But more generalized assessment systems could be designed to gather and use not only employment test data and competency data but also performance data, training and development data, compensation data, job history and progression data, background data, and health data. This level of integration would require organizations to carefully specify requirements for data confidentiality and privacy, data access, and data use. Of course, these are not new requirements.

However, e-enabled systems are likely to require a reconsideration of these data requirements because e-enablement frequently is part of other strategic changes that may give employees more access and ownership of their own data and may invite HR strategists to analyze new combinations of data such as performance and health data. These considerations of systems integration are rooted in the design of the core employee database that would jointly support multiple applications. Certainly, large scale, commercially available HR management systems such as PeopleSoft and SAP represent e-enabled solutions to integrated HR systems and processes.

"Free Market" Versus Regulation

An important but sometimes subtle issue that organizations should address in the design of e-enabled selection systems is the degree of regulation that will be imposed on the system processes and user capabilities. (This point is separate from the related point about legal risk management which, itself, may impose regulations on the systems and users.) Because selection processes govern employee movement, organizational stability may suggest certain regulations.

At one end of the spectrum, systems may be designed to be open, free market systems in which all employees have unfettered access and all managers have unlimited ability to make the personnel decisions most important to their local organizations. Consider, for example, an e-enabled assessment system that serves the purpose of advertising internal vacancies, gathering employee skill data, and enabling managers to evaluate, select, and offer jobs to the most qualified employees. An open, free market system would place few if any limitations on employees' access to the posted vacancies or their ability to provide skill information to be considered for the vacancies. Similarly, managers' access to candidates and their ability to select and offer candidates jobs would not be limited. In this approach, the embedded pressures of supply (of skilled employees) and demand (available positions) would "govern" the operation of the system. The disadvantages of such an open system, however, are that it enables employees to move without regard to the investment of their current organization in their skills, it creates the uncontrolled possibility of understaffed organizations, and it tends to place relatively more of the burden of initial recruiting and staffing on organizations that happen to be dominated by "feeder pool" jobs.

Similar concerns can be seen in another application of assessment systems that is designed to develop, assess, and certify job skills which, when achieved, trigger automatic compensation growth. An open system that does not regulate employees' access to such development, assessment, and certification resources may result in an organization providing higher levels of compensation to more skilled employees than it can use at any one time.

Our experience has been that organizations typically choose to govern employees' access to and managers' use of systems that support personnel movement and compensation. This type of regulation typically takes the form of HR policies relating to time-in-title requirements, non-releasability options, candidate prioritization rules, approval requirements for movement or promotion, "ownership" of employees by "home" organizations, and the like. Generally, the purpose of these regulations is to control employee movement and progression to ensure (a) a fair return on organizations' investment in the development of employees; (b) a stable number of skilled workers; (c) equal opportunity and access for employees; and (d) a general homeostasis in the organization's workforce.

Of course, many factors, including an organization's culture, business strategy, industry, work climate, management-labor relationship, and HR strategy will determine the degree of regulation. But it is also likely to be true that the environment in which e-enablement becomes an attractive business strategy is an environment in which many of those factors will be changing. It is likely that an organization will be dissatisfied with e-enablement regulations that merely reconstruct existing policies and requirements. Organizations are more likely to identify appropriate policies and governance if they view the implementation of e-enabled HR systems as part of a larger change management process that is designed to capitalize fully on the capabilities of such systems to reduce costs and maximize the organization's use of human capital.

Technology Considerations

Perhaps the most important theme in this section is that the selection system's technology is merely a tool to support the company's hiring goals; technology should not be seen as an end unto itself. It is vitally important to recognize that technology simply (one hopes) makes the hiring support function easier and more efficient and effective. It is misguided to add technology to a selection process simply because competitors are doing it, because one's previous employer used it, or because it seems "cool." Technology should be employed because it complements the way the company does business and because it will allow HR to do its job better.

For example, one large, decentralized company contracted to develop a web-based hiring system for entry-level positions. The company was very interested in leveraging all the advantages of a centralized, high-tech solution. However, the initial roll out of the system revealed several issues. Most applicants were walk-ins (rather than recruited via the Internet) and the company's locations did not have connectivity. In addition, the managers administering the system did not have the computer skills required to operate a sophisticated applicant tracking and assessment system. Initial users were frustrated by low applicant flow as well as the difficulties in establishing connectivity at the locations. Realizing that the success of the project was in jeopardy, the project team decided to quickly introduce a paper-based alternate process to address the needs of the end users.

In hindsight, the company could have saved a great deal of money and user frustration by properly assessing the needs of the field and not developing a web-based driven process.

Choosing the Technology

One key decision point is which technology platform to utilize. Computerized testing started as applications on local PCs and has evolved into complex Internet-based applications. Today, companies have many options available based on their unique implementation requirements.

Local, un-networked PC-based applications are still in use by many organizations with diverse locations. These systems provide a consistent administration and scoring environment. However, maintaining a centralized database of test results is nearly impossible, as are rolling out updates to test scoring, cut scores, and test content. Vendors may be less inclined to offer this option due to the difficulty in monitoring test usage (that is, volume-based test licensing) and ensuring proper administration. These types of applications can be built either by a vendor or by internal IT resources.

The technology may be implemented as a new module within an existing company system (HRIS) or as an intranet application. For example, certain types of HRIS systems can be programmed to administer and/or score selection assessments. Alternatively, a typical web-based assessment tool can be implemented on a company's intranet. This approach allows for centralized databases of test results and easier roll out of scoring, cut score, and test content changes. These types of systems are usually "home-grown," as most test vendors are reluctant to support their products when used in these types of implementations. Therefore, these strategies are very dependent on the company's ability to allocate IT resources to the project as well as their ability to work closely together to ensure the usability of the final product.

The last implementation method is an Internet application administered via an application service provider (ASP) model by the testing vendor. This implementation model is becoming the most common method for implementing e-assessments via computer. It allows the company to completely outsource the implementation, maintenance, and support of the assessment(s). ASP implementation is often the least taxing on internal IT resources and easier to quickly implement in the short term for companies with reliable Internet access from most or all of its locations.

Table 3.1 provides some of the key decision points that influence which implementation method to choose and also indicates where each method falls in terms of each. As can be seen, no single approach is the clear winner. Rather, an organization must decide which consideration(s) are most critical; based on our experience, cost, ease of updating, and demands on internal IT resources are often at the top of the list.

Developing and Implementing the Technology Solution

In developing and implementing the technology solution, the following topics are critical: (a) implementation requirements; (b) cost considerations; (c) end-to-end versus modular solutions; (d) access channels; (e) professional standards; (f) user interface; and (g) data management.

Table 3.1. e-Selection Decision Points.

	Technology Alternatives		
Considerations	**PC-Based**	**Intranet (Internal to Company)**	**Application Service Provider (by Vendor)**
Cost	Low	Moderate	High
Centralized Databasing	Low	High	High
Ease of Updating	Difficult	Easy*	Easy
Support	Difficult	Moderate	Easy
Implementation Timeline	Moderate	Moderate*	Fast
Integration with Other HR Systems	Difficult	Moderate–Easy	Moderate–Easy
Demands on Internal IT Resources	Moderate–High	High	Low

*Entries fluctuate depending on the ability to quickly and easily task IT resources within the organization.

Implementation Requirements

Implementation of any new selection system is complex and the integration of technology makes that implementation more complex. In fact, the technology platform and its features, functions, and reliability can often determine the difference between a successful and an unsuccessful implementation. To the extent that all major stakeholders effectively participated in gathering and refining requirements, implementation can go rather smoothly. Their involvement is clearly an important step in implementing any new selection process.

The main difference between a successful and unsuccessful implementation process is that corporate and local IT resources must be engaged in the process early on. Often the company's own internal project managers are not aware of all the IT stakeholders who can make or break an implementation. IT resources within most companies are quite scarce. Therefore, it is important to get their buy-in as early as possible and rely on them to assist in identifying all the relevant IT stakeholders. Due to the fact that IT touches almost every part of a company today, the IT organization is often segmented. Including one IT group is often not enough to ensure a smooth implementation of a technology system. For example, the involvement of IT security, HRIS managers, network administrators, local desktop administrators, IT procurement, as well as other groups may be necessary.

Cost Considerations

The PC-based and internal administration models seem to be the least expensive in many instances due to their reliance on internal resources. However, the cost to the organization in terms of work hours could be great, as these resources are essentially creating a system from scratch. Once the system is complete, the ongoing support and maintenance of the system may be relatively inexpensive, depending on needed upgrades, system reliability, and similar features. ASP models are often more expensive, in terms of real cash outlay, due to the level of services provided by the vendor. However, the company must consider the cost and service levels provided by internal IT resources to determine the appropriate solution.

Undoubtedly, testing volumes aside, customization is the main factor that influences the cost of developing and implementing a technology tool to support selection. Numerous considerations can lead to the need for customizations, for example:

- *Look and feel*—to mirror other corporate applications (or websites), incorporate "branding," logos, or color schemes;
- *Types of applicant data collected*—name format, identifying information (name, address, EEO information, Social Security number);
- *Organization setup*—to match the company's divisional, regional, or HR administrative support structure and various access levels for local versus corporate administrators;

- *Hiring process*—if the technology is supporting multiple process steps, the alignment of the technology with established processes and procedures;
- *Customized versus existing assessment content*—although the majority of these costs will typically be from non-technology sources, implementing new assessment content requires a great deal of care and attention to detail;
- *Reporting*—often overlooked when defining requirements is whether existing reports are interpretable, useful, and otherwise appropriate for the proposed selection process;
- *Data transfers and systems integration*—with other applicant tracking systems and HRIS, including data uploads of scheduled or registered candidates, current employee data, company location data, as well as download of applicant data;
- *Platform integration*—ensuring that the technology tool will run successfully on the company's existing IT platforms and hardware; and
- *Volume*—based on a per-head model or unlimited use license for a set time period.

Other factors that may influence cost are functionality and features, up-time requirements, maintenance and other support requirements, and hosting agreements.

End-to-End Versus Modular Solutions

Companies will consider purchasing an end-to-end solution versus a modular solution, depending on their current processes and existing systems. Considering the relative ease of integrating technology solutions, standards in data transfer protocols, and increased security in data management, companies can create a very workable solution from a number of products and services offered by various vendors. Choosing the best pieces from a number of different sources, the company can create a highly customized solution. However, managing multiple vendors and ensuring proper coordination among them can be very challenging.

In the early years of computerized selection and assessment, modular solutions were most popular. Vendors concentrated on ensuring that their specific assessments and technology implementations were sufficient for clients' needs. Given that most products today are at least sufficient for most implementations, vendors are now broadening their offerings to give more end-to-end solutions to their clients. Many vendors are creating partnerships with other vendors in the supply chain so that they are able to provide a full-service offering to their current (or potential) clients. Alternatively, other vendors are merging or developing capabilities in other areas to accomplish this goal.

Companies with existing relationships with vendors for different parts of the hiring process may wish to continue those partnerships. For example, one large employer utilizes three different vendors for their hiring process. The company has successfully created a cohesive team among the vendors to develop a seamless process whereby candidates never know that they are being passed back and forth to different systems. One vendor takes in applicants via a telephone application system and passes that information to the applicant tracking vendor. The applicant tracking system passes the applicant to yet another vendor's system to administer a web-based assessment. Finally, the candidate is returned to the applicant tracking system (along with results in real-time) to complete the process.

Certainly, client companies are interested in streamlining vendor management and attaining economies of scale in purchasing outsourced services. Therefore, companies are more often seeking one vendor who can deliver a total end-to-end solution (and often other services such as performance management, government HR-related reporting, and benefits and compensation management).

Access Channels

Before the rise of e-selection, applicants would report to the potential employer at a specified date to complete the steps involved in the selection process. Now, with e-selection, applicants can enter a selection system through a variety of means. Table 3.2 describes the standing of the most common e-selection *access channels* with regard to several *key considerations* in selection system design and administration. There are five major access channels that we will review here:

- *Testing Centers Within Existing Business Locations*—Applicant goes to organization's location and takes assessment. Employees administer assessment(s) and organization provides any required technology.

- *Third-Party Testing Centers*—Applicant goes to third-party location, where third party proctors assessment and provides any necessary testing technology.
- *Interactive Voice Response (IVR)*—Applicant calls IVR system, listens to assessment questions, and responds via voice or touch tone to recorded questions.
- *Anywhere Access via the Web*—Applicant logs onto assessment website from a time and location of his or her choosing. No test administrator.
- *Semi-Proctored Environments*—Applicant goes to organization's field location (branch or store) and completes assessment in public area of the location. No proctor, but applicant is visible to employees and/or customers.

As can be seen in Table 3.2, there are a number of considerations, and no access channel is clearly more desirable than the others. Rather, an organization must decide how important each of the key considerations is given their situation and design their e-selection process accordingly.

For example, organizations administering cognitive ability test items should strongly consider the degree of control over the applicant's behavior and testing environment when deciding on an appropriate access channel. This is important because it is possible that applicants would receive help from friends if the test were taken via "anywhere access" over the web. Because cognitive ability items have objectively correct responses, this erodes confidence in the organization's inferences concerning the applicant's true standing on the construct of interest. Alternatively, items that do not have an objectively correct response, or those that are less transparent, might be better candidates for anywhere access. This specific concern has already spawned efforts to develop new item types that are more amenable to these unproctored environments (Schmidt, Russell, & Rogg, 2003).

The above example points out some of the complexities involved in choosing an access channel and also suggests a key way in which access channels can be aligned with an organization's overall selection strategy. In particular, an organization can decide to use different access channels for different steps in the selection process based on how important each consideration is, given the testing procedures under consideration as well as other relevant

Table 3.2. Access Channels.

	Existing Business Locations	Third-Party Testing Centers	Interactive Voice Response (IVR)	Anywhere Access via the Web	Semi-Proctored Environments
Control Over the Applicant's Behavior	High	Moderate–High	Low	Low	Moderate
Convenience for the Applicant	Low	Moderate	High	High	Moderate–High
Provider Technology Infrastructure Requirements	High	Low	High	High	High
Administration Technology Requirements	High	High	Low	Moderate	High
Content Flexibility	High	High	Low	Moderate	High
Control Over the Testing Environment	High	Moderate	None	None	Moderate
Logistical Requirements for the Organization	High	Moderate	Low	Low	High
Cost	Moderate	High	Low	Moderate	High
Potential to Turn Customers into Employees	Low–High*	Low	Low	High	High

*Depends on whether customers typically go to business locations (retailers).

factors (logistical and technology constraints, applicant volumes). Typically, screening items, where minimum, objectively verifiable qualifications are evaluated (for example, holding a valid driver's license for a job that requires driving) would be more amenable to anywhere access via the web or interactive voice response due to low concerns about candidate behavior, higher applicant volumes that make the initial technology investment more worthwhile, and a need for a relatively simple type of item content. On the other hand, an Internet-based work sample administered by computer toward the latter stages of a selection process might be more amenable to one of the other three access channels listed because it would be administered to fewer applicants, have restrictive technology requirements, be important to control the applicant's behavior during the simulation, and be able to pair it with follow-up in-person interviews. As can be seen from these examples, while these emerging access channels provide great flexibility to organizations and applicants, a variety of factors must be considered before their true value can be leveraged.

Some examples of these considerations include:

- A large geographically diverse food service organization desires to do some quick prescreening of applicants prior to face-to-face interviews. HR leadership knows that there is no connectivity in the restaurant and that the applicant pool probably does not have ready access to the Internet. Therefore, they opt for an IVR screening system that prequalifies candidates for an interview. Managers can check to ensure the candidate was, in fact, qualified on the prescreening. The corporate office can monitor usage via reports and data feeds from the vendor.
- Other companies use web-based or IVR systems to prescreen applicants before scheduling them for an onsite testing session.
- Retailers typically have Internet connectivity and room for in-store kiosks. These companies often opt for fully web-based processes administered to walk-in candidates utilizing sophisticated kiosk computers with touch screens in a semi-proctored environment. Often the company offers a parallel process over the Internet for applicants who prefer to apply from home.

- Hiring for blue-collar positions has not typically taken place over the Internet, based on an assumption that these candidates do not have access. However, recently we have not seen Internet access to be a barrier for virtually any applicant pool. The challenge for blue-collar processes is that these candidates typically are not "walk-ins," but are usually invited in for large testing sessions with scores of candidates in a single session. The challenge for those events is more often the organization's ability to provide proctored computer facilities to that many applicants at one time.
- Finally, companies that place more emphasis on cognitive skills and technical knowledge (telecommunications, for example) may require assessment in a fully proctored setting, but do not wish to take on the labor and facilities costs for in-house testing. More often, these companies are outsourcing proctored testing to a third-party testing center that may actually administer assessments for many different companies at one location.

Professional Standards

The most critical thing to remember is that e-assessments are subject to the same professional standards as other assessments. Just as it is risky to implement a paper assessment without proper validity evidence, it is risky to implement an e-assessment without proper validity evidence. The Internet has simply made access to these types of assessments easier than ever. However, we liken this to the availability of regulated drugs from so-called discount websites without a physician's prescription. Use at your own risk!

Consequently, in this section we will focus on the specific standards that are especially pertinent to issues that arise from the new challenges associated with e-assessments, with an emphasis on those found in the Society for Industrial and Organizational Psychology's *Principles for the Validation and Use of Personnel Selection Procedures* (SIOP, 2003) and the *Standards for Educational and Psychological Testing* (American Educational Research Association, American Psychological Association, and National Council on Measurement in Education [AERA, APA, NCME], 1999). The professional standards outlined in these publications are the major standards espoused by industrial/organizational psychologists who are likely to be constructing e-assessments. In addition, we refer readers to the American Psychological Association's *Psychological Testing on the Internet* task force report (Naglieri et al., 2004).

In our view, the most critical areas requiring special attention are administration and test security. This is because e-assessments largely examine the same underlying constructs as more traditional assessments (see our earlier discussion on equivalence in the testing channels section). Regarding administration, several sentences of the Standards capture the essence of the challenge facing e-assessments. "When directions to examinees, testing conditions, and scoring procedures follow the same detailed procedures, the test is said to be *standardized* [emphasis added]. Without such standardization, the accuracy and comparability of score interpretations would be reduced. For tests designed to assess the examinee's knowledge, skills, and abilities [KSAs], standardization helps to ensure that all examinees have the same opportunities to demonstrate their competencies. Maintaining test security also helps to ensure that no one has an unfair advantage" (AERA, APA, NCME, 1999, p. 61).

Standardization that parallels traditional assessments is truly impossible to achieve with some e-assessment access channels. Specifically, anywhere access via the web and semi-proctored environments, by their very nature, do not offer standardized testing environments; however, the Standards suggest that standardization is of most concern with regard to KSA testing, as opposed to personality or biodata testing. Hence, practitioners should carefully consider whether KSA testing is appropriate via anywhere access to the web or in semi-proctored environments (we do not see this as a concern with IVR due to its limited content flexibility). This is because it is extremely difficult to control not only the test environment, but more importantly, whether the applicant is receiving inappropriate aid from another person, using prohibited assistance devices (for example, a calculator), or even is, in fact, the person taking the test. Clearly, any one of these concerns could seriously call into question the integrity of the results, and this last issue is squarely addressed by the Principles: "The identity of all candidates should be confirmed prior to administration" (p. 86).

On the other hand, technology can aid the organization's efforts to standardize a selection process. In very decentralized organizations, individual hiring managers may pick and choose which components of a selection process to utilize. The technology used to administer the process can be configured to require a test score or a score on each interview question before the hire can be processed in the payroll system (or associated HRIS).

Second, test security becomes an issue as well. For instance, the Standards say that "test users have the responsibility of protecting the security of test materials at all times" (p. 64), and the Principles contain similar language: "Selection procedure items that are widely known or studied in an organization are usually less effective in distinguishing among candidates on relevant constructs" (p. 89). Clearly, this becomes virtually impossible to enforce with anywhere testing via the web, and perhaps to a somewhat lesser extent, on-site semi-proctored environments. This is because an applicant can very easily retain copies of all the test materials by taking screenshots, copying items down, or other means. While the organization delivering the test content certainly has an intellectual-property-based incentive to maintain test security, anywhere testing via the web largely requires abandonment of this principle. Clearly, the organization must make an informed decision about whether insecure test content outweighs the convenience of remote web testing (and many organizations have already decided that it does). We think this will give rise to efforts to develop valid, job-related items that are either opaque or clearly objectively verifiable in order to minimize this concern.

Other important, although less critical, areas for additional attention in e-assessments that were not discussed at length here include e-assessments for applicants with disabilities, the potential of excluding large portions of an applicant pool without convenient access to a particular access channel (such as anywhere access over the web), the increased complexity involved in validating the accuracy of scoring procedures, and maintaining security of large e-assessment databases with confidential applicant information. The interested reader should also see the APA's Internet Task Force report (Naglieri et al., 2004) for an extended discussion of these and other relevant issues.

User Interface

Just like websites and computer applications in general, user interfaces for e-assessments vary widely. This is because there are no commonly accepted standards for the look and feel of e-assessments. Thus, interfaces can vary from simple web pages with text-based questions and radio button style response options to engaging multimedia experiences. More typically, however, the look and feel of e-assessments tend to be in between these two extremes, that is, "professional"-looking interfaces that are not designed to be glamorous. This helps keep development costs and bandwidth requirements to a minimum while conveying that the organization takes its assessments seriously.

That said, in our consulting practices, we have seen an increasing interest in developing engaging applicant experiences in organizations' e-assessments. This is most typically accomplished by developing rich, multimedia assessments that are not only designed to impress applicants, but also to convey a realistic preview of the job at the same time. For instance, such an assessment for a call center job might include realistic voice interactions and a computer interface that closely mimics what a customer service representative might use on the job. Thus, these high-fidelity experiences form two purposes—assessment and applicant attraction or attrition based on the job preview. Although this requires more resources than traditional e-assessments, we believe this trend will continue to increase in the years to come.

Data Management

Traditional assessments require very little technology. Typically, all that is required is a word-processed document that can be administered to applicants. Alternatively, e-assessments have substantial technical requirements that can add a number of complexities to assessment implementation. In this section, we will discuss three key issues: assessment setup, quality assurance/control, and reporting.

Regardless of the interface used (see the user interface section above), e-assessments are almost invariably stored and deployed using relational databases such as Oracle or SQL server. This means that, unlike spreadsheet programs like Microsoft Excel, which store data in a single table, assessment content and examinee data are stored in multiple tables. For instance, in our consulting practices, we have seen relational databases that include up to several dozens of tables for complex work simulations. Clearly, designing relational databases of this size adds significant time to development efforts.

The first key implication of this complexity is that quality assurance becomes critically important, as well as very challenging. This is mainly because, rather than simply reviewing a list of items in a document, someone has to actually test-drive a beta version of the software. This occurs because the staff who created the content is almost never expert in the database systems delivering the test, providing ample room for errors. This not only must be done to ensure the content is 100 percent correct, but also to ensure that the item scoring, scale scoring, and related cutoffs are correct as well. For lengthy assessments, this can require substantial amounts of time. For example, many dozens of trials are often required to validate scoring systems, and even then, unless all possible scoring combinations are attempted, there will invariably be situations that occur in practice when the assessment is deployed to tens or hundreds of thousands of candidates that have not arisen in testing. One approach to accelerate the testing process is to develop interim scoring "utilities" or "simulations" that expedite the entry of applicant data. Of course, the downside of such utilities is that there can be disconnects between the utilities and the final implemented version of the e-assessment. Clearly, this adds substantial time, expense, and complexity to e-assessment deployments and revisions.

One area in which e-assessments clearly shine is reporting and analysis. Because data are stored in computer systems, it is possible to design real-time reporting and analysis processes to vastly accelerate the decision-making process for individual applicants, as well as overall process flow. Taking this one step further are online *business intelligence* platforms that allow users to flexibly perform online, real-time analysis of data or to generate custom reports using simple point-and-click tools. For example, applicant data collected via an IVR system may be downloaded for reporting by the company's HRIS or accessed via a web-based business intelligence reporting system. The accessibility of the data for reporting makes auditing the selection system much easier for HR leadership. Thus, managing the process and ensuring compliance and consistency can be made easier with technology.

The flip side of this is that candidate data might not be stored in a format that is readily available for analysis. Rather, a programmer might need to restructure the data in a flat file, or the data analyst might be required to do this on the desktop. Either approach adds to the time required, potential for error, and complexity of desktop-based analyses.

Finally, data standards are beginning to emerge in HR in general, and these standards will likely begin to govern integration of systems in e-assessment and selection. Specifically, extensible mark-up language (XML) was designated by the HR-XML Consortium and the Object Management Group as the standard for passing data between various HR systems (Weiss, 2001). While these standards will likely be transparent to the end user (as well as to most HR buyers), the result will be increased ease in linking modules from various vendors to create the best e-enabled selection process. For example, the HR director may like the functionality of a certain applicant tracking system, prefer the content of a different vendor's assessment products, and at the end of the day need to put all the data into her company's HRIS. Having all systems and vendors "communicate" via XML will reduce the time needed to coordinate integration of the various modules into the total solution. From an industry perspective, ease in systems integration will encourage partnerships among vendors with complementary services.

Tips and Guidelines

As Tippins (2002) discussed, the most valid of selection systems can be invalidated by shoddy implementation. The same is true with e-assessment selection processes. Technology adds a level of complexity to implementation that can make the whole project go very well or very wrong. In our experience, there are several important steps an organization can take that will ease the design and implementation:

- Involve internal IT resources early.
  Describe your plans to them and have them assist in the
      RFP process if you are planning to use a vendor or assist
      in design if you are building internally.

Ask internal IT to consult on service levels and support issues. They likely have experience with these agreements with other vendors.

Leverage contacts in IT to determine all the various IT reviews and approvals that may be needed to ensure that the project can proceed (for example, security review, network accesses, web services).

- Remember the real purpose of the hiring process and the needs of the key stakeholders. Do not allow technology to drive the organization's purpose, strategy, or policy in designing the new selection system.

- Gather input from key stakeholders early and ask for feedback from them often during the design process.

Carefully document your current process and gather requirements on what all stakeholders need from the process and what they would like to change.

Once the final "dream process" is finalized, request feedback from key stakeholders again. This is often best done in a face-to-face meeting so that stakeholders can discuss and negotiate needs and desires directly rather than having to work through a messenger. This process also allows others to assist in solving problems that may seem "mutually exclusive."

Begin the technology design process after all major stakeholders have approved these requirements. The project will more likely stay on time and within budget if the major process decisions have already been made.

- Be realistic and fair about project timelines. As for most projects, expect "slippage" in the timeline on your end as well as the vendor.

Create a carefully planned work plan and timeline at the beginning of the project—and expect it to change almost immediately. Look for ways to make up the time at later steps in the project, but don't count on being able to make up all the time.

Hold the vendor to the project timeline, within reason. Forgiveness for slight delays by the vendor will go a long way when you need to accelerate other steps due to delays on your end.

When delays are caused by the customer organization, do not expect the vendor to make up all of the time by accelerating their work. The vendor may be able to make up some of the time, but pushing for the system to be launched early may result in errors that can cause the whole process to lose credibility.

- Create a true partnership among the key project team members and other stakeholders. As for most projects, it is important to create a culture of partnership that encourages easy and open flow of information.
- Allow appropriate time to quality check the technology tool and train new users—then add some more.

    Avoidable errors that could have been detected and resolved earlier will undermine the acceptance of the new process.

    If users are not properly trained, they will not use the new process and tools. Their frustrations with the system will become known and erode support for the project.

- Avoid the temptation to make that one last little change or addition.

    As we mentioned earlier, customization is expensive. Customization at the last minute before a big implementation is deadly! Establish a moratorium on changes in the last two to four weeks of development—and stick to it!

    If last-minute changes are a must, delay the implementation launch until the change is fully tested and confirmed to be functioning as planned.

Asking these questions and following these tips will allow most organizations to avoid the most common pitfalls in technology implementations. Although following all our advice doesn't guarantee a perfect project, it will help most organizations avoid the expensive mistakes.

To better illustrate these points, we can provide an example of a very smooth and successful implementation:

Company A is a large decentralized organization that implemented a selection system via the Internet and in-store kiosks. The locations all had high-speed Internet connectivity maintained for other business purposes by the corporate IT department. In addition, the users were already using computer systems in their jobs every day. The kiosks were purchased and specifically designed for the hiring application. In fact, the kiosks were dedicated to the hiring process application. The IT team worked collaboratively with the vendors to configure and test the applications, connectivity, systems interfaces, and anticipated candidate loads. The organization and vendors were open and honest about challenges and issues so that all parties could work together to solve any potential barriers to success. The organization's IT resources tested the applications in a central lab to identify and rectify major issues. Later, the applications were tested again at the actual hiring locations prior to training. While the vendors were creating customized systems and content, the organization's HR team built process maps and scripts for how the new system would be integrated into current workflows. The implementation team from the organization conducted one week of training and orientation at the hiring location on the actual hardware prior to launching the new process. The implementation team stayed on site and monitored live candidate activity daily for the first few weeks of implementation. Daily status calls were held between the end users, the organization's implementation team, and the vendors to uncover and immediately address any issues. The organization also created a help desk for user questions and problems immediately. All the preparation and care that went into this implementation fostered strong field support, acceptance, and high compliance.

Future Technology Developments

One thing is sure about e-selection technology—expect it to keep changing. The first wave of innovations is likely to be seen (and is already emerging) as an integration of the various systems involved in the selection process, such as integration of prescreening, testing, interviewing, offer, and other selection steps into an overall applicant tracking system. Integration can be accomplished through partnerships, mergers, or an expansion of services by current incumbent firms. Integrated services usually allow for more convenient, faster, and cost-effective service delivery.

Companies will continue to desire to make the application process more convenient and more efficient. Despite some of the complexities discussed earlier in this chapter, unproctored Internet-based testing will become more prevalent, and organizations will want to measure more aspects of performance in less time. These demands will almost certainly prompt innovations in novel item types designed to reduce transparency. These new item types should allow for reliable and valid unproctored Internet testing. In addition, assessment developers will strive to create more engaging experiences for applicants to increase interest and measure constructs in novel ways.

Finally, general computer technology changes will certainly affect the future of e-selection. High-technology companies are already looking for ways to incorporate new technologies, such as mobile computing devices (Palm Pilots®, Internet-enabled cell phones). However, these advancements may be further off due to limited screen size and low resolution of these devices. As pure assessment delivery becomes stable and established, organizations will increasingly focus on the applicant experience. They will put a greater focus on multimedia applications, which may make assessment "fun" for candidates (perhaps trying to limit faking by getting candidates to forget they are applying for a job). These new multimedia assessments may begin to mask situational judgment tests as "reality" television shows or computer decision-making games (such as The Sims or SimCity). High-tech simulations of plane cockpits or other vehicle controls could serve as assessments of candidates' ability to understand directions and problem solve, as well as of reaction time and manual dexterity. Someday soon, we will even likely see true virtual reality work simulations that include "day in the life" scenarios that are part assessment and part realistic job preview.

As technology begins to drive the development of new assessments, I/O psychologists will be challenged to research the equivalence, fairness, and job relevance of the constructs being measured. In addition, researchers will seek to understand and demonstrate the ways that these assessments can solve existing problems in selection (such as faking and face validity) and solve new issues brought about by the assessments (such as construct validity and fairness).

Designing and Managing e-Selection Processes

Implementing an e-selection process entails most of the decisions involved in a traditional paper-and-pencil program. Thus, the current section highlights many of the elements that would be addressed during the design and implementation of any new assessment system, whether technology-focused or not (also see Tippins, 2002, for an excellent treatment on implementing large-scale selection programs in general). This section also includes a special focus on the improvements e-selection offers over paper-and-pencil assessment.

Organizations planning an e-enabled employment selection system must consider a variety of procedural requirements, including processes to design up-front; vendor selection and project steps; assessment steps and protocols for the test event; feedback to candidates and internal clients; methods of processing candidates after testing; and management of the candidate flow and test program itself. We now turn to the design issues, which are listed in Exhibit 3.4 also.

Designing the e-Enabled Selection Process

Flow Chart Current Process

A useful first step in understanding the scope of the work is to make a flow chart of the current assessment process for pre-employment and/or employee development. An example of a pre-employment assessment process is shown in Figure 3.1. Various assessment steps, decisions, and outcomes are shown, and the graphic lends itself to an understanding of the e-selection inputs (types of assessments) and outputs (pass/fail results and whether the candidate remains in the applicant pool). Figure 3.1 also illustrates how e-selection might be included in the process.

Exhibit 3.4. Key Issues for Designing e-Selection Processes.

- Design the selection process step-by-step from every user's point of view: candidate, recruiter, test administrator, hiring manager, information technology manager, HR researcher/administrator.
- Make use of instantaneous and automated information flow to improve each user's e-selection experience.
- Establish policies and consistent procedures for restricting access to the test and results.
- Protect proprietary and sensitive information as you would for a paper-and-pencil testing program.

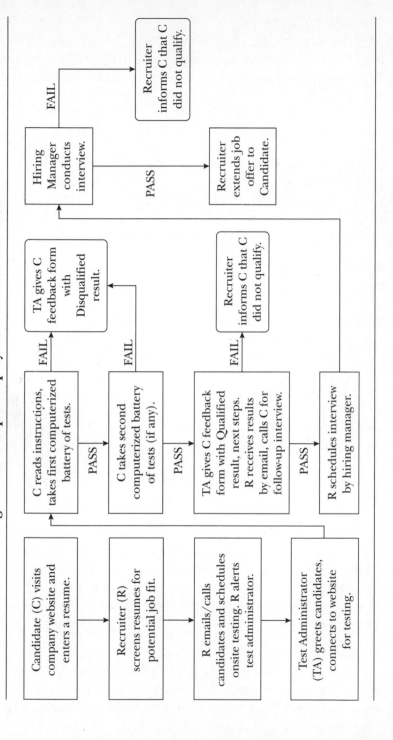

Figure 3.1. Sample Employment Process Flow Chart.

Flow Chart New Process

Next, the organization should draft the desired process flow that will result from the e-selection implementation(s) under consideration. Process improvements, efficiencies, and cost savings should be evident from the diagram. For instance, some steps in the new process may involve less staff time and may be easy to make, such as changing from a team of proctors who usher in candidates, distribute test materials, and read test instructions to a single monitor who oversees a testing room while also attending to another task. The monitor also needs no inventories of test booklets, answer keys, or other materials. Scoring and processing candidates will be easier than paper-and-pencil processes, and precision and efficiency replace cumbersome and sometimes error-prone manual procedures.

Users

In drafting the new flow, it is important to consider how the various stakeholders and clients will use the system. Gilliland and Cherry (2000) provide a very insightful discussion of the "customers" of selection programs and their differing needs and objectives. Larger organizations will benefit by assembling task teams to represent the interests of various client groups impacted by e-selection. Clients include the HR users of the system, such as recruiters, administrators, research staff, and the company's technology experts (for example, HR network administrators). To a lesser extent, it may be beneficial to involve managers from the operating business functions, such as hiring managers and staff trainers and senior-level supervisors who will benefit indirectly from the assessment system. Other clients may be represented in absentia. Examinees are important clients not only because they are users of the system, but because they may be customers and/or shareholders and will form opinions about the organization based on reactions to the assessment process. It may be worthwhile to survey examinees about the usability of the e-selection system soon after it is up and running. Finally, outside organizations such as unions and federal compliance agencies may also be considered clients of the assessment process.

Scoring Systems

The process flow will include implicit assumptions about the methods of scoring assessments and using the results. For example, e-selection should allow scoring to be rapid or instantaneous, test results should be readily combinable with other tests results, and score reports should be available that are readily interpretable and printable for administrative use. These assumptions should be checked. Similarly, the choice of various technology-enabled scoring methods (automated PC-based methods and/or self-scanning of test answer sheets; scanning and scoring by a vendor organization; web-enabled scoring and distribution of results) have variable effects on the availability of results and the timing of next steps in the assessment process. Organizations considering e-selection should also take into account the long-term effects of decisions to retain legacy systems (for example, database management systems that must converse with the new system) and modes of administration (using both paper-pencil and e-selection).

Equivalence

Organizations that are transitioning from existing paper-and-pencil selection procedures to e-enabled versions of the same procedures will have to address the measurement equivalency of the previous paper-and-pencil assessments and the new e-enabled assessment procedures. Even organizations whose e-enabled selection system is novel and not designed to be an alternative form of a previous paper-and-pencil system may have a need to know the measurement equivalence of the e-enabled scores and corresponding paper-and-pencil assessments. Paper-and-pencil alternative assessment procedures may have to be identified for fail-safe reasons—the network crashes—or for manual delivery alternatives that would deliberately not use the e-enabled system, such as mass testing.

Measurement equivalence is usually important for two reasons. First, the degree of equivalence will affect the transferability of any previous validation evidence that may have been accumulated. Second, for practical reasons it is very likely to be important to know the scores from the e-enabled assessments that are administratively equivalent to scores from paper-and-pencil versions of the same (alternative) assessment procedures. Adequate measurement equivalence is necessary to treat two scores as administratively equivalent. Two scores from two different assessment procedures are administratively equivalent if they produce the same outcomes.

This issue of equivalence applies both to ability tests and to self-report personality and biodata inventories. For ability tests, substantial research has shown that the computerization of paper-and-pencil tests does not change their measurement characteristics except for speeded tests (Mead & Drasgow, 1993). For assessments in which socially desirable responding is an issue, such as personality inventories and biodata inventories, two recent meta-analyses have reached similar overall conclusions that responses to computerized measures do not appear to be any more or less prone to socially desirable responding than responses to paper-and-pencil measures (Dwight & Feigelson, 2000; Richman, Kiesler, Weisband, & Drasgow, 1999). Furthermore, the earlier trend for computer administration to yield less socially desirable responding than paper-and-pencil administration appears to be lessening over time. Later research tends to show smaller differences between computer and paper-and-pencil administration. However, these overall results appear to change when instruments are not administered anonymously, as is the case with employment assessments. In that case, there is some evidence that computer administration may increase socially desirable responding compared to paper-and-pencil administration. In any case, users should not assume that computerized personality assessment will counteract the motivational effect of applying for a job, and users should not assume that computer administration will reduce socially desirable responding compared to paper-and-pencil administration. Overall, the equivalency research results are clearer for ability tests than for personality and biodata inventories.

In most e-enabled selection programs, the organization will have a need to equate the computer administration scores with paper-and-pencil scores from the same tests or highly similar tests. While this equating is most meaningful when the two measures are known to have measurement equivalence, equating that is useful for administrative purposes may also take place, even if measurement equivalence is unknown or not high. Score equating is a process of calibrating the scores on a computer-administered assessment to be administratively equivalent to scores on the paper-and-pencil counterpart. This is a scaling process, not a process for inducing measurement equivalence. Two useful calibration methods are equipercentile equating by which computer and paper-and-pencil scores at the same percentile rank in their corresponding distributions of scores are equated and equiprediction equating by which computer and paper-and-pencil scores that predict the same criterion score are equated. Measurement equivalence aside, equiprediction equating is more meaningful because the equating is based on equal outcomes that are of interest to the organization. In most cases, however, the organization will not have the data available to perform equiprediction equating and will revert to some other equating method such as equipercentile equating.

Administrative Decisions

From a process flow chart, such as shown in Figure 3.1, it is important to identify the decision rules that will be required to evaluate the outcome of each step. Organizations must make choices about how to use the assessment scores. For instance, will test results be expressed as quantitative scores or profile interpretations, with recommendations from a vendor about the "match" of that profile with the vacant position? Will there be pass/fail cut scores, or will decisions be made top-down? Or will results be grouped into bands, such as "definitely hire," "possibly hire," and "definitely reject"? Might two or more test scores be considered additively, such that a lower score on one part compensates with a higher score on another part ("compensatory" scoring)? Or would each step in the assessment process be a requirement that must be met, in sequence, upon conditionally qualifying on the previous step (a "multiple hurdles" approach)? (For further discussion on these topics, see Guion, 1998, and Tippins, 2002.) In general, the more complicated the decision rule, the more beneficial the use of e-selection will be in processing candidates.

Another outcome from the assessment process is the information that should be known about the candidate. The data to be tracked are the same as for paper-and-pencil testing, for example, has the candidate been tested previously, and if so, has sufficient time elapsed that a re-test is reasonable? Has the candidate held the job previously or for other reasons should be grandfathered or exempted? As the size and complexity of the testing program increases, the availability of readily accessible testing databases (for example, a testing and tracking system) becomes increasingly important.

Managing the e-Enabled Process

Preparing to Test: Processes to Arrange in Advance

As shown in Figure 3.1, the first testing step may occur before the organization has had any formal contact with the candidate. That is, the company may wish to prescreen candidates, particularly if there are many applicants for a small number of job openings. Options include websites for entering a résumé and answering questions about desired work, web-delivered assessments such as biodata and work attitudes, telephone-based assessments the candidate takes using the touch-tone keypad, and in-store kiosks with electronic applications. The next step often involves automatically notifying an HR manager or recruiter of the results. For instance, some companies have a system whereby if a candidate qualifies on the self-administered test at an in-store computerized kiosk, an HR representative is automatically summoned for a follow-up interview and any further testing.

It may be worthwhile to prepare candidates in some way for the exam. Possibilities include general information about the organization's testing program, descriptions of tests required for various jobs the company hires for, or practice examinations applicants can take so that they are familiar with the instructions (as is permitted for college-entry SAT and ACT exams in the United States). Possible reasons for permitting practice include reducing test anxiety and equalizing levels of familiarity with test instructions between re-testers and first-time examinees. Such test information may or may not be necessary and is a matter of choice for the organization. Many assessment systems provide practice test items, tutorials, or other instructions to take just before the test that will be sufficient for candidates to reduce test anxiety and provide any last-minute preparations that might be required.

When scheduling candidates, there should be an opportunity to self-identify the need for disability accommodation on testing. Ideally, administration instructions during testing should also mention special accommodation as a follow-up—whether read by an instructor or appearing onscreen—so that candidates have ample opportunity to identify their special needs. Technology may be able to accommodate the needs of the examinee with longer test times or verbal instructions read by the computer in lieu of written material.

Some organizations will consider administering assessments without a proctor or method of identifying and observing the candidate (for example, remote testing outside of a controlled environment). For developmental assessments that result in private feedback to the participant and do not qualify/disqualify, label the candidate, or otherwise involve high-stakes outcomes, unproctored or remote assessment may be convenient and cost-effective. However, for selection purposes, knowing the identity of the candidate and ensuring standardized testing conditions may be essential—especially for ability tests. Nevertheless, some organizations do opt to do some unproctored assessments (questions answered at an in-store kiosk) or remote assessments (biodata items administered over the telephone or Internet). Ideally, any remote, unproctored assessments should be followed by assessments in a controlled, supervised setting.

Test/Event Administration

Certainly, test administrators will need to become familiar with the new characteristics and capabilities of e-selection tests, as well as new issues that are created or solved by the use of technology. Test administration issues include usability, test access, feedback, and scoring. The Principles (SIOP, 2003) includes guidelines for administering selection procedures that apply equally well to paper-and-pencil and e-selection.

Usability issues are important when testing both inexperienced and experienced computer users. Some companies that have implemented computer-based or Internet testing have encountered examinees who are unfamiliar with computers and do some surprising and legendary things (for example, stepping on the computer mouse, thinking it is a foot pedal) and others may simply experience some anxiety associated with the computer that interferes with their ability to perform well on the tests. It is important to know the applicant pool in order to determine whether some mouse training or other instruction should be part of the testing system, particularly if the candidates are applying for work with little or no computer experience, and therefore may be expected to be less than proficient.

Computerized testing systems must also be built for the experienced computer user, with test security in mind. That is, the test should not permit examinees to take the test dishonestly (use the calculator when taking an arithmetic test or access the Internet), compromise the test items (cut/paste or print the contents of the screen), or interrupt the test (reboot the computer by pressing a combination of keys). All non-essential functions of the keyboard, mouse, or other controllers should be locked out.

It is also important to pay attention to test timing. First, a caveat about test timing is in order. Not all timed tests operate correctly, particularly if the test is administered over the Internet, where bandwidth can affect the operation of the test clock or timer. When creating a test or choosing a vendor product, it is very important to check the timer and be certain that it does not run slowly/quickly or continue running out when the test is loading, taking time away from the examinee unfairly. On an encouraging note, computerized tests provide a certain administrative freedom at the test site, particularly if the tests are self-administered at a computer station, such that simultaneous start and end times may not be necessary. The traditional mass-testing event with verbal instructions to "Put your pencils down" may be replaced by quietly ushering candidates in to take their exams and visit the proctor when they are finished.

Note that a good vendor product should not pose many technical difficulties that might require restarting the test. Obvious technical problems such as a loss of power should be infrequent and, even so, should be anticipated, such that the test software stores answers and permits continuity even if power is lost temporarily or the test is interrupted for other reasons.

Managing access to the test is a critical role for the test administrator. With paper-and-pencil testing, test booklets are generally numbered and kept under tight control of a test administrator. Similarly, some vendors restrict access to web-delivered tests by essentially numbering each test with a "key" or identifier so that the test can be taken only once. And well-developed computerized tests will lock out non-test functions that would permit candidates to compromise test items by cutting/pasting or printing text, just as they would prevent other types of cheating described above.

Automated test delivery and immediate scoring can speed the test process. Immediate scoring enables the selection system to combine test events into a single score, providing a more complex picture than has often been possible in real time. Previously, a multiple-hurdles, and often multiple-day, process was required due to the need to wait for manual scoring or interpretation of results. The organization must plan how to use this information. As with paper-and-pencil testing, organizations also have a variety of choices of feedback, such as whether to give candidates detailed information versus qualified/disqualified (or even to provide feedback onscreen after a section is completed; this is useful for developmental assessments and less so for employment tests), and whether to make the proctor available to answer face-to-face questions versus emailing or sending results by mail, et cetera. Feedback should be available in a printable format so that each candidate will have proof of his or her result in exchange for the time invested in testing.

After the Test/Event

Knowing immediately whether or not the candidate has qualified for the next assessment step is very useful in processing candidates. Examinees may move immediately to the next pre-employment step. Recruiters need not wait for results; the assessment system may notify them, such as by sending an email with the afternoon's candidate results with an interview roster. Alternatively, recruiters may search a database of just-arrived score reports.

Computerized testing produces a database of searchable score results and other test characteristics, such as specific tests delivered, history, and dates of testing. All are useful for various administrative functions, such as generating reports of passing rates and other hiring statistics and for integrating with the company's HR database. For example, the recruiter will know when the candidate tested and whether it is too soon to retest (per the organization's policy), and will know whether the candidate's test records qualify him or her for other positions in the organization. Further, depending on the candidate's level of performance, the on-file results might qualify him for one or more positions other than the one for which he was testing. As was described earlier, the organization must create decision rules for the use of test records, for example, whether to use the highest score or the most recent score (Tippins, 2002), as well as who will have access to the database and who will be able to modify records.

Managing the Applicant Flow and Test Program

Related to the use of a test database, the organization may manage the application process effectively by tracking the number of candidates available to test, the number who have qualified on one or more steps, expected pass rates, and so forth. This enables recruiters to know when to source more candidates or to stop (for example, if previously qualified candidates who were not offered positions due to a temporary hiring freeze could now receive an offer).

Finally, some computerized test delivery software permits electronic management of accounts (such as ordering and managing access to test inventory online, and using the interface to grant others privileges to view test information online). This feature is especially useful for large testing programs.

The preceding section introduced a variety of important issues that may be considered when designing an e-selection system. Key questions are shown in Exhibit 3.5.

Exhibit 3.5. Some Questions to Ask About e-Selection Systems.

Inventory and Administrative Rights: How will tests be inventoried/ordered/purchased? Is this process simple/automated? Who has administrative and record-sharing rights? Can these rights be delegated?

Access and Security: How will a candidate gain access to tests—open access versus privilege-based? What will be the provisions for test security and standardization of the test environment? How will the test system guard against tampering?

Ability to Apply Test Policies: Will the test system permit special disability accommodation (for example, extended time on the test)? Will information be stored/applied to determine who should be tested (former incumbents, people who took the test recently and were disqualified)?

Scoring: What scoring options will be available (for example, can individual results be combined into an overall test battery score with a choice of scoring weights and algorithms)? Will it be possible to apply norms to scores automatically?

Results: When/how will test results be available—storage, communication with other HR systems, interpretable and printable score reports? What information will be collected for analyses of EEO results, pass rates, and test functioning (race/gender, identifying information, test date, location, item-level data)? What information will be exported, and in what data format?

Vendor Management and Partnership

Although technology-savvy companies may opt to develop some e-selection tools on their own, few companies would consider implementing an entire e-selection system without the aid of a vendor specializing in these services. Just as the implementation of an e-selection process follows the same general guidelines as an assessment process without technology, managing a vendor of technology follows the same steps as managing a vendor of other services. Steps include defining the scope of work; negotiating a contract and project plan—including stipulating who will be accountable for delivering products and services and what the criteria are for acceptable work—and monitoring timelines and milestones as the project progresses.

Scope of Work

After the organization maps the process flow (as shown in Figure 3.1), the scope of work for the e-selection implementation begins to come into focus. Elements of the scope of work will include a description of the product and service deliverables, with reference to the process flow, as well as anticipated deadlines for completion of each deliverable. Frequently the deadlines are divided into phases, such as a small pilot test and analysis of outcomes, followed by a general rollout and a series of updates. With e-selection implementations, it is important to include ongoing maintenance and client staff training in the scope of work. Rarely does the project end with the first release of the software.

Negotiating the Contract

When seeking to contract services to a vendor, many companies issue a request for proposal (RFP), with either a detailed set of guidelines and expectations or a call for general proposals written at each vendor's discretion. It is best to be as specific as possible about the work expected from the vendor so that neither party is surprised later by the other's requirements and ability to deliver. All reasonable proposals will detail timelines, consulting expenses, and any special charges the vendor will recover from the client. Both client and vendor must provide opportunities for fielding questions about the work to be performed and the solutions offered. Companies often provide a deadline for vendor queries and require vendors to present their ideas. Due to the complexity of the services involved and the need for numerous interchanges to learn about the company's current technology and the vendor's ability to customize a solution, creating and revising the proposal can be an iterative process for both client and vendor.

While the organization and its vendors share responsibility for mapping the new process onto the existing one, some areas of responsibility are more clearly assignable to one party or another. The client organization is responsible for proper use of the assessment system, such as meeting the hardware, software, and network requirements; ensuring standardized test conditions; and using assessment products consistently and fairly. The vendor is responsible for quality assurance on the test delivery, scoring accuracy, and delivery of score data and reports. Such work should not be placed on the client organization's shoulders.

Service Level Agreements

Performance standards for the vendor are defined in specific service level agreements (SLAs) between e-selection vendors and their clients. These "agreements" are exhibits or attachments within the actual contract or statement of work and include performance objectives or goals. It is very important for vendors and clients to clearly articulate needs and services as well as agree on objective measures to evaluate performance.

Some common SLAs are listed below:

- *Availability/uptime* is defined as number of outages, duration of each, and total outage time for some predefined period (usually one month). When developing this SLA, it is important for the customer to determine when the system will be used and require acceptable uptime within those hours. It will be inefficient to require the vendor to agree to uptime outside of normal hours of use (and therefore more expensive for the customer).
- *Scheduled downtime* for maintenance is another SLA that will be negotiated between the vendor and customer organization. Both companies will typically have standard "maintenance win-

dows" that fall during off or low usage hours and are easily coordinated.

- *System performance* metrics are as unique as the functionality of the particular system under consideration. For example, SLAs may be set to govern scoring completion time and transaction response time (the interval from when the user requests a page to when he or she receives the last byte of the required page).

- *Technical support* should be a part of any standard set of services provided. However, there is a wide range of services that may or may not be included here. For example, support hours should reflect the hours of use; contact with the vendor's help desk may be open to all users or filtered through a central communication team within the customer's organization; and vendors may limit the number of support hours within a specified period (typically a year). In addition, customers should work with vendors to define problem routing processes, resolution times, follow-up reports (for example, root cause analysis), and escalation procedures.

Managing Milestones

Although it is obvious that timelines for implementation should be realistic, organizations and their vendors too often share a tendency toward wishful thinking—the organization's frequent unfamiliarity with the technical issues involved in implementing the program, coupled with the vendor's desire to win the business, sometimes result in failing to meet ambitious deadlines. As early as possible in the discussions about the scope of work, organizations and consulting companies should review timelines for reasonableness and discuss what will be done if certain deadlines are not met, and how to keep the project on track. Later, these discussions can be built into the contract, including consequences of failure to deliver on schedule.

During the development and implementation of the assessment system, the client will have responsibilities and accountabilities as well as the vendor. For instance, various portions of the assessment may require client input as subject-matter experts (feedback as users of the new testing system or on HR processes). SME cooperation is essential to meeting key milestones.

Ongoing Maintenance

When the software, hardware, and technology infrastructure are complete, the organization and its vendors will be required to collaborate further to see that training is effective and that ongoing maintenance concerns are met (for example, software updates to improve usability, document procedures, or provide additional services). Note that once the assessment system is up and running, working with the vendor should be expected to involve some loss of control for the client organization, such as the inability to modify the assessments without assistance from an outside software expert. The client organization must accept this delegation of work, as must any company that outsources services and expertise.

Finally, when designing and managing an e-selection process, consider the tips and guidelines shown in Exhibit 3.6.

Exhibit 3.6. Tips and Guidelines for Designing and Managing e-Selection Processes.

1. Know your own selection process and have an idea of your desired state before you shop for a vendor. The e-selection end state must be of value to your stakeholders; it will be difficult to defend the implementation against later criticism if the reasons for implementation decisions are not clear or appear to be more convenient for the vendor than for your company.

2. Research the vendor's products as many ways as possible. Beyond speaking to references and trying out demo versions offered by the vendor, ask to see e-selection systems currently running on other client sites. Ask an existing client for an "inside tour" of a working e-selection system. Try out the sites to get the candidate's experience, examine the online application, try out the in-store kiosk, or dial into the IVR application system.

3. Use the data to show the value of e-selection. Virtual storage allows the collection of vast amounts of data, not only about the candidates and hiring process, but about individual and group- or organization-level performance results.

4. Know that the implementation is never finalized or immutable. The vendor will have periodic upgrades and improvements, both vendor-initiated and as a result of your comments and suggestions, and ongoing management, training, and technical support is integral to your continued success.

References

American Educational Research Association, American Psychological Association, and National Council on Measurement in Education. (1999). *Standards for educational and psychological testing.* Washington, DC: American Psychological Association.

Dwight, S. A., & Feigelson, M. E. (2000). A quantitative review of the effect of computerized testing on the measurement of social desirability. *Educational and Psychological Measurement, 60,* 340–360.

Gilliland, S. W., & Cherry, B. (2000). Managing "customers" of selection processes. In J. Kehoe (Ed.), *Managing selection in changing organizations: Human resource strategies* (pp. 158–196). San Francisco: Jossey-Bass.

Guion, R. M. (1998). *Assessment, measurement, and prediction for personnel decision.* Mahwah, NJ: Lawrence Erlbaum.

Mead, A. D., & Drasgow, F. (1993). Equivalence of computerized and paper-and-pencil cognitive ability tests: A meta-analysis. *Psychological Bulletin, 114*(3), 449–458.

Naglieri, J. A., Drasgow, F., Schmit, M., Handler, L., Prifitera, A., Margolis, A., & Velasquez, R. (2004). Psychological testing on the internet: New problems, old issues. *American Psychologist, 59,* 150-162.

Richman, W. L., Kiesler, S., Weisband, S., & Drasgow, F., (1999). A meta-analytic study of social desirability distortion in computer-administered questionnaires, traditional questionnaires, and interviews. *Journal of Applied Psychology, 84,* 754–775.

Society for Industrial and Organizational Psychology. (2003). *Principles for the validation and use of personnel selection procedures* (4th ed.). College Park, MD: Author.

Schmidt, D. B., Russell, D. P., & Rogg, K. R. (2003, April). *Reducing call center associate turnover through effective and focused selection procedures.* Paper presented at the Society for Industrial and Organizational Psychology 18th Annual Conference, Orlando, Florida.

Tippins, N. (2002). Issues in implementing large-scale selection programs. In J. W. Hedge and E. D. Pulakos (Eds.), *Implementing organizational interventions: Steps, processes, and best practices.* San Francisco: Jossey-Bass.

Weiss, J. R. (2001). Six things you should know about XML. *The Industrial-Organizational Psychologist, 39*(2), 30–34.

CHAPTER 4

Research-Based Guidelines for Designing Distance Learning

What We Know So Far

Eduardo Salas
Renee E. DeRouin
Lisa N. Littrell

As Horton (2000, p. 6) aptly pointed out, "Web-based training is part of the biggest change in the way our species conducts training since the invention of the chalkboard or perhaps the alphabet. The development of computers and electronic communications media has removed barriers of space and time. We can obtain and deliver knowledge anytime anywhere." The advent of the World Wide Web has provided us with greater flexibility in the way we design and implement training than ever before. However, web-based training is only one small part of today's training technology. For instance, in recent years, satellite, video, audio, audiographic computer, and multimedia technology have been applied to organizational development programs, allowing organizations to provide training for employees simultaneously around the globe (Leonard, 1996). The use of these various technologies for training make up what are referred to as "distance learning" methods.

Corporate and government investment in distance learning has skyrocketed over the last few years. For instance, in 1999, organizations spent $3 billion on technology-delivered training. In 2001, this expenditure was estimated to jump to $8.2 billion, an increase in investment of approximately 170 percent in two years (Moe & Blodget, 2000). With regard to e-learning, one type of distance learning, organizations reported spending approximately $2.2 billion on the development and implementation of this training method in 2000. Those expenditures were expected to rise to $14.5 billion in 2004 ("The Payoffs of e-Learning," 2003).

The popularity of distance learning stems from its convenience. Distance learning allows employees to access training modules on demand from any location around the world. Moreover, it has been linked with substantial cost savings. Cisco Systems reported savings of 40 to 60 percent after implementing distance learning methods (Gill, 2000), Dow Chemical of $34 million (Brayton, 2001), IBM of $400 million (Mullich, 2004), and Hewlett-Packard of eleven months of training and $5.5 million (Horton, 2000). These benefits make distance learning an obvious solution to the challenge of training a global workforce in need of continuous skill updating. However, despite its advantages, research suggests that distance learning is not always more effective than traditional forms of instruction, such as classroom instruction (Alavi, Yoo, & Vogel, 1997; Russell, 1999; Webster & Hackley, 1997). In fact, Gale (2003) suggests that distance learning can be detrimental to organizational development if improperly implemented.

One reason for this may be that distance learning programs are not always developed according to standardized, experimentally tested procedures but instead are often simply adaptations of other training tools used by the company (for example, text materials transported into Microsoft PowerPoint and Word and placed on the web; Barton, 2001) or modifications of training programs offered by distance learning vendors (for example, click2learn.com, Smartforce, Teach.com, Learningbyte International, Learnframe, DigitalThink, Inc.; see www.distance-learning-list.com for an inventory of distance learning providers). As a result, organizations would benefit from a theoretically derived and empirically validated set of guidelines for the design and delivery of distance learning systems (Salas & Cannon-Bowers, 2001).

The purpose of this chapter is to provide applied researchers and training practitioners with literature-based guidelines for the design and delivery of distance learning systems. In developing these guidelines, we draw from the science of training literature (for example, Salas & Cannon-Bowers, 2001; Tannenbaum & Yukl, 1992) and from the theoretical and research literature on distance learning within educational (where most experimental work is performed) and organizational settings. However, because the focus of this chapter is on the implementation of organizational distance learning systems, our emphasis is on the findings from workplace distance learning studies.

In order to provide readers with an understanding of what distance learning in organizations actually involves, we begin with a definition and description of distance learning. Then, we offer thirteen guidelines for the design of distance learning programs within workplace organizations and provide literature support for each of these recommendations. We conclude with directions for future needs of distance learning research and practice and with an overall summary of how these recommendations might be used to improve the effectiveness of distance learning systems.

What Is Distance Learning?

Distance learning is "the desired outcome of distance education" (Kaplan-Leiserson, 2002, para. 78), although the terms "distance learning" and "distance education" are often used interchangeably. Distance education has been defined by the American Society for Training and Development (ASTD) as an "educational situation in which the instructor and students are separated by time, location, or both. Education or training courses are delivered to remote locations via synchronous or asynchronous means of instruction, including written correspondence, text, graphics, audio- and videotape, CD-ROM, online learning, audio- and videoconferencing, interactive TV, and facsimile" (Kaplan-Leiserson, 2002, para. 77). Many other terms are used in reference to distance learning technology, including distributed, online, distance, Internet- and web-based training (Salas, Kosarzycki, Burke, Fiore, & Stone, 2002). This has resulted in a rather fragmented understanding of distance learning, which as Kosarzycki, Salas, DeRouin, and Fiore (2003) point out, might be due to the rapid pace at which this technology has developed.

Distance learning is a broader concept than e-learning, which is primarily considered to be associated with electronic and computer-based learning methods (OneTouch Systems, Inc., 2003). As a result, distance learning encompasses both electronic and non-electronic forms of instruction (Kaplan-Leiserson, 2002). Because of its flexibility, distance learning offers several benefits over traditional forms of instruction, including the ability to train employees quickly and efficiently around the globe, use the most knowledgeable instructors for high-quality training, provide updates to training material as necessary, increase the responsibility trainees have for learning, and add trainees or instructors without much supplementary cost (Burgess & Russell, 2003). In addition, distance learning drastically reduces the indirect costs of training (for example, costs associated with travel to training facilities, hotel accommodations for trainees, lost work time for employees attending training) that have estimated to account for 80 percent of organizational training costs (Kozlowski, Toney, Mullins, Weissbein, Brown, & Bell, 2001).

How Can Distance Learning Be Improved?

As many organizations report, distance learning can be a viable method for training workplace skills (Brown, 2001; Gopher, Weil, & Baraket, 1994; O'Hara, 1990). However, this requires that it be designed in a way that facilitates effective learning. In this section, therefore, we discuss thirteen research-based guidelines for the design of successful distance learning programs (see Table 4.1 for a summary of these guidelines).

Guideline 1: Only provide distance learning when you are sure it meets the organization's needs.

Before distance learning is adopted as a training approach, it is important that organizations examine whether distance learning is an appropriate training strategy for the particular training need. Often and unintentionally, organizational management wants distance learning to work in a situation for which it is either inappropriate or infeasible. However, distance learning is not ideal for every training endeavor within an organization. Consequently,

Table 4.1. Research-Based Guidelines for Distance Learning.

Guideline	Description	References
Only provide distance learning when you are sure it meets the organization's needs.	Before distance learning is chosen as the strategy for delivering training, it is necessary to consider the organization development problems that it will address and the manner in which it can help solve these problems.	Gale, 2003; Kiser, 2002; "The Payoffs of e-Learning," 2003; "Ten Tactics to Make e-Learning 'Stick'," 2003.
Take into consideration human cognitive processes when designing distance learning programs.	Distance learning should be designed so that learning modules are consistent with the tenets of cognitive learning theory, a theory that explains how the mind processes environmental stimuli.	Clark & Mayer, 2003.
Enhance the learning experience by including both graphics and text in the presentation of learning topics.	Using multiple forms of media in distance learning is advantageous, because past research has demonstrated that individuals learn the most when they are actively engaged in the learning process; active learning is facilitated when both graphics and text are used in distance learning, because individuals are forced to make relevant connections between the words and the pictures.	Clark & Mayer, 2003; Mayer, 1989; Mayer & Anderson, 1991; Mayer & Gallini, 1990; Mayer, Steinhoff, Bower, & Mars, 1995.
Include learning games.	Learning games are typically computer games that have been adapted to train specific workplace skills; these games can be beneficial to learning in that they: (1) increase the appeal of online training; (2) make the idea of "tests" less frightening; (3) facilitate discovery learning; and (4) offer trainees substantial amounts of practice in workplace skills.	DeVeaux, 2001; Horton, 2000, 2002.

Keep learners engaged.	One of the primary reasons why learners drop out of distance learning programs is the failure of many online courses to keep learners engaged; this problem, however, can often be remedied by a simple change in the focus of the distance learning program.	Horton, 2000; Moshinskie, 2001; Salas & Cannon-Bowers, 2000; Skipper, 2000.
Offer a blended approach.	Offering a combination of training techniques will likely satisfy both employees who prefer to work online and employees who prefer classroom instruction.	Goodridge, 2001; Masie, 2002; Mullich, 2004; Phillips, Phillips, & Zuniga, 2000; ASTD & The Masie Center, 2001.
Allow for interaction between trainees and for communication between trainees and facilitators.	Distance learning programs can allow for interaction between trainees and for communication between trainees and facilitators through asynchronous and synchronous communication tools and by building factors into the program such as virtual communities and interactions with expert sources and facilitators.	Davis, 2003; Green, 2003; Salopek, 2002; Shepherd, 2003; "Ten Tactics to Make e-Learning 'Stick'," 2003.
Offer computer-based, distance learning methods to computer-savvy trainees or train learners on computer basics before offering computer-based training.	Distance learning that employs computer-based instruction will likely be most suitable for trainees with high levels of prior experience with computers; however, one way to bring trainees with lower levels of computer experience up to the level of trainees with more extensive experience is to provide instruction on basic computer skills before trainees begin computer-based, distance learning.	Brown, 2001; Schelin & Smarte, 2002.

Table 4.1. Research-Based Guidelines for Distance Learning, Cont'd.

Guideline	Description	References
Provide distance learning for hard-skill training but supplement it with other forms of instruction for soft-skill training and for training on such abstract topics as workplace ethics.	Distance learning appears to be particularly appropriate for the training of explicit, factual-based knowledge, for soft-skill training, and for training on such abstract topics as workplace ethics; however, distance learning might best be administered by supplementing it with other training approaches (lecture, role play).	Mullich, 2004; Welsh, Wanberg, Brown, & Simmering, 2003.
Offer trainees control over certain aspects of instruction.	Trainees in distance learning programs might benefit from control over both the context of training examples/practice problems and the amount of instruction; however, it might be better to withhold some types of control from trainees, such as control over pacing, sequencing, and provision of optional content, because research has not shown these types of control to be consistently positive.	Freitag & Sullivan, 1995; Gray, 1989; Judd, Bunderson, & Bessent, 1970; Lai, 2001; Ross, Morrison, & O'Dell, 1989; Ross & Rakow, 1981; Steinberg, Baskin, & Matthews, 1985.
When offering trainees control over instruction, make sure that trainee preparation, system design, and workplace conditions facilitate successful use of that control.	In order to ensure that increased learner control will lead to better training outcomes, certain conditions should be met before trainees are granted this control, such as providing instructions on how to use learner control and why, allowing trainees to "skip" rather than "add" extra instruction, and promoting use of learner control through supervisor support of this instructional feature.	Baldwin & Ford, 1988; DeRouin, Fritzsche, & Salas, 2004; Gay, 1986; Hicken, Sullivan, & Klein, 1992; Rouiller & Goldstein, 1993; Salas & Cannon-Bowers, 2000, 2001;

		Steinberg, Baskin, & Matthews, 1985; Tannenbaum & Yukl, 1992.
Guide trainees through the distance learning program.	Tools, such as advanced organizers and cognitive maps, may help trainees to have a better understanding of the core elements of training and, simultaneously, to traverse a distance learning program more easily.	Bell & Kozlowski, 2002; Cannon-Bowers, Rhodenizer; Salas, & Bowers, 1998; Mayer, 2004.
Make the program user-friendly.	The course content of distance learning must be divided into small, manageable sections and each web page within the program should be limited to no more than two hundred words.	Mullich, 2004; Zeidman, 2003.

before distance learning is chosen as the strategy for delivering training, it is necessary to consider the organizational development problems that it will address and the manner in which it can help solve these problems. In addition, the costs of distance learning, its feasibility given the organizational infrastructure, and its usefulness must be discussed before a distance learning program reaches the initial design phase ("Ten Tactics to Make e-Learning 'Stick'," 2003).

Furthermore, according to the same source, distance learning courses should be designed with a specific job in mind. Many organizations make the mistake of buying a distance learning program before they consider the objectives of the program. However, the phrase "one size fits all" does not apply to distance learning, and organizations are often forced to make their distance learning needs fit the purchased program. One company, the Royal Bank of Scotland, was able to avoid this problem by conducting a thorough analysis of existing distance learning programs before making the switch from classroom to online training (Kiser, 2002). The Royal Bank decided to create its own "homegrown" web-based/CD-ROM program with the help of a custom e-learning developer, Epic Group. According to Lars Hyland, the Epic Group account manager, "The system didn't offer the full range of functionality written on the advertisements of a lot of LMS [Learning Management System] vendors, but it met 80 to 90 percent of the bank's actual needs" (Kiser, 2002, p. 34). Because the Royal Bank did not choose to adopt an off-the-shelf program whose customization would have cost even more time and money, the company was able to develop a program that appropriately matched the organization's training needs and that could later be rebuilt for added functionality.

Guideline 2: Take into consideration human cognitive processes when designing distance learning programs.

Distance learning should be designed so that learning modules are consistent with the tenets of cognitive learning theory. Cognitive learning theory explains how the mind reacts to sensory information in the environment. In order for sensory information to be processed and stored in long-term memory, several events have to occur. First, the critical information from the environment needs to be recognized. Second, working memory has to be cleared so that room is available for rehearsal (an essential component of learning) of this critical information. Third, the new auditory and visual information has to be consolidated and then integrated with the information already present in long-term memory through rehearsal in working memory. Fourth, the knowledge and skills gained from the integration must be retrieved from long-term memory and placed into working memory when needed. Fifth, meta-cognitive skills (that is, skills in how to manage one's cognitive processes) must guide and direct all of the above events (Clark & Mayer, 2003).

The design of distance learning programs should take into account each of these cognitive events. For instance, in order for critical information in learning modules to be recognized, instructors should ensure that this information is presented via vibrant colors or lists of learning objectives. To reduce the load on working memory, distance learning designers should omit irrelevant pictures and sounds and be concise in their wording of text. In order to consolidate the information from the eyes and ears and to integrate it with existing information, pictures on the screen should be combined with text and sounds and active practice should be encouraged. To improve retrieval and transfer, the practice exercises and examples in the distance learning program should incorporate material from the actual job. And last, in order to enhance meta-cognitive monitoring, the distance learning program should include self-checks on learning progress (Clark & Mayer, 2003).

Guideline 3: Enhance the learning experience by including both graphics and text in the presentation of learning topics.

Using multiple forms of media in distance learning is advantageous because past research has demonstrated that individuals learn more from a combination of graphics and text than from text alone (Mayer, 1989; Mayer & Anderson, 1991; Mayer & Gallini, 1990). Active learning is facilitated when both graphics and text are used in distance learning, because individuals are forced to make relevant connections between the words and the pictures (Clark & Mayer, 2003). However, the illustrations that accompany the text must enhance the material presented in the text rather than distract the learner. Graphics can be used to teach content types, organize topics, demonstrate relationships, and present case studies (Clark & Mayer, 2003).

Typical distance learning programs that use both graphics and text present the textual information and graphical illustrations separately (Clark & Mayer, 2003). That is, the individual must first read the text and then scroll down to view the graphics. Learning would be enhanced if the text and graphics were presented in a more integrative fashion. Instead, the text should be placed as closely as possible to the graphical illustrations used to enhance textual meaning. Research supports this assertion in that several studies have revealed that learners receiving integrated information presentations outperform learners receiving material in which the text is separated from the graphics (Mayer, Steinhoff, Bower, & Mars, 1995; Moreno & Mayer, 1999).

Guideline 4: Include learning games.

Another way in which distance learning can be improved is through the use of learning games. Learning games are typically computer games (arcade games, quiz-show games, crossword puzzles) that have been adapted to train specific workplace skills. However, learning games can also involve tools as simple as email, chat, and Internet forums through which groups of employees collaborate on training topics (for example, the galactic wormhole game in which players "travel" back and forth in time and discuss how relevant, work-related issues would change depending on the time period considered) (Jasinski & Thiagarajan, 2000). According to Horton (2002), games can be beneficial to learning in that they: (1) increase the appeal of online training; (2) make the idea of "tests" less frightening; (3) facilitate discovery learning (that is, allow trainees to uncover the patterns and relationships in information themselves); and (4) offer trainees substantial amounts of practice in workplace skills. Learning games also allow trainees to actively participate in distance training without taking their focus away from the training content (Horton, 2000).

One place where learning games have been applied extensively is in military training. Because many of today's military recruits have extensive experience with video games, the military now uses digital war games, such as Joint Force Employment, Marine Doom, Spearhead II, and Falcon 4.0, as instructional tools for military personnel. These games serve to capture recruits' attention and, at the same time, provide them with skills that can be transferred to the battlefield (DeVeaux, 2001).

Through the use of learning games, learners are likely to become more engaged in the learning process and more motivated to succeed than they would in online courses that rely solely on text as a means of conveying information. However, several guidelines should be followed in the choice or design of a learning game for organizational distance learning (see Horton, 2002). First, success in the game should indicate learning of the desired material. If success in the game is not related to mastery of the required knowledge, skills, and attitudes (KSAs), then the game is not a useful method of presenting and testing information. Second, the game should always be a challenge to the learner. As the learner progresses through the game, the game should increase in difficulty. This technique ensures that the learner will continue to work hard during the learning game and that he or she will not lose interest partway through its completion. Third, the game should provide the learner with continuous and useful feedback. This feedback will allow learners to gauge their performance and to make changes to their strategies and/or methods as the game is played. Fourth, the game should not be too difficult for the learner to understand or play. If the game requires rules and instructions that are too complicated for learners to comprehend, they are likely to give up on the game or to quit the training program altogether. Fifth, the game should be flexible and adaptable to training needs. This characteristic of the learning game allows it to be altered when new technology becomes available, when training content has to be changed, or when the game has to be played by individuals or entire classrooms at once (Horton, 2002).

Guideline 5: Keep learners engaged.

Motorola reports that a significant gap exists in the number of employees who register for their e-learning courses and the number of employees who actually complete them (Moshinskie, 2001). In addition, estimates suggest that as many as 80 percent of employees who sign up for online training programs drop out before the programs end (Flood, 2002). This attrition rate is troubling because one of the basic benefits of distance learning is greater accessibility to instructional material. If this increased accessibility actually reduces the number of people who attend employee training, then the usefulness of distance learning for employee development may be called into question.

One of the primary reasons why learners drop out of distance learning programs is the failure of many online courses to keep learners engaged (Skipper, 2000). This problem, however, can often be remedied by a simple change in the focus of the distance learning program. In his review of the literature and discussions with distance learning experts, Moshinskie (2001) found that distance learners are most likely to be engaged when they are able to see the benefits of training to on-the-job performance. As a result, learner engagement in e-learning can be enhanced simply by tying training material to requisite job skills. One way in which this might be accomplished is to describe how the training objectives are related to workplace KSAs (Salas & Cannon-Bowers, 2000). This information can be provided in the instructions trainees are given before training begins.

In addition to linking training objectives to job skills in the instructions, Horton (2000) recommends that distance learning tasks actually require the development of some form of intellectual property that learners can use after completing the training course. For instance, the course could provide employees with training on how to write action plans or business proposals that could later be utilized within the company. In addition, the training could involve the creation of a computer program that could afterwards be applied back on the job. The development of these various forms of intellectual property will help trainees see the relevance of training to workplace KSAs. As a result, they will find themselves more engaged in the learning process and will be less likely to quit before training is completed.

Guideline 6: Offer a blended approach.

Although distance learning is often one of the most efficient ways to deliver training, it is sometimes not the most preferred. A report by ASTD found that 62 percent of employees surveyed preferred classroom training to e-learning (ASTD & The Masie Center, 2001). In addition, in their review of the literature on distance learning, Phillips, Phillips, and Zuniga (2000) found that most employees prefer face-to-face instruction over distance learning methods.

One way to remedy this problem is to offer a blended approach to learning. In blended approaches, distance learning (typically computer-based, e-learning) is combined with classroom instruction to create experiences that capitalize on the best of both worlds: the cost effectiveness and on-demand availability of distance learning and the face-to-face interaction and socialization features of classroom training (Goodridge, 2001; Masie, 2002). Because distance learning is best used to convey explicit knowledge, such as product information or principles regarding customer satisfaction, it is typically used for the delivery of content information to trainees. Face-to-face instruction, in contrast, is typically used for the delivery of workplace skills due to its ability to convey tacit knowledge, such as judgment, personal awareness, interpersonal skills, and growth (Mullich, 2004).

One organization that has had success with the blended learning approach is IBM. Studies have revealed that, when compared to traditional classroom instruction, IBM's blended learning approach reduced training costs by one-third and increased learning outcomes by 500 percent (Mullich, 2004). Although the effectiveness of the blended learning approach over and above distance learning alone has yet to be determined, it appears that offering a combination of training techniques will likely satisfy both employees who prefer to work online and employees who prefer classroom instruction. However, as Hofmann (2001) points out, "Determining the right blend [of classroom and distance learning techniques] isn't easy or to be taken lightly" (p. 18).

Guideline 7: Allow for interaction between trainees and for communication between trainees and facilitators.

In a survey of online learning conducted by the 2001 Campaign for Learning, results indicated that only 3 percent of respondents preferred learning alone (Linne & Plers, 2002). In addition, research has shown that adults learn better in situations in which they are members of a community of learners (Davis, 2003). As a result, many organizations have incorporated synchronous and asynchronous communication tools into their distance learning programs. Synchronous communication tools typically involve the use of chat rooms or threaded discussions that allow trainees to ask and answer questions about training topics in "real time." In contrast, asynchronous communication tools, such as message boards, permit trainees to post questions or answers that can be accessed later by other trainees (Selix, 2001).

In a study comparing the use of these two communication tools within a distributed learning environment, Alavi, Marakas, and Yoo (2002) found that email, an asynchronous communication tool, was a significantly more effective method of interaction between trainees than a more advanced asynchronous and synchronous messaging system. In particular, the authors found that the use of email for communication between trainees led to better learning outcomes than the more advanced system. One reason for this might be that the advanced system was so complex that trainees spent more time trying to understand the communication tool than they spent working on the training task; as a result, the less complex communication tool (email) was more effective in transmitting information from one trainee to another than the sophisticated asynchronous/synchronous messaging tool.

In addition to asynchronous and synchronous communication tools, distance learning programs can also be made more interactive by building factors into the program, such as virtual communities and interactions with expert sources and facilitators (Shepherd, 2003). At Mattel, for example, best practices in business are shared through a web-based operations university in a way similar to that of a virtual community (Green, 2003). When one Mattel factory develops an innovative idea, that idea is posted to the web so that factories around the world can be alerted to and apply this new idea in their own facilities. In addition, it is essential that distance learning programs incorporate an online tutor or facilitator into the design to provide technical support ("Ten Tactics to Make e-Learning 'Stick'," 2003). Jennifer Hofmann, president of InSync Training Synergy, recommends the use of two facilitators for synchronous learning events in which audio and video are employed, one facilitator for controlling visuals and troubleshooting and one for presenting instructional content (Salopek,

2002). According to Hofmann, "[This technique] helps to change the voices up to keep learners engaged" (Salopek, 2002, p. 18). These various methods for facilitating interaction among trainees have yet to be supported by empirical research, although they are likely to facilitate a sense of community among learners, which can lead to improved learning outcomes (Davis, 2003).

Guideline 8: Offer computer-based, distance learning methods to computer-savvy trainees or train learners on computer basics before offering computer-based training.

Although distance learning has been found to be an effective training method, it is not necessarily the best training method for everyone. Certain types of trainees (for example, trainees with computer experience) might perform better in distance learning environments than others do. One study (Brown, 2001) found that computer experience was significantly related to post-training test scores. Specifically, trainees with more computer experience performed better on the training post-test than did trainees with less computer experience. It is likely that distance learning that employs computer-based instruction will, therefore, be most suitable for trainees with high levels of prior experience with computers.

One way to bring trainees with lower levels of computer experience up to the level of trainees with more extensive experience is to provide instruction on basic computer skills before trainees begin computer-based, distance learning. This instruction may be presented in the form of a tutorial that trainees complete before training. In order to determine who needs to complete the tutorial, a brief quiz on computer knowledge may be administered before training. Trainees who pass the quiz may continue on to the main topics of the distance learning program, whereas trainees who do not pass may be presented with the training on computer skills.

Jabil Circuit, an electronics manufacturing company, found that the effects of low computer experience on distance learning outcomes could be ameliorated by including computer training and e-learning in their classroom courses (Schelin & Smarte, 2002). According to Michael McGinnis, the training manager at Jabil Circuit, "The way we introduced e-learning to our campus was to make it part of our classes. This enabled computer-illiterate personnel to learn how to operate the computer, and it had great results in the training . . ." (Schelin & Smarte, 2002, p. 22). In addition, Jabil Circuit only included less-sophisticated technologies (for example, Microsoft PowerPoint) in their distance learning platform when it was first introduced. This allowed less computer-savvy employees to focus on the content of the instruction rather than on its various tools and functions.

Guideline 9: Provide distance learning for hard-skill training but supplement it with other forms of instruction for soft-skill training and for training on such abstract topics as workplace ethics.

As mentioned briefly in the discussion of blended learning approaches, distance learning appears to be particularly appropriate for the training of explicit, factual-based knowledge (Mullich, 2004). However, its use in the training of soft skills has been the subject of some debate (Welsh, Wanberg, Brown, & Simmering, 2003). For instance, distance learning may be inappropriate for training in interpersonal skills and teamwork. These skills often involve the use of nonverbal and verbal communication and may, therefore, require face-to-face interaction between trainees and between trainees and instructors. In addition, distance learning may be an ineffective training method for such topics as workplace ethics. Workplace ethics often involves a set of unwritten rules that vary depending on the circumstances involved. As a result, they are not typically hard-and-fast rules that can be delivered primarily via text format.

Although organizations and educational institutions, such as the Bank of America (Dobbs, 2000) and Loyola Marymount University (see http://careers.lmu.edu), have implemented distance learning approaches for the training of interpersonal and interviewing skills, and organizations such as Dupont have used distance learning techniques to teach workplace ethics ("Ethics Before It Was Fashionable," 2004), the use of distance learning for these topics might best be administered in a blended approach (as described above). In such cases, supplementing distance learning with other training approaches, for example, lecture or role play, might best provide for the training of soft skills and topics that are difficult to specify in concrete terms.

Guideline 10: Offer trainees control over certain aspects of instruction.

Research findings from the educational psychology literature suggest that learners benefit from increased control during the learning experience. For instance, learners have been found to have greater satisfaction with multimedia learning programs when they are given control over the context of examples. Ross, Morrison, and O'Dell (1989) found that learners who were allowed to choose how their examples were framed (for example, in terms of educational, business, or sports contexts) were more satisfied with the learning experience and viewed more practice problems than learners who were not given control over the contexts of their examples.

Similar results have been found for learners given control over the amount of instruction. When learners in a computerized training program are allowed to specify whether they prefer a brief or a comprehensive training program before beginning training and are subsequently matched to this preference, they have been found to enjoy the training more and to perform better on training post-tests than trainees in programs unmatched to their preferences (Freitag & Sullivan, 1995).

These findings suggest that trainees in distance learning programs might benefit from control over both the context of training examples/practice problems and the amount of instruction (as indicated by preferences for a brief or comprehensive training program evaluated prior to the start of the training program). However, it might be better to withhold some types of control from trainees. The research findings for control over the pacing, sequencing, and provision of optional content (that is, the choice of whether or not to view more examples/practice exercises during training) has not been shown to be consistently positive. In fact, such control has been found to lead to significantly reduced training performance (Gray, 1989; Judd, Bunderson, & Bessent, 1970; Lai, 2001; Ross & Rakow, 1981; Steinberg, Baskin, & Matthews, 1985). As a result, organizations might choose to withhold giving trainees control over these instructional features until after they have demonstrated mastery of training topics.

Guideline 11: When offering trainees control over instruction, make sure that trainee preparation, system design, and workplace conditions facilitate successful use of that control.

In order to ensure that increased learner control will lead to better training outcomes, certain conditions should be met before trainees are granted this control (DeRouin, Fritzsche, & Salas, 2004; for a complete summary of these conditions, see the learner control guidelines in Table 4.2). First, steps should be taken to prepare trainees to take control. These steps may include providing instructions before training that describe the types and amount of control that trainees will be given during training and, more importantly, why they are given this control (Gay, 1986; Steinberg, Baskin, & Matthews, 1985). An example of how training instructions might fulfill these dual purposes is as follows: "In this training course, you are free to select the context of training examples. In other words, because you are the best judge of your own learning style, this program offers you a choice of the types of examples you would like to view. Your choices include business-related, military, and educational contexts. You can choose the example context that you believe will best help you to understand the topic in each example. This helps you to be in the driver's seat of your own learning experience" (DeRouin, Fritzche, & Salas, 2004, p. 152). By providing trainees with an understanding of the learner control they have and why this control is beneficial to their learning experience, they are more likely to accept and successfully utilize learner control within distance learning programs.

Second, the distance learning system should be designed so that trainees can effectively make use of the control they have. For instance, the learner control literature suggests that designing an instructional program so that learners are allowed to "skip" instruction is more beneficial than designing a program so that they are allowed to "add" extra instruction. Specifically, Hicken, Sullivan, and Klein (1992) found that learners who were given a comprehensive version of a program and were allowed to skip over certain

Table 4.2. Research-Based Guidelines for Offering Learner Control in Workplace e-Learning.

Guideline	Description	References
Preparing Trainees for Learner-Led Instruction		
Understanding learner control is half the battle.	Give trainees instructions that allow them to understand the control they have and how that control can contribute to improved learning outcomes.	Gay, 1986; Hicken, Sullivan, & Klein, 1992; Steinberg, Baskin, & Matthews, 1985.
Give it time.	Provide trainees with enough time in training to learn how to use learner control strategies.	Cronbach & Snow, 1981; Reeves, 1993.
Calibrate expectations.	Help trainees understand that adult training, especially learner-controlled training, is challenging.	Freitag & Sullivan, 1995; Gray, 1987.
Designing Learner-Controlled Training		
Offer help.	Trainees should be given tools during training that help them to diagnose their skill development.	Meta-cognitive/ self-regulatory training: Osman & Hannafin, 1992; Schraw, 1998; self-tests/ feedback: Brown & Ford, 2002; advisement/adaptive guidance: Bell & Kozlowski, 2002; Shyu & Brown, 1992; Tennyson, 1980.

Table 4.2. Research-Based Guidelines for Offering Learner Control in Workplace e-Learning, Cont'd.

Guideline	Description	References
What's good for one trainee may not be good for another.	Certain trainees may benefit more from learner control than others (for example, trainees with high ability, prior experience, and motivation).	Colquitt, LePine, & Noe, 2000; Gay, 1986; Kanfer & Ackerman, 1989; Lai, 2001; Tsai & Tai, 2003.
More isn't necessarily better.	The amount of control given needs to be matched to the amount necessary for effective training; with too much control, trainees' cognitive resources may become tied up in decision making rather than training content.	Freitag & Sullivan, 1995; Gray, 1987.
"Skipping" is better than "adding."	Allowing trainees to skip extra instruction rather than to add extra instruction during training may increase the amount of time spent on the optional portions of a program and still offer trainees control over the amount of instruction.	Hicken, Sullivan, & Klein, 1992.
Keep it real.	Trainees may benefit from control over the context of their examples, such as nursing, sports, and so forth.	Ross, Morrison, & O'Dell, 1989.
Footprints help ("You are here").	The training program may need to provide trainees with tools that allow them to pilot themselves through the program and utilize the control they have.	Cognitive maps: El-Tigi & Branch, 1997; Large, 1996; footprints, "return" arrows and "landmark" links: Nielsen, 1990.
Keep each instructional segment self-contained.	Trainees in learner-controlled training should not be required to remember too much material when transferring from one instructional segment to another.	Kearsley, 1988.

Share design control.	Trainees can be given some control over the program's design (for example, to open multiple windows at once and to control their size and location on the screen).	Kearsley, 1988; Park, 1991.
Be consistent.	The design of the training program should be relatively consistent so that trainees are able to better focus on learner control decisions.	El-Tigi & Branch, 1997.
Create smooth transitions.	In learner-led instruction, transitions between instructional segments are important so that trainees understand how the segments are functionally related.	Park, 1991.

Creating Workplace Conditions That Facilitate Successful Learner-Led Instruction

Promote it.	Organizations can promote learner-controlled training through supervisor support of learner-led instruction.	Baldwin & Ford, 1988; Rouiller & Goldstein, 1993; Salas & Cannon-Bowers, 2000, 2001; Tannenbaum & Yukl, 1992.
Organizational climate matters.	Some organizational climates may be more supportive of learner-controlled training than others. Organizations should first assess employees' receptivity to learner-led instruction prior to its implementation.	Rouiller & Goldstein, 1993; Theory Y cultures: McGregor, 1957; need for future research.
Make it matter.	Use of learner control strategies can be linked to organizational incentives to increase trainee motivation.	Colquitt, LePine, & Noe, 2000; Vroom, 1964; need for future research.

Source: Adapted from "Optimizing e-learning: Research-based guidelines for learner-controlled training," by R. E. DeRouin, B. A. Fritzsche, & E. Salas, 2004, *Human Resource Management, 43*, pp.150–151. Copyright 2004 by Wiley Publishers, Inc.

topics viewed more examples and were more satisfied with the computerized learning program than learners who were given an abbreviated version of a program and were allowed to add extra topics. By allowing trainees to skip rather than add instructional topics, they are less likely to pass over important information in the program; moreover, trainees are likely to feel more responsibility for their learning because they chose which topics to view and which to skip. These conditions may lead trainees to perform better on the overall instructional program and to focus more on the training content.

Third, workplace conditions must facilitate learner control. For example, the science of training literature suggests that supervisor support has a profound impact on training effectiveness (Baldwin & Ford, 1988; Rouiller & Goldstein, 1993; Salas & Cannon-Bowers, 2000, 2001; Tannenbaum & Yukl, 1992). Because supervisor support reflects how much the organization itself values training, trainees are more likely to invest themselves in the training experience if their supervisors consider training important.

Supervisor support of learner control is likely to have similar effects on its acceptance. If supervisors do not support learner control in distance learning, trainees are not likely to make use of this learning option. Therefore, it is important that supervisors promote the use of learner control in distance learning systems and its potential value in the learning experience.

Guideline 12: Guide trainees through the distance learning program.

Although the literature suggests that learners benefit from increased control over certain aspects of training, it is important that trainees still be given enough structure in the learning program that they are able to learn the skills necessary for effective performance on the job. The concept of "discovery learning" has been heralded by educational psychologists as the instructional wave of the future (Shulman & Keisler, 1966). Its roots in constructivism, a theory of learning in which learners are considered active participants (Steffe & Gale, 1995), discovery learning refers to the idea that students learn best by guiding themselves through the learning process, making mistakes that eventually lead to a better cognitive understanding of the subject matter. However, Mayer (2004) in a recent article in *American Psychologist,* argued that discovery learning as a purely exploratory, undirected means of learning is less effective than discovery learning in which structure and guidance are provided for learners. Mayer cited three areas of research supporting his proposition: discovery of problem-solving rules (1960s), discovery of conservation strategies (1970s), and discovery of programming concepts (1980s). In his examination of each of these three research areas, Mayer found that guided discovery by an instructor was more successful than pure discovery in which students themselves chose what and how to learn. As a result, he concluded that, as an instructional method, discovery learning is primarily effective when learners are directed through the learning process.

Distance learning is one form of training that is particularly amenable to discovery learning (Allen, 2002). Its ability to link learning modules to outside websites and to provide information in virtually any form (for example, graphics, computer animation, simulation) makes it an ideal environment for trainee-directed instruction. However, Mayer's (2004) review of the literature on discovery learning suggests that distance learning may be more effectively designed and implemented with guidance designating which topics to study during training. The science of training suggests that the use of tools, such as advanced organizers, may help trainees to have a better understanding of the core elements of training and, simultaneously, to traverse a distance learning program more easily (Cannon-Bowers, Rhodenizer, Salas, & Bowers, 1998). In addition, adaptive guidance in the form of recommendations about the material on which to concentrate may be presented to trainees throughout the training program to help them remain focused on appropriate topics (Bell & Kozlowski, 2002).

Guideline 13: Make the program user-friendly.

A survey conducted by researchers at James Madison University revealed that 36 percent of respondents cited poor design and mismatch of learning styles as the primary reasons for abandoning e-learning programs (Mullich, 2004). Thus, many elements must be incorporated into distance learning programs to make them more user-friendly. First, distance learning courses should be designed by experts. These individuals not only must possess an under-standing of course design, but they also must understand instruc-tional design principles (Zeidman, 2003). Second, the course content of distance learning must be divided into smaller, more manageable sections. This can be accomplished by dividing the course into lessons spanning no longer than fifteen pages (Zeid-man, 2003). Furthermore, each web page within the program should be limited to no more than two hundred words. These strategies help to ensure that learners are not overwhelmed by the sheer quantity of instructional material.

The quality of the course design can also be improved by in-cluding instructional pages at the beginning of each learning mod-ule (Zeidman, 2003). The first few pages of each course should include instructions regarding the use of the distance learning pro-gram. This procedure enables the user to practice navigating the interface before beginning course material. In addition, each page throughout the distance learning course should include links to a help page (Zeidman, 2003). This practice will make it easier for learners to solve problems as they progress through the course.

Future Needs in the Design and Delivery of Distance Learning Systems

In the creation of our distance learning guidelines, we found that much of the research literature focuses on how best to deliver dis-tance learning to trainees and on the cost benefits of distance learning over traditional forms of instruction. However, little re-search is devoted to such topics as evaluation, what works in dis-tance learning, standardization of the design and architecture of distance learning, and the application of distance learning to syn-thetic learning environments. Consequently, several needs exist for the future of distance learning research and practice.

First, *applied researchers should conduct more robust evaluations of distance learning systems.* The only way for organizations to truly know whether or not distance learning is effective is to experi-mentally evaluate the learning outcomes of trainees. Researchers, therefore, should move away from focusing primarily on the deliv-ery of distance learning to focusing on whether trainees learn in distance learning systems. A few recent attempts have been made to evaluate whether or not distance learning is an effective learning approach in workplace organizations and educational institutions (Alavi, Marakas, & Yoo, 2002; Brown, 2001; Gopher, Weil, & Baraket, 1994; O'Hara, 1990).

However, these research studies are few and far between. One reason may be that businesses traditionally do not allow researchers into their organizations to systematically evaluate the effectiveness of their distance learning systems. However, if we are to gain a better understanding of the consequences and benefits of distance learning to workplace training, businesses must open their doors to applied researchers.

Second, *researchers and practitioners must develop a catalog of what works in distance learning.* Although several practitioners have created "tips" and "tactics" for offering distance learning in organizations ("Ten Tactics to Make e-Learning 'Stick'," 2003), it is important that researchers and practitioners work together to produce an inventory of best practices in distance learning. Moreover, it is important that these best practices be linked to learning outcomes.

One attempt to bridge the gap between the research and practice of distance learning was Welsh, Wanberg, Brown, and Simmering's (2003) discussion of empirical and interview-based findings for distance learning. By combining a review of the distance learning literature with subject-matter expert interviews, they were better able to determine the most effective practices of distance learning initiatives and what practices are actually employed in workplace organizations. More alliances like this must be formed between researchers and practitioners in order to synthesize the results of empirical research with applied practice of distance learning systems.

Third, *practitioners need to standardize the design and architecture of distance learning so that distance learning is both created and presented in a consistent format.* This format should be based on the findings of the distance learning literature so that what has been found to be effective in distance learning research and practice is applied to its actual design and structure. The design and architecture, however, should be flexible and adaptable enough that organizations can incorporate their own learning techniques into the distance learning framework and can modify this framework to meet their specific organizational needs.

Fourth, *researchers must study the application of synthetic learning environments to distance learning.* Synthetic learning environments refer to the use of simulation and virtual reality in the training of complex tasks (Aidman, Galanis, Manton, Vozzo, & Bonner, 2002). Distance learning may involve the use of synthetic learning environments through the integration of simulation and virtual reality techniques into distance learning systems. The overall purpose of this integration is to make the learning experience more dynamic for trainees by having them interact with the program through hands-on tasks rather than text. As a result, trainees will likely learn more from the distance learning program than they would through more passive participation with the training material.

Conclusion

In their interview with subject-matter experts of distance learning programs, Welsh, Wanberg, Brown, and Simmering (2003) identified four themes about how distance learning will be applied in the future. These themes suggest that, in the next few years, synchronous learning tools will be employed more, blended learning approaches will become more widespread, distance learning technology will be improved and will become more easily accessible, and several aspects of distance learning (for example, the presentation of information, performance support, training, and collaboration with peers) will be more appropriately integrated. Although these four themes imply that distance learning programs will improve over the next few years, researchers and practitioners would still benefit from a list of research-based guidelines for the effective design of distance learning programs.

Therefore, in this chapter, we offered thirteen guidelines for the design and delivery of distance learning programs. These guidelines were based on relevant empirical and theoretical research on distance learning from both educational and organizational settings and from the science of training literature. The guidelines may be viewed by researchers and practitioners as both tools for practice and as avenues for future research.

Because distance learning will be increasingly adopted and applied by organizations in the next few years ("The Payoffs of e-Learning," 2003), it is important that organizations determine the most effective ways of designing distance learning programs. We hope that these guidelines will serve as a tool for the development of workplace distance learning courses as well as a stimulus for future research on the factors leading to distance learning success.

References

Aidman, E., Galanis, G., Manton, J., Vozzo, A., & Bonner, M. (2002). Evaluating human systems in military training. *Australian Journal of Psychology, 54,* 168–173.

Alavi, M., Marakas, G. M., & Yoo, Y. (2002). A comparative study of distributed learning environments on learning outcomes. *Information Systems Research, 13,* 404–415.

Alavi, M., Yoo, Y., & Vogel, D. R. (1997). Using information technology to add value to management education. *Academy of Management Journal, 40,* 1310–1333.

Allen, M. (2002, January). Discovery learning: Repurposing an old paradigm. *e-Learning, 3,* 19–20.

ASTD & The Masie Center. (2001). *e-Learning: "If we build it, will they come?"* Alexandria, VA: ASTD.

Baldwin, T. T., & Ford, J. K. (1988). Transfer of training: A review and directions for future research. *Personnel Psychology, 41,* 63–105.

Barton, K. (2001, January). Survey: Learning decisions benchmarking survey: The nuts and bolts of making e-learning. *Learning Decisions Interactive Newsletter.* [Retrieved March 2, 2004, from www.learning decisions.com/login/site/default.cfm]

Bell, B. S., & Kozlowski, S.W.J. (2002). Adaptive guidance: Enhancing self-regulation, knowledge, and performance in technology-based training. *Personnel Psychology, 55,* 267–306.

Brayton, C. (2001, October 1). The learning curve. The fragmented e-learning industry rallies around a new business case: The value chain. *Internet World.* [Retrieved March 2, 2004, from www.internet world.com/magazine.php?inc=100101/10.01.01ebusiness1.html]

Brown, K. G. (2001). Using computers to deliver training: Which employees learn and why? *Personnel Psychology, 54,* 271–296.

Brown, K. G., & Ford, J. K. (2002). Using computer technology in training: Building an infrastructure for active learning. In K. Kraiger (Ed.), *Creating, implementing, and managing effective training and development* (pp. 192–233). San Francisco: Jossey-Bass.

Burgess, J.R.D., & Russell, J.E.A. (2003). The effectiveness of distance learning initiatives in organizations. *Journal of Vocational Behavior, 63,* 289–303.

Cannon-Bowers, J. A., Rhodenizer, L., Salas, E., & Bowers, C. A. (1998). A framework for understanding pre-practice conditions and their impact on learning. *Personnel Psychology, 51,* 291–320.

Clark, R. C., & Mayer, R. E. (Eds.). (2003). *e-Learning and the science of instruction: Proven guidelines for consumers and designers of multimedia learning.* San Francisco: Pfeiffer.

Colquitt, J. A., LePine, J. A., & Noe, R. A. (2000). Toward an integrative theory of training motivation: A meta-analytic path analysis of 20 years of research. *Journal of Applied Psychology, 85,* 678–707.

Cronbach, L. J., & Snow, R. E. (1981). *Aptitudes and instructional methods: A handbook for research on interactions.* New York: Irvington.

Davis, J. (2003). The magic of blending e-learning, classic training. *Bank Technology News, 16,* 58–59.

DeRouin, R. E., Fritzsche, B. A., & Salas E. (2004). Optimizing e-learning: Research-based guidelines for learner-controlled training. *Human Resource Management Journal, 43,* 147–162.

DeVeaux, P. (2001, April). War games: Digital game-based learning transforms military training. *e-Learning, 2,* 30–32.

Dobbs, K. (2000). What the online world needs now: Quality. *Training, 37,* 84–94.

El-Tigi, M., & Branch, R. M. (1997). Designing for interaction, learner control, and feedback during web-based learning. *Educational Technology, 37,* 23–29.

Ethics before it was fashionable. (2004, February). *Corporate Legal Times, 14,* 23.

Flood, J. (2002). Read all about it: Online learning facing 80% attrition rates. *Turkish Online Journal of Distance Education, 3.*

Freitag, E. T., & Sullivan, H. J. (1995). Matching learner preference to amount of instruction: An alternative form of learner control. *Educational Technology, Research and Development, 43,* 5–14.

Gale, S. F. (2003). Making e-learning more than "pixie dust." *Workforce Management, 82,* 112–122.

Gay, G. (1986). Interaction of learner control and prior understanding in computer-assisted video instruction. *Journal of Educational Psychology, 78,* 225–227.

Gill, M. (2000). e-Learning technology and strategy for organizations. In K. Fry (Ed.), *The business of e-learning: Bringing your organization in the knowledge economy.* Sydney, Australia: University of Technology.

Goodridge, E. (2001, April 23). e-Learning blends in with classrooms. *Information Week, 834,* 97.

Gopher, D., Weil, M., & Baraket, T. (1994). Transfer of skill from a computer game trainer to flight. *Human Factors, 36,* 387–405.

Gray, S. H. (1987). The effect of sequence control on computer assisted learning. *Journal of Computer-Based Instruction, 14,* 54–56.

Gray, S. H. (1989). The effect of locus of control and sequence control on computerized information retrieval and retention. *Journal of Educational Computing Research, 5,* 459–471.

Green, H. (2003, November 24). Online extra: Taking Mattel from "atoms to electrons" [Electronic Version]. *BusinessWeek.*

Hicken, S., Sullivan, H., & Klein, J. (1992). Learner control modes and incentive variations in computer-delivered instruction. *Educational Technology, Research and Development, 40,* 15–26.

Hofmann, J. (2001, April). Blended learning case study. *Learning Circuits.* [Retrieved February 9, 2004, from www.learningcircuits.org/2001/apr2001/Hofmann.htm]

Horton, W. (2002). Games that teach: Simple computer games for adults who want to learn. In A. Rossett (Ed.), *The ASTD e-learning handbook.* New York: McGraw-Hill.

Horton, W. K. (2000). *Designing web-based training: How to teach anyone anything anywhere anytime.* Hoboken, NJ: John Wiley & Sons.

Jasinski, M., & Thiagarajan, S. (2000). Virtual games for real learning: Learning online with serious fun. *Educational Technology, 40,* 61–63.

Judd, W. A., Bunderson, C. V., & Bessent, E. W. (1970). *An investigation of the effects of learner control in computer-assisted instruction prerequisite mathematics (MATHS)* (Report No. TR-5). Austin, TX: Computer-Assisted Instruction Laboratory. (ERIC Document Reproduction Service No. ED053532)

Kanfer, R., & Ackerman, P. L. (1989). Motivation and cognitive abilities: An integrative/aptitude-treatment interaction approach to skill acquisition. *Journal of Applied Psychology-Monograph, 74,* 657–690.

Kaplan-Leiserson, E. (2002). e-*Learning glossary.* [Retrieved March 2, 2004, from www.learningcircuits.org/glossary.html]

Kearsley, G. (1988). Authoring considerations for hypertext. *Educational Technology, 28,* 21–24.

Kiser, K. (2002, July). Taking it to the bank: How the Royal Bank of Scotland group led one of the United Kingdom's first and largest online learning initiatives—and has been able to cash in on the results. *e-Learning, 3,* 32–36.

Kosarzycki, M. P., Salas, E., DeRouin, R., & Fiore, S. M. (2003). Distance learning in organizations: A review and assessment of future needs. In D. Stone (Ed.), *Advances in human performance and cognitive engineering research: Vol. 3. Human resources technology* (pp. 69–98). Greenwich, CT: JAI.

Kozlowski, S.W.J., Toney, R. J., Mullins, M. E., Weissbein, D. A., Brown, K. G., & Bell, B. S. (2001). Developing adaptability: A theory for the design of integrated-embedded training systems. In E. Salas (Ed.), *Advances in human performance and cognitive engineering research* (Vol. 1, pp. 59–123). Amsterdam: JAI/Elsevier Science.

Lai, S. (2001). Controlling the display of animation for better understanding. *Journal of Research on Computing in Education, 33.* [Retrieved February 25, 2004, from www.iste.org/jrte/33/5/lai.cfm]

Large, A. (1996). Hypertext instructional programs and learner control: A research review [Electronic version]. *Education for Information, 14,* 95–106.

Leonard, B. (1996). Distance learning: Work and training overlap. *HR Magazine, 41,* 41–47.

Linne, J., & Plers, L. (2002, November). The DNA of an e-tutor. *ITTraining,* 26–28.

Masie, E. (2002). Blended learning: The magic is in the mix. In A. Rossett (Ed.), *The ASTD e-learning handbook.* New York: McGraw-Hill.

Mayer, R. E. (1989). Systematic thinking fostered by illustrations in scientific text. *Journal of Educational Psychology, 81,* 240–246.

Mayer, R. E. (2004, January). Should there be a three-strikes rule against discovery learning? The case for guided methods of instruction. *American Psychologist, 59,* 14–19.

Mayer, R. E., & Anderson, R. B. (1991). Animations need narrations: An experimental test of a dual-processing system in working memory. *Journal of Educational Psychology, 90,* 312–320.

Mayer, R. E., & Gallini, J. K. (1990). When is an illustration worth ten thousand words? *Journal of Educational Psychology, 88,* 64–73.

Mayer, R. E., Steinhoff, K., Bower, G., & Mars, R. (1995). A generative theory of textbook design: Using annotated illustrations to foster meaningful learning of science text. *Educational Technology, Research and Development, 43,* 31–43.

McGregor, D. M. (1957). The human side of enterprise. *Management Review, 46,* 22–28.

Moe, M. T., & Blodget, H. (2000). The knowledge web. Merrill Lynch & Co. *Merrill Lynch—eLearning: The knowledge web part 4 corporate e-learning—feeding hungry minds.* [Retrieved February 25, 2004, from www.usc.edu/dept/education/globaled/hentschke/documents/ KW4.pdf]

Moreno, R., & Mayer, R. E. (1999). Cognitive principles of multimedia learning: The role of modality and contiguity. *Journal of Educational Psychology, 91,* 358–368.

Moshinskie, J. (2001). How to keep e-learners from e-scaping. *Performance Improvement, 40,* 28–35.

Mullich, J. (2004). A second act for e-learning. *Workforce Management, 83,* 51–55.

Nielsen, J. (1990). The art of navigating through hypertext. *Communications of the ACM, 33,* 296–310.

O'Hara, J. M. (1990). The retention of skills acquired through simulator-based training. *Ergonomics, 33,* 1143–1153.

OneTouch Systems, Inc. (2003). *FAQ: About e-learning.* OneTouch Systems Corporate Website. [Retrieved on February 8, 2004, from www.one touch.com/aboutel.html]

Osman, M. E., & Hannafin, M. J. (1992). Metacognition research and theory: Analysis and implications for instructional design. *Educational Technology, Research and Development, 40,* 83–99.

Park, O. (1991). Hypermedia: Functional features and research issues. *Educational Technology, 31,* 24–31.

The payoffs of e-learning go far beyond the financial. (2003). *HR Focus, 80,* 7–8.

Phillips, J., Phillips, P. P., & Zuniga, L. (2000). Evaluating the effectiveness and the return on investment of e-learning. *What Works Online: 2000, 2nd Quarter.* American Society for Training and Development. [Retrieved March 2, 2004, from www.astd.org/ASTD/Resources/ eval_roi_community/return.htm]

Reeves, T. C. (1993). Pseudoscience in computer-based instruction: The case of learner control research. *Journal of Computer-Based Instruction, 20,* 39–46.

Ross, S. M., Morrison, G. R., & O'Dell, J. K. (1989). Uses and effects of learner control of context and instructional support in computer-based instruction. *Educational Technology, Research and Development, 37,* 29–39.

Ross, S. M., & Rakow, E. A. (1981). Learner control versus program control as adaptive strategies for selection of instructional support on math rules. *Journal of Educational Psychology, 73,* 745–753.

Rouiller, J. Z., & Goldstein, I. L. (1993). The relationship between organizational transfer climate and positive transfer of training. *Human Resource Development Quarterly, 4,* 377–390.

Russell, T. L. (1999). *The no significant difference phenomenon*. Raleigh: North Carolina State University.

Salas, E., & Cannon-Bowers, J. A. (2000). Design training systematically. In E. A. Locke (Ed.), *The Blackwell handbook of principles of organizational behavior*. Oxford, UK: Blackwell Publishers Ltd.

Salas, E., & Cannon-Bowers, J. A. (2001). The science of training: A decade of progress. *Annual Review of Psychology, 52*, 471–499.

Salas, E., Kosarzycki, M. P., Burke, C. S., Fiore, S. M., & Stone, D. L. (2002). Emerging themes in distance learning research and practice: Some food for thought. *International Journal of Management Reviews, 4*, 135–153.

Salopek, J. J. (2002, February). Virtually face-to-face: Synchronous e-learning defies bandwidth barriers. *e-Learning, 3*, 16–19.

Schelin, E., & Smarte, G. (2002, April). Recognizing the champions: Real-life tales of e-learning triumph and innovation. *e-Learning, 3*, 12–24.

Schraw, G. (1998). Promoting general cognitive awareness. *Instructional Science, 26*, 113–125.

Selix, G. (2001). Improving blended learning. [Electronic version]. *e-Learning, 2*, 48.

Shepherd, C. (2003, September). e-Learning's neither a threat nor a panacea. *ITTraining*, 34.

Shulman, L. S., & Keisler, E. R. (Eds.). (1966). *Learning by discovery*. Chicago: Rand-McNally.

Shyu, H., & Brown, S. W. (1992). Learner control versus program control in interactive videodisc instruction: What are the effects in procedural learning? [Electronic version]. *International Journal of Instructional Media, 19*, 85–96.

Skipper, J. (2000, April). Distance learning barriers: ASTD study. *DL News*, IBM Corporation, p. 1.

Steffe, L. P., & Gale, J. (Eds.). (1995). *Constructivism in education*. Mahwah, NJ: Lawrence Erlbaum.

Steinberg, E. R., Baskin, A. B., & Matthews, T. D. (1985). Computer-presented organizational/memory aids as instruction for solving Pico-fomi problems. *Journal of Computer-Based Instruction, 12*, 44–49.

Tannenbaum, S. I., & Yukl, G. (1992). Training and development in work organizations. *Annual Review of Psychology, 43*, 399–441.

Ten tactics to make e-learning 'stick' in your dept. or center. (2003, June). IOMA's *Report on Customer Relationship Management*, 4–6.

Tennyson, R. D. (1980). Instructional control strategies and content structure as design variables in concept acquisition using computer-based instruction. *Journal of Educational Psychology, 72*, 525–532.

Tsai, W., & Tai, W. (2003). Perceived importance as a mediator of the relationship between training assignment and training motivation. *Personnel Review, 32,* 151–163.

Vroom, V. H. (1964). *Work and motivation.* Hoboken, NJ: John Wiley & Sons.

Webster, J., & Hackley, P. (1997). Teaching effectiveness in technology-mediated distance learning. *Academy of Management Journal, 40,* 1282–1309.

Welsh, E. T., Wanberg, C. R., Brown, E. G., & Simmering, M. J. (2003). e-Learning: Emerging uses, empirical results and future directions. *International Journal of Training and Development, 7,* 245–258.

Zeidman, B. (2003). Guidelines for effective e-learning. *Chief Learning Officer, 2,* 24–28.

CHAPTER 5

eHR and Performance Management

A Consideration of Positive Potential and the Dark Side

Robert L. Cardy
Janice S. Miller

Technology seems to offer us boundless possibilities and hope. Somehow, technological advances seem to bring with them visions of increased ease, efficiency, and fairness, while reducing the need for labor and providing more time for leisure. Technology, in the form of improved appliances and chemistry, is taking the drudgery out of housework. Similarly, the advent of the automobile afforded safe, convenient, and economical travel to virtually everyone. Further, the personal computer offered to level the playing field and bring instantaneous information to everyone, even those who might be housebound or in remote areas.

While there can be little doubt that technological advances, such as those described above, have improved our lives, they may not have lived up to their initial promises. Further, the advances have brought with them negative aspects that may not have been anticipated. For example, technological advances would be expected to reduce the time we spend doing housework. While over the years there has been a reduction in average time spent on housework for women, the figure has increased for men (Greenwood, Seshadri, & Yorukoglu, 2004; Institute for Social Research, 2002;). Changes in the amount of time spent in housework appear to have more to do with the labor market than with labor-saving devices. Further, technological advances in the form of labor-saving devices can actually increase the time spent in housework. At least in part, a reason for the counterintuitive relationship between technological advances and time spent in housework is that appliances bring with them their own set of tasks. They also make possible a higher level of performance and therefore change the standards for performance. For example, an "automatic" dishwasher may involve rinsing or pre-washing dishes. Since the dishwasher makes possible storage and daily washing of dishes, dirty dishes left in a sink is no longer acceptable in many households. The level of performance made possible by technological advancement has changed the standard for acceptable performance. Similarly, the automobile has made travel easier and more accessible to millions of people. However, auto accidents maim and kill drivers, passengers, and pedestrians on a daily basis. Further, auto advancements such as four-wheel drive and traction control hold forth the possibility of horrific accidents when the performance envelope is extended beyond its boundaries. As another example, personal computers offer information and communication, but we are far from paperless and viruses and spam now seem to be permanent fixtures on the computer landscape.

In sum, technology offers great positive possibilities, but negative outcomes, often unintended, can be part of the advancement. Further, technology now permeates our lives, and its role in performance management in the workplace is no exception.

Our purpose in this chapter is to consider the role of technology in performance management. We will consider the promise and potential of technology in this important area of management. We will also consider the sometimes not-so-obvious negative possibilities that technology can bring to performance management. Our hope is that a review of positive possibilities as well as the "dark side" can identify potentially beneficial applications of technology to performance management and identify potential costs and how they might be avoided.

The Positive Potential for Technology in Performance Management

In view of the fact that HRM centers on an organization's unique human and "inimitable" component, whereas technology is more standard and replicable, incorporating technology into HRM introduces some interesting and relevant concerns for practitioners. For example, to what extent is it productive to invest in technology relative to investments in employee development, mentoring, or career management? Or can technology actually support or accelerate positive outcomes in these areas? Does success depend less on how firms manage their technology than on how they manage their human assets? In short, the contrasts between "content" concerns and "process" concerns confronting HRM are intriguing issues to explore, as these contribute uniquely to the way organizations manage and develop their members.

The use of technology in performance management has the potential to increase productivity and enhance competitiveness. We believe that appraisal satisfaction is a key concept that is central to any discussion of technology and performance management. Clearly, gains technology makes are Pyrrhic victories if appraisal satisfaction does not improve as well. Contemporary attention to psychological variables such as appraisal satisfaction that underlie the appraisal process and user reactions to the performance management system have supplanted previous preoccupations with appraisal instrument format and rater accuracy (Cardy & Dobbins, 1994; Judge & Ferris, 1993; Waldman, 1997). In view of the uniqueness and competitive advantage that human resources provide, it is appropriate that organizations pay greater attention to questions of employee satisfaction and with how firms evaluate their performance.

We believe that appraisal satisfaction will remain a relevant concern, even when technology is a primary mechanism for the feedback process. Beyond this, appraisal satisfaction is also a critical concern when technology actually *becomes* the appraisal process. This is because an important link exists between satisfaction with appraisal processes and technology's potential as an effective force for change and improved performance.

Given that high-quality performance feedback should be one factor that helps organizations retain, motivate, and develop their employees, these outcomes are more likely to occur if employees are satisfied with the performance appraisal process, feel they are treated fairly, and support the system. Conversely, if ratees are dissatisfied or perceive a system as unfair, they have diminished motivation to use evaluation information to improve their performance (Ilgen, Fisher, & Taylor, 1979). In the extreme, dissatisfaction with appraisal procedures may be responsible for feelings of inequity, decreased motivation, and increased employee turnover.

Furthermore, from a reward standpoint, linking performance to compensation is difficult when employees are dissatisfied with the appraisal process. Noting this difficulty, Lawler (1967) suggested that employee opinions of an appraisal system might actually be as important as the system's psychometric validity and reliability. The question of appraisal satisfaction is a relevant concern in discussions of how technology interacts with performance management systems since, absent user satisfaction and support, technological enhancements are likely to be unsuccessful.

Technology as Content

Technology may contribute to performance management and thus to appraisal satisfaction in two primary ways. First, technology may facilitate measuring an individual's performance via computer monitoring activities. This frequently occurs as an unobtrusive and rote mechanical process that relies on minimal input from individuals beyond their task performance. Jobs that incorporate this type of appraisal technology are frequently scripted or repetitious and involve little personal judgment or discretion. Working in a call center or performing data entry are examples. In this instance, the very act of performing a job simultaneously becomes the measure of how well a jobholder accomplishes it. Keystrokes, time on task, or numbers of calls made are recorded and at once become both job content and appraisal content.

A second approach to technology and performance management changes the emphasis so that technology becomes a tool to facilitate the process of writing reviews or generating performance feedback. Examples here include multi-rater appraisals that super-visors or team members generate online, as well as off-the-shelf appraisal software packages that actually construct an evaluation for a manager. This particular technological approach occurs more often in the context of jobs that involve personal judgment, high discretion, and open-ended tasks for which real-time performance monitoring is not an option. Again, it is critical to consider these aspects of technology use in performance management within a framework of appraisal satisfaction. We will address the second application of technology to performance management in the next section of this chapter.

In 1993 computerized performance reports evaluated the work of approximately ten million workers in the United States (Hawk, 1994). Although estimates vary, by the end of the twentieth cen-tury this number may have reached at least twenty-seven million workers (DeTienne & Abbot, 1993; Staunton & Barnes-Farrell, 1996). Computerized performance monitoring (CPM) technology facilitates data collection by counting the number of work units completed per time period, number and length of times a termi-nal is left idle, number of keystrokes, error rates, time spent on various tasks, and so forth. The resulting data are attractive to employers who may opt to use the technique for workforce plan-ning, evaluating and controlling worker performance, and pro-viding employee performance feedback, our focus here.

Clearly, this use of technology in performance management has positive features from a manager's perspective. For one, CPM permits greater span of control because it facilitates accurate col-lection of performance data without requiring managers to spend significant time observing each individual worker's actual job per-formance. Similar to technology implemented in other organiza-tional processes (purchasing or manufacturing, for example), when firms apply technology to performance management they stand to benefit from prized gains in efficiency.

Trust is a critical issue that arises in connection with the use of CPM. Some describe trust as the essence of social exchange. That is, when mutual trust flourishes, so also does the extent of the exchange. Earley (1988) empirically demonstrated that computer-generated performance feedback enhanced worker performance if the individual trusted the feedback source. His study centered on telemarketers who either received CPM feedback that a supervisor provided or, in an alternate condition, accessed their CPM feedback directly. Results showed that an individual's performance and trust in feedback was higher for the self-generated than for the supervisor-generated condition. Although employees' direct access to feedback data had positive effects, the level of specificity of information available from CPM also led to performance improvements. The researcher found that specific information produced greater performance gains than more general performance feedback, as the latter had only limited value in enhancing performance.

Another way to interpret these findings is that self-efficacy increases when an individual takes control of generating his or her own feedback via technology rather than ceding this function to a supervisor. Enhanced control over one's work that comes from receiving feedback directly from a computer may be preferable to relying on the supervisor to manage the feedback process as an intermediary. It may be that computer-generated feedback that performers access and interpret on their own is less threatening than situations in which the person is a powerless and passive recipient of feedback from a supervisor.

More recently, Douthitt and Aiello (2001) approached CPM using a procedural-justice framework. In a laboratory study, they exposed participants to four feedback conditions in which participants experienced varying levels of control over the feedback they received. They found that the opportunity to participate in determining how one received feedback positively affected perceived procedural justice, and that this was more effective than actually having an opportunity to control or turn off the computer monitoring. One of the authors' conclusions was that heightened perceptions of procedural fairness provide positive return for the cost involved in establishing employee participation in a CPM environment. Thus, these researchers confirmed a growing awareness of the importance of allowing workers to retain control over some aspects of computerized feedback generation.

Organizations that invest in technology for performance improvement have wasted their resources if employees are uncomfortable with the system or are overwhelmed with the amount of data that is available. Therefore, formal training for users that will result in comfort and confidence with the system should be an essential part of CPM implementation. This is especially important if organizations allow employees access to their own CPM data.

To enhance perceptions of system fairness, practitioners should find a way to balance quantitative performance data with acknowledgment of system factors. For example, an employee who delivers high-quality customer service over the telephone could generate positive responses from the public that would foster return business, even though objective call duration data alone might not capture this fact, as more time spent on individual calls results in handling fewer calls daily. A CPM system that monitors call volume could cast this individual's performance in a negative light. However, a process that also incorporates acknowledgment of system factors—such as call complexity—would put work performance in perspective. Since this is the kind of performance that an organization seeks to encourage, finding an appropriate objective/subjective balance benefits not only the performer in terms of fairness, but the organization from an outcome standpoint.

In this vein, DeTienne and Abbot (1993) cautioned firms not merely to measure quantity via CPM but also to find ways to measure subjective aspects of job performance. A CPM process that includes provisions for acknowledging the situational constraints or system factors affecting performance may greatly enhance employee satisfaction with an appraisal process. Examples of constraints could include changes in workload based on fluctuations in employment level, introduction of new work processes, the specialized nature of some tasks, or shifting demand as a result of marketplace changes over which an employee has no control.

A system approach to CPM is appropriate because organizational researchers now recognize that individual-level variables do not operate in isolation, but interact with situational factors that surround working individuals. The system approach to performance management hails from Deming's (1986) assertion that 85 percent of performance variation comes from organizational systems. As most employee performance falls within a predictable range of behavior or is within statistical control, Deming believed that performance fluctuations were due to system inputs like poor training, inadequate technology, or other factors under management control.

In this framework, system factors may either facilitate or be detrimental to performance (Cardy & Dobbins, 1994). For example, economic factors, computer crashes, or task complexity variations could all influence CPM data. If firms find ways to incorporate situational constraints and system factors into CPM practices, then satisfaction with computer generated performance feedback need not suffer.

One way to pursue objectivity, while acknowledging system factors, is by incorporating CPM into a broader "Management by Objectives" (MBO) format. A key component of MBO programs is an emphasis on joint supervisor-subordinate determination of goals and performance indicators. As discussed above, employees respond with greater trust to an appraisal system in which they have had a voice. A CPM appraisal system does not preclude jointly set goals and agreement on measurement tactics. Practitioners may find that the upside potential for heightened trust that can lead to loyalty and commitment more than compensates for the time spent engaging in the MBO process in conjunction with CPM.

An additional important consideration is follow-up and establishment of a development plan after feedback delivery. Although CPM provides accurate performance feedback in quantitative form, its role and function appear to end there. To have a positive effect, data delivery must also include a developmental aspect that includes devising a plan for monitoring progress and achieving improved performance. Indeed, merely providing outcome measures without addressing how to interpret them—or establishing a program designed to elicit subsequent performance improvements—fails to fulfill the goals of a well-administered appraisal process.

One effective way to administer CPM feedback may be to borrow again from established MBO practices. For example, a supervisor might have a developmental meeting with an employee to review the CPM data, discuss tactics for raising performance, and jointly solve problems regarding current procedures. To make CPM a more positive experience, practitioners might consider exploring how to convey CPM data feedback in a way that involves interaction between supervisor and employee and is geared toward data interpretation and employee development, rather than simply overwhelming an employee with quantitative performance numbers.

An attractive feature of CPM is that feedback is more clearly related to work output and less to superiors' biased impressions (Shamir & Salomon, 1985). This contrasts with performance-management processes that may be highly political or that encourage individuals to practice impression management or other nonperformance tactics to improve appraisal outcomes. Despite a wide range of impression-management behaviors that employees may engage in to influence appraisal results, these behaviors are largely irrelevant in organizations that rely on objective CPM data. Certainly recipients of CPM performance feedback should feel confident that data are unbiased by nonperformance factors or political behaviors that can affect traditional performance appraisal in various ways (Longnecker, Sims, & Gioia, 1987). While this is clearly a positive feature of CPM from the standpoint of fairness, it does not tell the whole story.

There is growing research interest in CPM and its impact on employees and their performance, but few conclusions about personality and other individual-level variables such as demographic or biographical characteristics and their roles in CPM. There has been a surprising lack of attention to individual differences in technology acceptance, particularly in view of extant research on individual differences and technology implementation (Agarwal & Prasad, 1999). Both theory development and practice could benefit from discovering which personality traits or individual qualities provide the best fit for a CPM environment. There are two approaches organizations could use to explore this supposition.

First, the "Big Five" model of personality (Barrick & Mount, 1991) may shed some light on the type of individual who prospers in a firm that uses CPM to evaluate his or her performance. A starting point for this discussion comes from Earley's findings (1986, 1988) regarding the importance of employee participation in CPM practices. Along with increased trust and individual self-efficacy resulting from accessing one's own CPM data, personality factors may enhance success in this environment. For example, one relevant factor might be the Big Five concept of "openness to experience." Individuals high in *openness* tend to be broad-minded, motivated to learn, imaginative, and interested in new ideas. This willingness to try something new (that is, master the technology necessary to access one's own CPM data and benefit from it) seems consistent with the kind of CPM procedures Earley (1988) advocated.

Second, recent work exploring the relationship between worker age and technology has disclosed that age significantly influences workplace technology usage. In a recent longitudinal study, Morris and Venkatesh (2000) reported that, compared to older workers, the ease or difficulty of technology usage strongly influenced attitudes of younger workers toward a particular technology. They also found that social pressure to use a technology was a more important factor in determining older workers' attitudes toward usage. Consideration of these findings could have positive implications for satisfaction with performance management administered via CPM.

Technology as Process

In contrast to the performance management of routine or low-discretion jobs that CPM addresses, organizations also have the option to use software that can both generate appraisal forms and their accompanying narrative. In this case, technology becomes an aid that facilitates delivering performance feedback, rather than generating the actual content or data, as CPM does. This broadens technology options to the remaining jobs in an organization whose incumbents receive appraisals.

There are several ways to achieve technological enhancement of performance-management systems in these remaining jobs. One method incorporates appraisal as part of an overall enterprise resource planning (ERP) software system. Today many performance/competency management systems are part of ERP packages. The advantage of this macro approach is that it comprises a wide variety of enterprise data, including finance, operations, and sales/marketing. The ERP system permits viewing an organization in ways that otherwise would not be feasible by exploring the enterprise data and analyzing competencies for individuals, groups of workers, departments, and project teams. This allows HR practitioners to identify high performers, to spot skill and competency gaps, and to analyze pay relative to performance (Greengard, 1999). The ERP creates a continuous process, providing managers with easy access to information. The ERP can also adapt to fluctuations in subordinates' progress toward goals.

Once HR holds this information, it may provide training, coaching, and education so an organization remains competitive. The ERP methodology is also attractive from the standpoint of permitting a strategic approach to HRM—the HR practitioner can concentrate on developing an organization's unique human component, while the employees remain fully engaged in their work (Greengard, 1999).

Firm intranets or the Internet may also serve as key technological enhancements of the performance-management process. Novell Inc., in San Jose, California, anticipates reaching the point where employee evaluations are accomplished entirely online, creating a truly paperless system (Caudron, 1994). Increasingly, these tools serve as the method of choice for implementing multi-rater or 360-degree feedback. For example, a performance evaluation process might begin with email messages coordinating the program. Next, participants can nominate potential evaluators who provide feedback about them. When the process is web-based, the technology may actually impose limits on participation that prevent "popular" evaluators from being overwhelmed with requests to rate others. In addition, online systems prevent evaluators from receiving separate communications from all multi-rater participants. Instead they receive only one email message announcing whom they will evaluate. Assigned passwords then allow evaluators to enter a secure website and, complete evaluation questionnaires; feedback is collected and assembled into reports that participants receive electronically (Summers, 2001).

One highly attractive aspect of web-based appraisal technology is that organizations can evaluate more employees and evaluate them more frequently. The value of frequent appraisal is that the focus changes from appraisal as an annual (and perhaps adversarial) event to one that is an ongoing, real-time process geared toward development. Since employees both want and need feedback on their performance, frequent appraisals done in such a user-friendly manner should have a positive and immediate effect on job performance.

Web-based systems also offer training advantages. Rater training is often a standard feature of web-based appraisals, simultaneously saving the firm money for training costs and also enhancing the value of resulting feedback (Summers, 2001). In addition, feedback recipients can automatically access online development suggestions, training opportunities within their firms, and other related sources on the web. A web-based system may also allow users to track their own progress over a series of evaluations. This option is an attractive means for employees to bridge the gap between feedback and development planning.

Another way technology facilitates performance appraisal is through use of stand-alone software products designed to help compose an appraisal. Most of these software packages are relatively inexpensive and easy to use. One of the most appealing advantages of appraisal software is that it allows performance management to become paperless, simplifying the logistics of the appraisal process for evaluators, workers, and administrators (Bracken, Summers, & Fleenor, 1998).

A feature of some appraisal software packages is their ability to automate the more tedious parts of creating evaluations, which helps managers focus on the content of the evaluation rather than on the forms. Some programs allow users to click buttons on a screen for each rating and simultaneously create sentences and paragraphs of text. If ratings within an individual factor are high or low—or varied at both ends of the scale—the program prompts the evaluator to review the rating and to add his or her own comments to the evaluation (Adams, 1995).

As a means of assisting evaluators in writing narratives, some software products contain enormous databases of prewritten text, a feature allowing users to automatically upgrade to more positive evaluation or downgrade to more negative evaluation (Adams, 1995). Appraisal software may also include a coaching utility that provides information to evaluators about coaching individuals they evaluate. All these options have the potential to make the performance evaluation process less daunting to frontline managers, engineers, scientists, and others who often strongly resist spending time and effort on this activity. Since information technology can potentially save time and resources, it should free individuals to concentrate on tasks they are more qualified to perform. As a result, supervisors who can avail themselves of the benefits of online performance appraisals may be less reluctant to do them. Rather than viewing performance management as an unwelcome diversion from regular duties, the process should become a less onerous one that individuals learn leads to higher performance among those they supervise. One would expect increases in appraisal satisfaction when viewed from the ratee's perspective as well, since feedback will occur more frequently and be more informative.

Software packages also have the advantage of promoting adherence to legal guidelines. For example, technology-based systems allow evaluators to receive feedback reports regarding how closely they agree with others' ratings of the same participants (Bracken, Summers, & Fleenor, 1998). Thus a frame of reference for rating can be developed that increases accuracy. Similarly, online systems permit evaluators to compare their ratings with aggregated ratings others have produced on the same workers (Summers, 2001). Evaluators who receive this information may learn to eliminate rater distortion. In addition, an appraisal-software program is presently available that allows an evaluator to check whether protected classes of employees receive more harsh or lenient evaluations than their colleagues do. This package also includes an optional legal/language review utility that scans an evaluation for words that could lead to charges of discrimination or harassment.

While it is critical to deliver timely and accurate information so that performance improvements ensue and organizational learning takes place, individuals generally resist being a bearer of bad news. Consequently, managers often either postpone delivery of negative feedback or attempt to alleviate its impact through positive distortion or leniency. In a laboratory study, Sussman and Sproull (1999) investigated the possibility that computer-mediated communication increased honesty and accuracy in delivering negative information that had personal consequences for a recipient. They found that participants engaged in less distortion of negative information and were more accurate and honest when they used computer-mediated communication than when they used face-to-face or telephone communication. In addition, those receiving feedback in their study reported higher levels of satisfaction and comfort in the computer-mediated communication situation.

The psychometric features available in some appraisal programs include checks in the process that hinder evaluators from inflating ratings. A manager may feel more confident in feedback sessions—even when delivering bad news—if he or she is convinced of an appraisal's psychometric robustness and accuracy. Furthermore, ratees may also appreciate appraisal accuracy and value rewards that are determined more objectively and not on the basis of distorted ratings. Again, organizations will benefit in the long term from an elevated level of appraisal satisfaction inherent in this process.

Since online evaluation and appraisal software packages can make the appraisal process less onerous for evaluators, ease of administration may lead to more frequent, accurate, and ongoing feedback. In this way performance management may become more of a real-time, continuous process or "conversation" and less an annual event. Creators of a web-based 360-degree system believe that taking the multi-rater appraisal process online allows resources to be directed to value-adding activities such as feedback and development planning, and that online components therefore optimize face-to-face discussions (Bracken, Summers, & Fleenor, 1998). Indeed, more frequent feedback delivery enhances its potential to improve performance. Rater training available in performance-appraisal software helps solve the problem that supervisors may not know what to talk about or why they are even doing appraisals. Similarly, an online appraisal, like a traditional one, can be the basis for a meaningful conversation about performance between supervisor and subordinate. The online process should be more informative for all users so that supervisors will know what to discuss as well as why they are talking. As a result, they may be willing to deliver feedback to subordinates more often.

Information technology proponents recognize that the greatest impediments to success are often people related rather than information, technology, and systems related (Roepke, Agarwal, & Ferrat, 2000). Obviously, the human component is a central concern when organizations introduce technology to the performance-management process. After all, melding people and technology successfully is of critical importance to today's firms. While the potential for accelerating positive HRM outcomes through technology applications clearly exists, implementation that fails to consider trust, fairness, system factors, objectivity, personality, or computer literacy and training has negative implications for an organization's distinct and inimitable human component. Possible gains in efficiency, objectivity, or accuracy that a high-technology approach to performance management produces could turn out to be costly for firms if they bring about user dissatisfaction leading to diminished job attitudes, poor performance, or increased turnover. We turn next to a discussion of this "dark side" of the technology/performance management interface.

The "Dark Side" of Technology in Performance Management

As discussed at the outset of this chapter, technology can have unintended and negative consequences. In this section, we emphasize the potential negative characteristics that can result from applying technology to performance management. The negative outcomes are no more guaranteed than are positive outcomes. However, these negative aspects can be unintended costs that can accompany a technology-aided approach to managing performance. Thus, it is worthwhile to consider some of the major negative possibilities, with the hope that awareness of these negative possibilities can assist practitioners in avoiding potential problems.

This consideration of the "dark side" of a technologically aided approach to performance management is presently a more conceptual than an empirical discussion because little research has been done from this perspective. Nonetheless, we provide a structure for these comments using the framework appearing in Figure 5.1. This framework distinguishes between two major types of performance management. On the one hand, performance management can occur at a more macro level and consist of allocating labor to projects or jobs. On the other hand, performance management can occur at a more micro level and involve performance measurement and development of individual or team performance. The micro category of performance management is probably the category most I/O and HRM people tend to think of. However, line managers often approach performance management from a more macro perspective of combining labor and other resources in order to assure adequate performance on various initiatives. Thus, the framework directs our attention at both micro and macro levels of performance management.

**Figure 5.1. Content and Process
of Performance Management.**

		Focus	
		Content	Process
Macro (Labor Allocation)		**Cell 1** Reductionism	**Cell 2** Arbitrary Top-Down
Micro (Individual/Team Performance)		**Cell 3** Relevance Discriminability	**Cell 4** Distance Trust Intent

(Performance Management — row label)

The second factor included in the framework is "focus," which refers to the content or process of performance management. With a focus on *content*, the primary concern is with the "what" of performance management. Content issues primarily have to do with criteria and what is measured. With a focus on *process*, the primary concern is with the "how" of performance management. Process issues primarily have to do with how managers carry out performance management.

Depending on whether performance management is at a macro or micro level and whether our focus is on content of process, there are four possible combinations. We next consider each of these four cells that result from crossing the performance management and focus factors. This framework provides a convenient way for categorizing, discussing, and thinking about possible negative outcomes.

Cell 1: Macro and Content

Technology has recently made some important strides when it comes to allocating human resources to projects. Separate HRM functions, such as hiring, training, and benefits, have seen the application of software and the development of web-based approaches. However, it is at a more macro level, a level that cuts across and integrates various management functions, where development and corporate funds seem to be focused. Software that integrates across all areas of an organization and captures the entire enterprise would seem to hold the promise of wringing out all of the potential advantages of a technological approach, such as greater speed, clarity, efficiency, and improved planning capabilities, among others. We will next broadly consider enterprise resource planning and then look at potential content problems that may accompany this approach.

Enterprise resource planning software is meant to provide managers the information technology needed for real-time assessment of the status of orders and where materials are in the system. Further, and perhaps most important, the technology can provide the information needed to realize new projects or strategic direction. For example, paired with a human resource information system, the competencies of employees can easily be electronically catalogued. Breaking down a project into its component tasks and then identifying the competencies needed for those tasks allows a manager to identify employees who have the skills that best position them to make the project a success. The electronic approach allows management to determine the type of labor needed and its likely cost. Enterprise resource planning vendors, including SAP, Oracle, IBM, Infinium, PeopleSoft, Lawson, Austin-Hayne, and others, have developed sophisticated capabilities to accomplish these objectives. Estimates of how long a project may take to complete or to get up-to-speed can be made and return-on-investment estimates can be generated. We are not far from a system in which labor is brought together to accomplish particular projects and then reconfigured in a different fashion for another project. "I'll take one from column A and two from column B for this project." "I'll put in my labor order for the next project as soon as I finish running the numbers." Technology is theoretically providing the means for maximal efficiency by taking, essentially, a Chinese takeout approach to managing initiatives.

The electronically assisted approach described above is certainly rational. The tasks needed, associated competencies, and employees (portrayed as boxes of competencies), can all be represented as a flow of boxes on a computer screen. Putting the various components together in cyberspace can allow examination of the bottom-line impact of varying combinations and amounts of the components. How can labor be most efficiently allocated? How should labor be assigned so that it results in the greatest productivity? How much more competitive, then, could we be in the marketplace? Certainly these are rational business questions and the ability to answer them is wonderfully enhanced by the use of technology. What could be wrong with this picture of management nirvana?

We believe that problems associated with the software-based approach to management don't really reside in the software. The problems stem from the mindset that underlies or is engendered by the software-based approach. Specifically, the software approach seems to be the computerization of scientific management. The central concept here is reductionism. If projects or jobs can be unbundled into their component tasks, then the discrete competencies needed to perform each component can be identified. The competencies available in the labor force can then be assigned in the most efficient and productive manner possible. A firm that employs this approach is Stride Rite Corporation, in Cambridge, Massachusetts (Caudron, 1994). Certainly, this general approach has been with us for many years. However, competitive pressures and technology are combining to result in reductionism and allocation on a much more rapid basis.

In the extreme, employees may be thrown together on a short-term basis and never even meet each other because their project is conducted virtually. What makes a manager think that people can be successfully allocated like this? For one thing it is because labor and other pieces of the service or production function are portrayed as separate factors on an electronic display. But are the competencies so separable and easily reconfigured? The problem, of course, is that even though factors can be conceptually portrayed as independent and separable features, operationally it may be the bundle of factors that is the meaningful unit. In other words, the configuration may be more important than the separate figures. Put in terms that we are probably all familiar with from the Gestalt school of thought, "The whole is more than the sum of its parts." This truism was originally directed at perception, but it may apply just as well to organizational life.

A real-life example may clarify why it may be compelling but dysfunctional to manage by separating parts from a whole. Consider the case of an unnamed book publisher. A cost-conscious and computer-savvy editor had laid out all of the tasks associated with publishing another edition of a text. Timelines and budgets were in place for each piece of the puzzle, from revising each chapter to the instructor's manual and video cases. One of the pieces that could be broken out as a separate task was editing the text. Of course, good project planning would indicate that costs could be minimized and efficiency and ROI maximized if only new material (for example, inserts and cases) would be copy edited. A copy editor was asked to do his job without having access to the entire text, only the new material. Thus, the context, the terms that may already have been defined, and the overall voice and style of the text were not part of the editing process. You can imagine the difficulty caused by this approach. The reductionistic approach of breaking out all of the tasks was supposed to result in cost savings and efficiency. It must have been a compellingly attractive cost saving item on the computer screen. Unfortunately, the computer analysis was wrong, and the forest was almost lost for the trees. Viewed as partners in the process rather than as boxes to manage, people could participate out of commitment rather than compliance or fear. Yes, productivity and profit are important, but so are people. As a contrast to reductionism, we generically refer to this alternative perspective as the *holistic* approach.

A holistic approach might differ in a number of important ways from the common reductionistic approach. Some of the contrasts that may be important distinctions are presented in Table 5.1.

**Table 5.1. Contrast Between
Reductionistic and Holistic Approaches.**

Reductionistic	Holistic
Feature	Gestalt
Process	Outcome
Control	Trust
One Way	Many Possibilities
Component Boundaries	Discipline or Project Boundaries

The *reductionistic* approach focuses on the features or components that make up the overall process. It is by focusing on and controlling the steps in the process that a positive outcome will be achieved. The emphasis is on control, even though an ostensibly liberating technology is used. That same technology can be used to collect various and fairly invasive measures of performance. In addition, the reductionistic approach ends up, perhaps by default, assuming that there is one way to successful performance. That is, a certain set of competencies, perhaps defined in behavioral terms, are specified as required for effective performance. This competency model serves as the screen and template for success. The boundaries in the reductionistic approach are defined by the components. The limits to someone's job are clearly drawn (often literally on a computer screen), and marching orders and domains are clearly separated.

In contrast, a *holistic* approach focuses on the whole, which may include employee well-being and development, as well as profit. The focus in a holistic approach would, somewhat ironically, seem to be on the outcome, not so much on the process. For example, a holistic approach might lead to discussion with employees about the competitive environment in which the organization operates and exploration of what the organization may need to do in order to survive and be competitive. The focus may be on the overall outcome, but employees would be trusted to find means to achieve those ends. In contrast to the reductionistic approach, the holistic approach would allow for a variety of paths to success. Given a sufficiently organic, empowered, and flexible approach toward how the process of work is structured, people find where their skills and style best fit and what roles they can best play. In most work situations, the reality is that there are a lot of paths to success, and great variance in styles and in patterns of strengths and weaknesses can be observed across successful people. Some people are best with concepts, and others seem best with details. Some people are quantitative and technically oriented, while others are more people oriented and are gifted with exceptional interpersonal skills. However, people find ways to compensate and deal with their deficits and make the most of their strengths. There are numerous paths to success. Finally, in a holistic approach the boundaries constraining or defining an employee's responsibilities and activities are handed to them by their function or discipline or by the project. For example, responsibility in a job may capture or include aspects that, in a reductionistic approach, are clearly in the domain of another component. However, the holistic approach allows for employees to more broadly define their responsibility based on logic and common sense as to what is best for the overall project.

The above contrasts highlight some of the distinctions between the reductionistic and holistic approaches to managing work. It is interesting to note that the reductionistic approach, fueled by software capabilities, would seem to be contrary to the desires of most upper-level managers. A summarization of the ideal workplace for most people in upper management is to have a fluid and flexible workplace that can quickly adapt to changing competitive pressures. However, a reductionistic approach compartmentalizes and fixes structure and labor contributions. This end—that seems to us to be at variance with what top management would really like to achieve—is brought about by the seductive rationale of reductionism and the promise of increased efficiency all quickly and easily laid out in an electronic fashion. Once the component system is in place, there is little doubt that increased speed should be a benefit. Quality of the overall product or service? Well, that depends on whether all of the parts that were separated and done independently fit together into a seamless whole. Further, it must be assumed that the whole isn't more than the sum of its parts.

As can be seen in the above discussion, the reductionistic approach can conceptually lead to greater efficiency, but can operationally lead to increased costs and other negative outcomes. Allocating labor to the various parts of the production or service function conveys to employees that they are just another cog in the process. Enterprise software provides the capability to push this approach to the extreme. Projects can be broken into their component parts and each part can be managed to minimize costs and maximize productivity. Looking at each step in a production or service function as simply a separate component can dehumanize what really exists within those components.

Related to the potential problem of reductionism, technology-aided macro performance management tends to result in content that is made up of physical characteristics rather than psychological or social components. Viewed as units of labor that can be shifted around as needed, the human resource tends to be seen as sets of quantities: How many? What kind? What types and level of skill? However, physical concerns, such as how the workers may get along together, whether they will psychologically mesh, and whether they will be committed to each other and to the project may be important issues. These psychological and social factors, while easily ignored with technology, can play a critical role in determining bottom-line issues such as quality, productivity, and profit.

Cell 2: Macro and Process

Using technology to assist in managing performance at a macro level also can bring with it potential problems in regard to process. How is labor allocated to a project? We are going to make some gross generalizations here, but we think they capture an important and representative distinction between a nontechnological and a technological approach. In a *nontechnological* environment, labor assignment is often the result of negotiation between a manager/ supervisor and a worker. A new project or a sudden increase in demand may result in a manager discussing the needed labor with workers to see what may work out in terms of balancing production needs against worker schedules and preferences. Volunteers may even be requested. If assignments are made by the manager, they would usually be open for some discussion and negotiation.

In contrast, a *technologically aided* approach removes the decision making from the managers and workers. How many units of what kind of labor as well as when and where they should be assigned can all be electronic outcomes. It is difficult to negotiate with software. The technological approach to macro performance management can thus be seen, particularly from the worker's perspective, as top-down and arbitrary.

Cell 3: Micro and Content

Managing performance at an individual or team level rests on measuring performance. The critical content of performance management at an individual or team level is criteria. In other words, what are the standards? What is being measured? The answers to these questions are at the heart of it. The criteria signal what is important and guide the feedback and development efforts that are directed toward the worker or team of workers. Using technology in the management of individual or team performance can influence these criteria in ways that may be unintended and negative.

Technological assistance for individual or team level performance management can range from online rating scales to computer-aided creation of performance dimensions and feedback. There are increasing numbers of websites that, for a fee, guide managers through the process of identifying performance dimensions. If you don't have dimensions already developed, the website will offer a set or help you develop your own—on the spot and online. Further, depending on the pattern of evaluations, the software or the website will generate narrative prose to serve as feedback to the worker.

An electronic version of rating scales is a convenience, but the use of software to generate dimensions is much more substantive and potentially problematic. The "dark side" content issues we discuss next are directed at this more substantive application of technology to performance management.

Potential content problems with the technology-aided approach center on criteria. Specifically, do the characteristics of performance being evaluated really capture the core or important facets of the job? In other words, are the performance measures relevant? There are at least two ways in which the relevance of performance measures can be undermined with the application of technology. First, generic performance dimensions can be selected or custom dimensions can be created online. This on-the-spot and quick process is made possible through technology, but it is a far cry from the recommended approach of deriving performance dimensions from a thorough job analysis. The use of online performance management tools does not preclude the use of a thorough job analysis, but this background work would likely be sidestepped, particularly by organizations that are in competitive and rapidly changing environments. The technological approach allows for the quick solutions that are needed in dynamic environments. However, the cost of this speed may be reduced relevance of the measures. In the extreme, the measures can be created at the time of the evaluation. Workers certainly might question the relevance and fairness of criteria that were unknown and were not available to guide their efforts.

A second means by which technology can reduce the relevance of performance measures has to do with what technology allows us to measure. For example, the average number of keystrokes per hour, the average duration of phone interactions, and so on can now be fairly easily measured with technology. However, just because these measures are available or easily obtained doesn't mean they should be measured. Do measures such as speed of keystrokes and duration of phone calls really capture, for example, the speed or quality of customer service? Probably not. However, because technology makes such measures possible or readily available, our fear is that they will be embraced as operational performance measures. Such measures, though, may be a better reflection of what is technologically possible than of what is really important about the job.

In addition to relevance, technology has the potential to negatively affect the discrimination among performance measures. Specifically, technology brings with it the capability of measuring characteristics at a level that may not have been possible before. For example, not only can speed be measured, but it can be measured at a fine-grained level of keystroke rate, and there will be variance across workers on this measure. Setting aside the relevance issue that we just discussed, a critical issue is the meaningfulness of this variance. To coin a phrase, the use of technology can lead us to make mountains out of molehills.

Cell 4: Micro and Process

The process of individual or team performance management revolves around how things are measured and how performance feedback is conveyed to people. With a technologically aided approach, the performance management process can be a source of difficulty. A "dark side" process issue is the perceived distance between a worker and the evaluator. Technology can act as a third and intervening party between them. For example, an evaluator may not be able to explain why the software generated certain conclusions and recommendations. All the evaluator may know is the judgments that were entered into the program. How the data were massaged and the rationale for any results is not directly observable. This "black box" effect can be used by evaluators to duck responsibility for some of the performance management outcomes. However, workers will quickly perceive a distance between management and their performance feedback. As such, we would expect this problem to lead to less regard for people in the evaluation role and reduced leadership or managerial power.

A related problem is the extent to which workers will trust the evaluations and associated feedback. If workers know that software generates their performance feedback, they would be expected to discount and distrust the conclusions and recommendation. Even if workers are not privy to details of how the performance management system works, the types of measures and any inability of the evaluator to explain aspects of the system or its results would be expected to lead to lower trust of the performance management system and its results.

Finally, the types of measures and the precision of measurement can lead workers to question the very intent of the performance management function. Fine-grained measurement of discrete activities or behaviors, particularly if viewed as not really capturing important aspects of job performance, can lead workers to question the intent of evaluation and feedback. Specifically, while management would like to think that the purpose of performance management is primarily to improve performance, workers may think otherwise. The technologically aided approach can result in workers concluding that the performance management system is there to trip them up. Far from being a partnership focused on maximizing performance, technology can help divide managers from workers and instill an adversarial climate.

Recommendations for Practitioners

To make best use of the positive facets of technology while avoiding the "dark side" potential discussed here, we suggest the following:

1. Monitor employee satisfaction with appraisal via periodic surveys or focus groups.
2. Bolster trust in feedback by allowing employees direct access to feedback data and some level of control in CPM processes.

3. Balance quantitative performance data with allowance for system factors.
4. To elevate trust, consider incorporating an MBO format and development plan where computer monitoring systems are in place.
5. Be aware of potential relationships between demographic and personality factors and workplace technology usage, and be willing to adapt as appropriate.
6. Provide evaluator training if performance appraisal software does not offer it as part of the package.
7. Take a holistic approach to enterprise management that includes employee well-being and development as well as job competencies and profit.
8. Allow employees to broadly define their responsibilities on projects and teams rather than being "compartmentalized."
9. Continue to use a thorough job analysis rather than selecting generic performance dimensions and criteria that are not relevant to your organization.
10. Avoid allowing technology to intervene between an evaluator and a worker. Do not replace face-to-face discussion with reliance on computer-generated feedback.

References

Adams, J. T., III. (1995). Four performance packages add ease and speed to evaluations. *HRMagazine, 40,* 151–155.

Agarwal, R., & Prasad, J. (1999). Are individual differences germane to the acceptance of new information technologies? *Decision Sciences, 30,* 361–391.

Barrick, M. R., & Mount M. K. (1991). The big five personality dimensions and job performance: A meta-analysis. *Personnel Psychology, 44,* 1–16.

Bracken, D. W., Summers, L., & Fleenor, J. (1998). High-tech 360. *Training & Development, 52,* 42–45.

Cardy, R. L., & Dobbins, G. H. (1994). *Performance appraisal: Alternative perspectives.* Cincinnati, OH: South-Western.

Caudron, S. (1994). HR leaders brainstorm the profession's future. *Personnel Journal, 73,* 54–60.

Deming, W. E. (1986). *Out of the crisis.* Cambridge: MIT Initiative for Advanced Engineering Study.

DeTienne, K. B., & Abbot, N. T. (1993). Developing an employee-centered electronic monitoring system. *Journal of Systems Management, 44,* 12.

Douthitt, E. A., & Aiello, J. R. (2001). The role of participation and control in the effects of computer monitoring on fairness perceptions, task satisfaction, and performance. *Journal of Applied Psychology, 86,* 867–874.

Earley, P. C. (1986). Trust, perceived importance of praise and criticism and work performance: An examination of feedback in the United States and England. *Journal of Management, 12,* 457–473.

Earley, P. C. (1988). Computer-generated performance feedback in the magazine-subscription industry. *Organizational Behavior and Human Decision Processes, 41,* 50–64.

Greengard, S. (1999). Putting HR software to work. *Workforce, 9,* 4–10.

Greenwood, J., Seshadri, A., & Yorukoglu, M. (2004). Engines of liberation. *Review of Economic Studies.*

Guest, D. E. (1987). Human resource management and industrial relations. *Journal of Management Studies, 24,* 503–521.

Hawk, S. R. (1994). The effects of computerized performance monitoring: An ethical perspective. *Journal of Business Ethics, 13,* 949–957.

Ilgen, D. R., Fisher, C. D., & Taylor, M. S. (1979). Consequences of individual feedback on behavior in organizations. *Journal of Applied Psychology, 64,* 349–371.

Institute for Social Research. (2002, March 12). *U.S. husbands are doing more housework while wives are doing less.* [Available at www.umich.edu/~newsinfo/Releases/2002/Mar02/r031202a.html.]

Judge, T. A., & Ferris, G. R. (1993). Social context of performance evaluation decisions. *Academy of Management Journal, 36,* 80–105.

Lawler, E. E. (1967). The multitrait-multirater approach to measuring managerial job performance. *Journal of Applied Psychology, 51,* 369–381.

Longnecker, C. O., Sims, H. P., Jr., & Gioia, D. A. (1987). Behind the mask: The politics of employee appraisal. *Academy of Management Executive, 1,* 183–193.

Morris, M. G., & Venkatesh, V. (2000). Age differences in technology adoption decisions: Implications for a changing workforce. *Personnel Psychology, 53,* 375–403.

Roepke, R., Agarwal, R., & Ferrat, T. S. (2000). Aligning the IT human resource with business vision: The leadership initiative at 3M. *MIS Quarterly, 24,* 327–353.

Shamir, B., & Salomon, I. (1985). Work-at-home and the quality of working life. *Academy of Management Review, 10,* 455–464.

Staunton, J. M., & Barnes-Farrell, J. L. (1996). Effects of electronic performance monitoring on personal control, task satisfaction, and task performance. *Journal of Applied Psychology, 81,* 738–745.

Summers, L. (2001). Web technologies for administering multisource feedback programs. In D. W. Bracken, C. W. Timmreck, & A. H. Church, (Eds.), *Handbook of multisource feedback.* San Francisco: Jossey-Bass.

Sussman, S. W., & Sproull, L. (1999). Straight talk: Delivering bad news through electronic communication. *Information Systems Research, 10,* 150–166.

Waldman, D. A. (1997). Predictors of employee preferences for multi-rater and group-based performance appraisal. *Group and Organization Management, 22,* 264–287.

CHAPTER 6

e-Compensation
The Potential to Transform Practice?
James H. Dulebohn
Janet H. Marler

In most U.S. organizations since the 1990s, the employment relationship has shifted from being lifelong with career management provided by the organization into being more short-term with employees having to manage their careers as they move between multiple organizations with flatter organizational structures. As a consequence, the role of compensation has become an important management tool for attracting, retaining, and motivating the talent needed to be competitive. In this chapter we discuss how e-compensation tools have the potential to transform the administration of existing compensation plans to better adapt to the dynamic demands of this evolving competitive landscape.

In the past, firms primarily hired employees at the lowest organizational levels, placed workers on career tracks, trained them for higher-level jobs, and promoted from within. The focus at that time for most jobs was on internal equity of compensation and less on external competitiveness. Today, however, organizations hire at all levels. Consequently, they must pay more attention to external market rates of compensation, thus increasing the demand for market salary data as well as tools to access, analyze, and communicate this data to hiring managers and to employees.

Through e-compensation tools organizations can adapt to shifting demands for information. e-Compensation tools enhance the practice of designing and administering compensation programs in a dynamic and competitive environment in three key ways. First, e-compensation tools can increase *access* to critical compensation information without the need for sophisticated or dedicated IT staffs and sophisticated technology infrastructures. They can simply access key information electronically on an as-needed basis. Second, e-compensation tools enable round-the-clock *availability* of meaningful compensation information to senior managers, HR managers, and employees. Third, e-compensation tools can *streamline* cumbersome bureaucratic tasks through the introduction of workflow functionality and real-time information processing.

Human Resource Information Systems and e-Compensation

e-Compensation represents a web-enabled approach to an array of compensation tools that enable an organization to gather, store, manipulate, analyze, utilize, and distribute compensation data and information. The term *e-compensation* connotes web-based software tools that enable managers to effectively design, administer, and communicate compensation programs. What distinguishes e-compensation from previous compensation software is that e-compensation is web-based, rather than client-server based or stand-alone PC-based. Using an Internet browser, the Internet and the World Wide Web, individuals access electronically distributed compensation software, databases, and analytic tools from anywhere—their office, their home, on vacation, on the other side of the globe.

Most HRIS systems provide data storage, transaction processing (that is, automated handling of data for HR functional activities), and management information system (MIS) functionality (that is, functionality to convert raw data from transaction processing systems into a meaningful form; an example would be reporting total compensation of each direct report to the manager). Systems that are web-enabled also allow related data entry and data processing to be performed remotely by managers and employees (for example, through self-service portals and workflow functionality), and other stakeholders through an Internet browser. For example, a manager can review a list of the proposed merit increases for his or her direct reports.

Many human resource information systems, however, do not yet provide integrated analytic features needed for compensation planning and decision support, such as the ability to also see related real-time competitive market salaries. Instead, the compensation functionality provided by most software focuses on database administration and record keeping related to compensation activities such as payroll, merit pay increases, and benefit enrollment. Migration and effective use of web-enabled integrated compensation design and analysis capabilities are still in their infancy. Many larger organizations have implemented sophisticated human resource information systems (HRIS) from enterprise resource programs (ERP) vendors such as PeopleSoft, SAP, Oracle, and Lawson, yet these ERP HRIS systems have yet to provide a full suite of integrated analytic features needed for compensation planning and decision support.

While large-system vendors such as PeopleSoft have been adding analytic tools and some compensation planning functionality to their HRIS system software, this is the exception rather than the rule. Therefore, e-compensation planning software programs are typically add-ons to a larger HRIS system or separate systems altogether. This is illustrated in Figure 6.1. The figure portrays the typical HRIS, which does not provide capabilities to perform compensation system design. HRIS systems generally provide administrative functionality at the transactional processing and management information system levels. It is through add-on software programs, or stand-alone programs, that HR specialists are able to perform higher-level functions such as designing compensation systems that represent more strategic activities. e-Compensation add-ons allow HR managers to focus on important strategic compensation issues.

e-Compensation and Strategic Design

Whether computerized or manual, the process of designing, adjusting, and administering organizational compensation systems is based on procedures for establishing internal equity, external equity, and individual equity. Internal equity refers to establishing the relative

Figure 6.1. Current e-Compensation Systems.

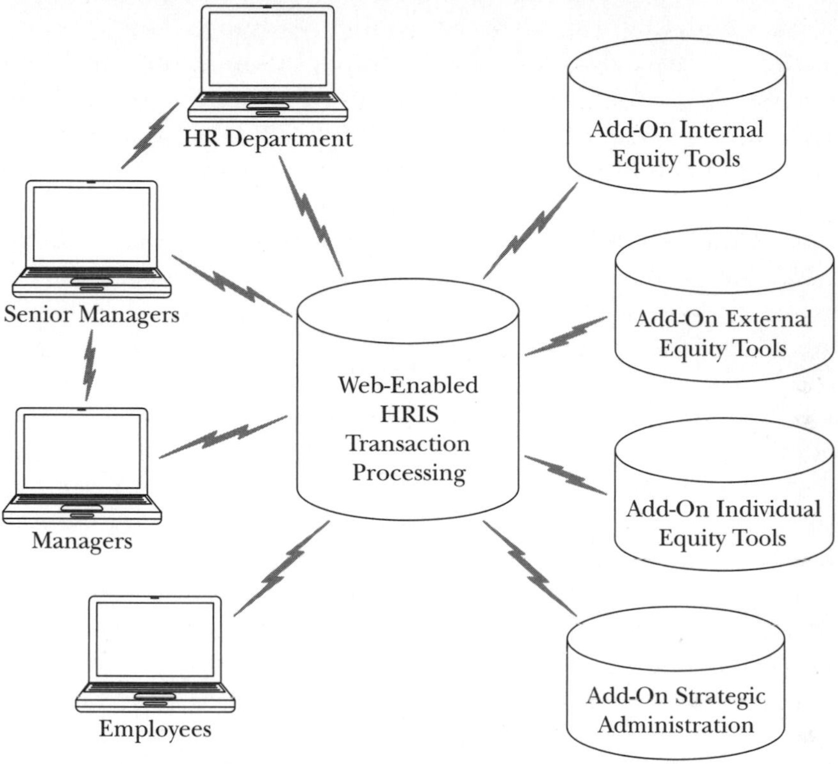

worth of jobs inside the organization. External equity, or external competitiveness, involves determining an organization's pay in relation to the external labor market. Individual equity involves recognizing and rewarding individuals for their contributions.

An organization's compensation system consists of policies and practices that address how the organization establishes and maintains internal, external, and individual equity. This configuration of policies and practices is considered strategic if it supports achieving critical business goals, including how the cost of total compensation is controlled, managed, and communicated.

We review how e-compensation tools can reduce the challenges inherent in designing and implementing an effective compensation system. To do this, we organize our discussion around using e-compensation to better achieve internal equity, external equity, individual equity, and strategic administration. Within this framework, we highlight some of the available software that, as noted earlier, are typically stand-alone compensation systems or HRIS add-on programs. We also illustrate how e-compensation technology can: (1) facilitate access to sophisticated databases and decision-support tools; (2) enable round-the-clock availability of key compensation information; and (3) streamline processes. At the end of each section, we conclude with challenges that HR managers still need to address despite advances in technology.

Objective One: Internal Equity

Researchers have shown that employees' perceptions of fairness affect their work-related attitudes, such as job satisfaction and organizational commitment, and their behaviors, such as turnover and productivity (see Dulebohn, 1997; Rynes & Gerhart, 2001). Consequently, an important consideration to organizations is that the pay differentials between jobs should accurately reflect differences between positions in terms of their requirements, responsibilities, and complexities. An organization's pay structure should logically convey that jobs with greater requirements and responsibilities are paid more.

Organizations achieve internal equity through performing job analyses and job evaluations. Job analysis is a systematic process of collecting information about jobs: identifying and describing what knowledge, skills, abilities, and other characteristics are required to do a job. Drawing on the output of job analyses, job evaluation is a formal procedure for hierarchically ordering a set of jobs or positions with respect to their value or worth, usually for the purpose of setting pay rates. The outcome of job evaluation is a rating of a job's worth (*not* rating the incumbent), and ultimately provides a rationale for paying jobs differently inside the organization.

While there are several job evaluation methods, the most widely used approach in larger companies is the point method. This approach evaluates jobs based on a set of compensable factors that represent what the organization wants to pay for. A compensable factor is an element of skill, ability, responsibility, or competency that can be described at various levels. For each compensable factor, a scale is devised representing increasing levels of worth. Each level is assigned a given number of points. The range of possible points is constant across all jobs. Each job is rated on each factor separately and is assigned point values. After rating all jobs, the end result is a job structure or hierarchy, which ranks all the organization's jobs based on their total point values (that is, summation of point values received for each compensable factor level).

e-Compensation Tools for Establishing Internal Equity

The job evaluation process is associated with bureaucracy, hierarchy, and over-attention to internal structure to the detriment of flexibility and market competitiveness. But while external competitiveness garners greater attention when labor markets are tight and competition for talent fierce, achieving internal equity can be critical to successfully managing mergers, acquisitions, and reorganizations. Keeping existing employees productive and maintaining morale is best achieved by managing internal equity and meshing disparate compensation systems in a systematic and equitable way. Consequently, despite declining popularity, job evaluation is essential to deriving and maintaining pay structures that promote fairness and reduce perceptions of inequity.

Thompson and Hull (2003), executives of Link HR Systems, believe that intranet/Internet-based technology will transform the job evaluation process and restore its earlier popularity. The range of products that use the Internet and web access to enhance either job analysis or job evaluation illustrate how e-compensation tools can transform designing and maintaining internal equity policies from a bureaucratic hassle to an effective automated competitive practice. The Internet and web access make best practices more accessible and available and can also streamline existing internal equity practices.

Increasing Accessibility
Internet technologies level the playing ground by making available expert information to a much broader audience. For example, HR managers can electronically access advanced job analysis techniques

developed by well-regarded experts such as Personnel Systems and Technology Corporation's (PSCT) web-based job analysis tools. Subscribers to PSCT do not need sophisticated hardware or to be HR specialists in job analysis or job evaluation (www.pstc.com). For example, subscribers can access PSCT's flagship job analysis instrument, the Common Metric Questionnaire (CMQ), a web-based questionnaire designed and validated by I/O researchers to accurately describe both managerial and nonmanagerial occupations (www.cmqonline.com). PSCT also offers web hosting and reporting services to administer online tests and surveys, custom web-programming, and test design.

Knowledgepoint (Shair, 2001) (www.knowledgepoint.com), a subsidiary of CCH, offers another job analysis product accessed over the web. The advantage of Knowledgepoint is that it provides low-cost access to an extensive job description library, along with search capabilities. Knowledgepoint's web-accessed software and database illustrate how e-compensation makes sophisticated "knowledge management" databases available to even smaller companies, potentially reducing competitive advantages larger organizations have.

A caveat to these marketed online compensation tools, however, is that it is hard to determine the value of the information before you pay. For example, while William M. Mercer Inc.'s description of its eIPE job evaluation tool provides screen shots, descriptions, and demos to convey in more detail what you are purchasing in advance, it still costs money to acquire (www.imercer.com). Job evaluation tools and information are easily available on the web, but are not necessarily low cost.

Not all job evaluation tools on the web carry hefty price tags. With patient searching, if you have time, at the other end of the spectrum, organizations can find free web-based services such as HR-Guide's job evaluation tool. This interactive web-based tool found at www.hr-software.net/cgi/JobEvaluation.cgi provides an online point-method job evaluation instrument. Using this tool, an HR specialist can specify the number and type of compensable factors; the number of levels within each factor; and the points associated with the factors. Completely free, customizable, and simple to use, this tool is a quintessential example of the value of sharing resources and knowledge on the web.

Increasing Availability of Job Analysis and Job Evaluation Tools

Web-based compensation software increases the accessibility of information, making it available 24/7 using corporate networks, servers, PCs, and handheld devices. Managers and employees have access to key information to make completing a job analysis or job evaluation project relatively easy. Furthermore, best practices in both these activities are built into the software. For example, JPS Management Consulting (www.jpsmanagement.com) provides web-enabled standardized questionnaires that collect information from a constituent manager or job incumbent. Because the system is web-enabled, HR specialists can electronically distribute them to target employees or managers via the corporate intranet. Intranet technology, therefore, enables the responsibility for job evaluation to be decentralized to the desktop of the hiring manager, if desired.

Streamlining the Process

With online JPS Management Consulting Questionnaires, once the manager completes the online survey, the data is automatically collected and summarized. A standardized job description is automatically generated, converted to job evaluation format, and given a job evaluation point score. Because production, distribution, collation, and analysis are all automated and electronically distributed, the HR specialist is freed from multiple time-consuming and transactional tasks to spend more time on careful design and on developing practices that leverage the job evaluation information.

Challenges to Achieving Web-Enabled Internal Equity

Web-enabled technologies can increase the amount of information available to decision makers and speed up the process of developing and distributing this information. There are several factors, however, that can hamper companies from fully realizing the potential of web-enabled internal equity tools. First, most of these tools are not generally integrated across software packages. While there are a growing number of software programs in the market that support the design and maintenance of internal equity policies and practices, relatively few are currently both integrated and web-enabled. A survey of compensation administration software conducted by Advanced Personnel Systems in 2003 reveals that, of the thirteen web-based products with software supporting internal equity practices, only three companies also integrated external equity, individual equity, or administration practices (Advanced Personnel Systems, 2003).

InfoTech Works Inc. provides one of the few integrated web-based compensation software solutions that automates and integrates internal equity and external equity software applications and can be used stand-alone, over an intranet, or over the web on an outsourced basis. The job evaluation module automates any point-factor plan, including Hay or modified Hay point plans. Its job evaluation software comes bundled with market pricing modules, a salary range/bands module, and salary budgeting and records management modules. The job evaluation data are then used to create grades or bands and to interface with the other modules.

A second challenge facing organizations in implementing these e-compensation tools is that these tools are only as good as the data they access. This means there must be organizational commitment to gather, manage, and maintain accurate and relevant data. Organizations often assume IT tools will save money through reduced headcount, but many find that database software still requires employees' time to collect and manage more data. Third, proper training is required to ensure user acceptance and competent use of the technology. Companies frequently skimp on this aspect of software implementation to their detriment. Fourth, some users find data entry tends to be slower and less flexible using web applications than client-server-based software, particularly with nonlinear processes (that is, moving around to various screens without losing data). Faster servers and networks, however, are alleviating this early criticism.

Finally, while web-based software tools increase access to and distribution of information, the quality and efficiency with which decisions are made still remain ultimately with the manager. Thus, web-based technology makes information accessible and available and can streamline the whole process, but it is still ultimately a tool to be used by, not to replace, a HR specialist.

Objective Two: External Equity

Organizations have to offer competitive rates of pay if they wish to attract and retain competent employees (Barber & Bretz, 2000). While job evaluation provides an acceptable approach for determining relative worth of jobs within an organization, the organization still has to ensure that the value they attach to the job is competitive outside, in the external labor market. External equity, or external competitiveness, refers to an organization's pay in relation to the external labor market. Managing external equity is essential because employees also compare their pay to the pay for similar jobs in competitor organizations (Dulebohn, 2003). If an organization does not consider policies on external equity in its compensation designs, it stands to lose valuable employees and will fail to attract new ones.

Organizations establish external equity in compensation system design through conducting wage and salary surveys whereby data are gathered on the amount competitors are paying for key or benchmark jobs. Salary survey data provide organizations with a basis for evaluating their rates of pay as compared to their competitors. The process for conducting wage and salary surveys includes several steps. First, organizations determine on which benchmark or key jobs to gather wage or salary data. In practice, organizations do not gather market data on all jobs. Instead they gather survey data for a number of key jobs, which typically have the following characteristics: the jobs are defined quite precisely; the content of the jobs is relatively stable over time; and the jobs occur frequently in the organization and in competitive organizations that will be surveyed. The jobs chosen are representative of the range of jobs in the job hierarchy produced from the job evaluation.

In the second step, organizations determine which organizations to survey. The selection of survey companies depends on the product and labor markets in which the organization competes for talent. After relevant competitive organizations are chosen, the organization must verify that the job descriptions of the surveyed competitor organizations closely match the benchmark jobs the organization wishes to price. If necessary, the organization has to make adjustments to the collected wage data. For example, if an organization's job does not include supervision of subordinates, but a comparison job does, this has to be factored into the wage analysis.

Finally, an organization must also consider the date at which the wage survey data were collected. If the data are old, it may need to be adjusted (that is, aged) using the CPI or a similar index to account for price changes in the external market. Once the data are carefully matched and adjusted, only then can compensation analysts use the wage survey data to compute central tendency statistics. These metrics are then used to determine how competitive a particular job within the organization is compared to its competitive counterparts.

e-Compensation Tools for Managing External Equity

Online salary survey data is what most people think about when the term e-compensation is used. Online surveys and salary survey websites give users, both employer and employee, electronic access to salary information formerly available only on paper-published survey statistics for benchmark jobs (Gherson & Jackson, 2001). Since their introduction a few years ago, web-enabled surveys have proliferated. Salary survey websites are easy to use, easy to access, and increasingly used by both companies and employees.

Increasing Accessibility of Competitive Information

In facilitating the collection and distribution of benchmark job survey information, the Internet has accelerated a shift from focusing on internal equity to a greater emphasis on achieving external competitiveness. The outsourcing of these activities is also common. Salary survey participation, job matching, managing of salary surveys, and job pricing are some of the most frequently outsourced compensation practices (Brink & McDonnell, 2003).

With the increased accessibility and management of salary survey information, even smaller organizations with smaller HR staffs can develop relatively sophisticated external market analyses. Spreadsheets are available for download from the Internet that provide forms for consolidating multiple salary surveys along with automated features such as aging and weighting data. Compensation consulting firms that collect the salary survey information also make available downloadable spreadsheets that save hours in matching jobs, summarizing, and auditing data (Brink & McDonnell, 2003).

Increasing Availability of Salary Data

The salary survey data available over the Internet, while accessible 24/7, nevertheless does not represent real-time data. Much of the survey data published on the web represent the collation of job data that may be as much as two years old. Few consulting organizations have found it cost-effective or feasible to update their survey information more frequently than annually. Furthermore, few participating organizations have the manpower to support this effort. Thus, while the data are online, available, and accessible, they are not as yet real-time.

Streamlining the Process

Several specialized software vendors, such as Advanced Information Management Inc., HR Web Solutions International, and InfoTech Works Inc., and HR consulting companies, such as Mercer Human Resource Consulting LLP, Aon Consulting, and Watson Wyatt Worldwide, offer web-based systems that integrate external market and internal compensation data into a centralized database that also provides customized manager self-service access. These systems enhance the organization's ability to manage their external competitiveness by providing decision makers with relevant market salary information to compare against internal total compensation. They also speed decision making with the automation of the review and approval process.

Managers can now access their direct reports' salary history along with comparative market data derived from several salary surveys. Based on this information they can make salary increase and adjustment decisions that are within budget guidelines and are consistent with market competitiveness. Moreover, the process is further automated by workflow technology that electronically routes compensation decisions to senior managers and HR for approval. Interfaces with HRIS and payroll databases further automate the process. As a result, decision-making effectiveness, efficiency, and execution are enhanced.

Challenges to Achieving Web-Enabled External Equity

One of the challenges that compensation specialists face in having easy access and availability of market data is using it wisely. Easy web access to market information does not eliminate the necessity to be careful consumers of information. Users must still evaluate the quality of the market data, and this includes considering the quality of survey data, the quality of the benchmark job matches, survey age, sample size, and relevant competitive market. Some of the newer websites capitalizing on increased interest in market salary data do not always provide sufficient information for consumers to fully evaluate the quality of the data.

Another challenge is to integrate market data into an existing HRIS system such that the HRIS database includes current relevant market information on well-matched benchmark jobs. The challenge is both technical and organizational. From a technical perspective, the challenge is to create data-integration interfaces, which transfer data across different database platforms without errors. Organizationally, the challenge is to maintain a consistent sample of benchmark jobs that are well matched to the salary survey jobs. Without careful management of the plethora of accessible market information, compensation managers run the risk of distributing poor-quality data that will only enhance the efficiency with which *poor* decisions are made. Thus while the Internet and web-based technologies increase accessibility, availability, and efficiency of information access, HR managers must still critically evaluate the quality of the data, manage its integration across information technology platforms, and ensure that the timeliness and integrity of data is maintained.

Objective Three: Individual Equity

Achieving individual equity means managing comparisons individuals make relative to others working the same job inside their organization or to themselves, based on their contributions to the job (their performance, seniority, responsibility, and so forth). The concept is based on Adams's (1965) theory of inequity that focuses on the causes and effects of perceptions of wage inequity. Adams posits that individuals evaluate the fairness of their outcomes using an equity rule whereby they compare their own input-outcome ratios to a referent or comparable other, which is typically someone working a similar job in the organization. Individuals perceive equity or fairness when the ratio or balance of their outcomes to their inputs is equal in relation to the relative inputs and outputs of the referent other. In contrast, inequity exists when the ratios are perceived as unequal.

Adams asserts that perceptions of unequal ratios (resulting from either under- or overpayment) result in a state of inequity distress or psychological uneasiness that motivates individuals to engage in actions that will remove the dissonance and restore perceptions of equity. According to Adams (1965), "The presence of inequity will motivate [the] person to achieve equity or to reduce inequity, and the strength of motivation to do so will vary directly with the magnitude of inequity experienced" (p. 283). Workers will attempt to achieve equity through actions such as altering inputs, altering outcomes, adjusting their evaluations of their inputs and outputs, by using psychological justifications, or by withdrawing from the organization (for example, by engaging in negative behavior). In contrast, perceptions of a balance between input and output ratios result in evaluations that an outcome distribution is equitable, and this evaluation contributes to satisfaction and other positive individual and organizationally related attitudes and behaviors.

The terms "internal" and "external" in internal equity and external equity highlight the focus of comparison (in the former it is other jobs within the organization; in the latter it is the external labor market). The term "individual equity" best reflects what Adam had in mind in his theory of inequity—individuals making comparisons of their pay in relation to others in the organization working similar jobs. In establishing individual equity, organizations must have mechanisms in their compensation systems that reward individuals for their performance and their contributions to the organization.

Structurally, wage grades and wage ranges allow organizations to pay individuals differently based on differing productivity, despite having similar jobs. A wage grade is a horizontal grouping of different jobs that are considered substantially equal for pay purposes. Successive wage grades represent increasing amounts of job evaluation points, based on compensable factors such as responsibility, skill, knowledge, ability, and so forth. The accepted practice in designing wage grades is to use equal wage grade point intervals. This is accomplished by dividing the total job evaluation point amount by the number of grades needed to reflect differences in point values for groups of jobs. For example, a ten-grade structure consisting of 1,000 total points would have 100 points for each grade width.

Grades enable the compensation designer to treat jobs of similar value identically in the wage determination process. Grades also enhance an organization's ability to move people among jobs within a grade without changing in pay. Finally, grades enable an organization to recognize different individual performance in similar jobs.

The most widespread practice that U.S. organizations use to formally recognize individual differences in performance is merit pay programs. In practice, however, the determination and allocation of merit increases is a time-consuming and complex process. While pay grades provide some measure of structure and control in this process, it nevertheless is incumbent on the organization to keep them updated, equitable, and competitive. Merit increases must also be evaluated in terms of their effect on external competitiveness and internal equity.

There are two approaches to managing the merit pay programs. In a centralized approach, first, salary budgets are centrally determined based on factors such as average labor market rate increases, ability to pay, competitive market pressures, turnover, and cost of living. Once these factors are analyzed and an overall target salary increase is budgeted, the second step is to consider individual differences in productivity and merit. To capture this aspect but still maintain internally equitable pay structures, compensation managers develop merit increase grids as guidelines. In this system, centralized HR specialists rather than operational managers exercise greater control over salary increase decisions.

In a more decentralized approach, managers across the organization forecast the pay increases they expect to recommend in the coming year to retain their key employees and to remain competitive. These data are rolled up to form the organization's salary budget. This bottom-up approach allocates more discretion and control to line managers. HR managers are simply responsible for rolling up the information and ensuring the data are accurate and the resulting budget produced in a timely fashion.

Both approaches are widespread, and commercial products facilitate either approach although compensation managers should determine which administrative approach is built into the product to ensure a better fit with their organization's existing practices.

e-Compensation Tools for Achieving Individual Equity

Most large organizations rely on their HRIS to provide most of the information needed to administer pay increases based on individual merit. This includes accurate headcounts, current compensation levels, pay structure, pay history, pay survey information, and performance history. The challenge, however, lies in accessing data that is notoriously disparate, driven by multiple homegrown legacy systems, or spreadsheet processes and further complicated by multiple merger and acquisition activities. The result is often an environment in which organizations have islands of information that make the gathering and standardizing of compensation information extremely difficult (Weir, 2003). Most compensation administrators today are still conducting their salary or merit increase process using Excel spreadsheets and email, or by sending out the spreadsheets on paper. This process is time-consuming, prone to errors, and not very secure (www.aimworld.com/press_52902.html).

Streamlining the Process

Two firms, PeopleSoft and Kadiri, Inc., offer comprehensive web-enabled compensation planning software that coordinate and integrate information from internal pay structures and external market data to effectively and efficiently implement individual equity policies. PeopleSoft, an ERP software vendor, offers an HRIS module that is better leveraged in centralized structure. Kadiri, Inc., a specialized compensation software vendor, favors a more decentralized approach.

PeopleSoft Corporation is a comprehensive enterprise-wide resource planning software vendor known for its particularly strong Human Capital Management (HCM) module. As part of this HCM module, PeopleSoft includes a total compensation component that allows HR managers to budget and administer a compensation system that includes salary plans/grades/steps, multiple pay components such as base pay, spot awards, and geographic wage differentials, variable compensation plans such as stock options, and benefits. Their HCM module also interfaces directly with two self-service compensation modules, one for managers and one for employees.

The manager self-service module gives managers, upon proper authorization, access to their direct report employee records residing in the centralized PeopleSoft HRIS database, which includes compensation history, current total compensation, and job history. Managers also may request salary changes for their employees that include not only salary increases but also bonus allocations or spot awards. These salary requests are then electronically routed through a workflow routine to a more senior manager for approval before the database is updated.

Kadiri, Inc., has a web-enabled add-on software product that facilitates the salary budgeting allocation and approval processes. By integrating several key web-enabled technologies: self-service, workflow, and knowledge management, Kadiri TotalComp allows compensation specialists to gather information from their HRIS, configure it, add additional information such as pay survey data, and develop various budget allocation scenarios before placing it in an accessible central data repository. Through a centralized data repository, managers can access the comprehensive information necessary to make efficient, effective salary allocation decisions. This includes salary budgets, allocation guidelines, and employee salary and performance metrics for base, variable, and equity compensation. Managers can use this information along with an integrated compensation HR metric modeling tool to evaluate various allocation configurations before making a final decision. Upon completion of this process, managers submit their allocations electronically to senior managers, who complete a review before it is routed back to compensation managers for final review and integration into the organization's HRIS and financial plans.

Web-enabled compensation planning software can deliver significant savings through reduced decision-making time, more accurate data, and reduced errors. Using Kadiri to automate, streamline, and communicate compensation practices, one financial services company reduced their planning cycle from thirteen weeks to five weeks and reported over $10 million in cost savings from reduced hours spent by both line managers and compensation managers in the planning process (www.kadiri.com).

Objective Four: Strategic Administration

Compensation managers have to demonstrate how compensation decisions support achieving organization success. Administrative practices should ensure that policies on internal, external, and individual equity are properly operationalized in the day-to-day management of individual compensation and that this effective implementation supports overall business objectives. Effective compensation administration also ensures that total compensation costs are controlled and total compensation decisions are clearly communicated to employees. Both activities are critical to the success of any compensation design.

e-Compensation Tools for Compensation Administration

Planning and controlling compensation costs in a PeopleSoft system is more effective if there is a well-organized, defined, and centralized HR function. Control in a PeopleSoft compensation administration package builds control mechanisms within the software, therefore leaving less managerial discretion. Thus PeopleSoft automates the salary change approval process but does not provide built-in knowledge management capability that would guide or empower managers to make their own compensation decisions. Instead the choices are built upfront into centralized and standardized software routines.

In contrast, Kadiri, Inc.'s flagship product, Kadiri TotalComp, combines the attributes of both centralized and decentralized managerial structures. Kadiri's software enables centralized control over compensation design so that standardized compensation structures, guidelines, and pay allocations are consistent with overall business strategy and objectives. Decentralized decision making, however, is also facilitated with the distribution of a compensation knowledge management system. The knowledge management system reinforces company policy and objectives by providing managers with consistent, customized decision-making guidance.

In both approaches to compensation administration, HR managers have access to comprehensive compensation metrics that facilitate managing the organization's cost of labor within a strategically designed competitive framework. In both examples, however, these tools do not replace the need for compensation specialists who can optimize the potential these tools offer.

The communication of compensation policies using e-compensation tools provides another excellent example of the importance of developing an effective sociotechnical interface.

Communicating Compensation Policies

A compensation plan, no matter how brilliantly designed, will not accomplish its objectives without a communications strategy that is just as brilliantly designed (Fitzgerald, 2000). Even with the most meticulously planned and managed compensation system, communication to employees can make the difference in how compensation decisions are received and how favorably employees respond. For example, Jones and Scarpello's study of employees in a large county government found that perceptions about the fairness of the pay communication procedures contributed uniquely to the prediction of organizational commitment (Bergman & Scarpello, 2002).

There are four basic steps to designing a compensation communication plan. First, senior managers must set the objectives of the communication plan and the strategy for achieving these objectives. Second, HR specialists develop the content of the communication. Third, the content is distributed in a form and media that best achieves the communications objectives. Fourth, the effectiveness of the communication plan is evaluated.

Unfortunately, setting communication objectives is frequently ignored in a rush to get information out (Milkovich & Newman, 2002). However, it is important to have a clear idea of what the communication is meant to achieve. Is it meant to communicate the value of the employment relationship and thereby increase employee commitment and reduce turnover? Or is it meant to communicate how an employee can earn greater compensation by pointing out the motivational aspects of the compensation system? Is it meant to direct attention to valued behaviors? Is it meant to establish expectations about the nature of the employment relationship? Defining specific objectives is important because, without them, no matter how fancy the web-based technology, objectives cannot be achieved that have not been articulated.

Once objectives are articulated, managers must define a communications strategy. Will using ESS capability be the most effective communication vehicle? Will the targeted audience have access, know-how, and confidence to find and use the information? For example, PeopleSoft's HCM self-service module allows employees access to their personal compensation history through a feature that allows them to navigate via a web-based portal to their relevant data. Employees have viewing capability but cannot update or change the database. This may enhance communication or increase frustration if employees cannot find someone to answer questions.

Is it better to market an organization's total rewards or is it more effective to simply provide them with all the details and facts, as is the case in PeopleSoft's employee self-service module? A Towers Perrin study found that higher performing companies are more likely to share the details of their compensation programs such as salary ranges and grades with employees (Gherson & Jackson, 2001). Ultimately, compensation strategy and communication objectives should guide the electronic content and distribution practices.

e-Compensation Tools and Compensation Communications: Facilitating Strategic Administration

Web-based technologies communicate total compensation and can provide depth, flexibility, and connectivity that make the technology highly valuable for employee and employer. Employees' perceived value of the employment relationship is enhanced by the inclusion of a vast array of components; these range from base pay, stock options, paid time off, insurance, sabbaticals, and retirement plans to often-forgotten expenses such as seminars, conferences, training sessions, tuition reimbursement, car allowances, uniforms, and safety equipment. Presentation in the form of graphs and charts or illustrations can drive home the "a-ha" factor. Thus, with carefully crafted content and targeted distribution, web-based communication software can facilitate the dissemination of critical information and manage how employees perceive the value of employment relationship employees. Moreover, this vast amount of information can be personalized to each employee. For example, Nerheim & North (2001)of Hewitt indicate that, whereas a standard benefits statement offers four to twelve pages of information, a web-based tool can easily provide three to five times the content at a click and can be accessed 24/7.

Electronic communication offers several crucial advantages relative to print. First, the rapid online turnaround time gets information to employees far sooner than print, minimizing outdated information. Second, a website can be refreshed multiple times annually, resulting in total compensation communications that is fresh and relevant year around. Third, online publication results in substantial savings on paper and publication costs. Finally, websites can provide links to sites where employees can take action to grow their base pay or ensure they have enough money for retirement.

The comprehensive nature of such a website doesn't simply serve to convey data. It can help employees better understand the reciprocal nature of the employment relationship and how to maximize individual financial opportunities and also convey to employees the connection between personal behavior and business results.

Challenges to Web-Enabled Strategic Administration

Web-based technologies enhance and facilitate the compensation communication process but do not replace the need for well-designed content. While the steps involved in managing compensation communications have not changed, web-based technologies are changing the cost, quality, and speed with which these steps are executed. Best practice in total rewards today entails getting relevant information to employees, managers, senior management, and HR staff so they can make real-time informed decisions on a collaborative basis (Martin, 2001). As a result, more than ever before, an organization's communication practices can have a profound effect on how employees respond to an organization's compensation practices and whether the organization indeed gets what it pays for.

HR specialists still need to develop the content because they understand the key objectives and design features of the compensation system. As Michael Snipes of Allstate Insurance notes, "You must connect the dots for employees as to how they play in the larger corporate picture. Employees must understand their role in earnings per share in order for them to understand the last piece in the puzzle—what's in it for me and how can I benefit" (Berger, 2000, p. 23).

Conclusion

Compensation plays a critical role in organizations today. The decline in lifelong employment relationships and internal labor markets has increased the prominence of competitive compensation in attracting and motivating critical human capital. This necessitates a closer linkage with the external market and the tools to make rapid changes in compensation in order to remain competitive and attractive to current incumbents and prospective employees. e-Compensation tools provide HR managers with the ability to effectively adapt compensation systems to meet these challenges, to manage and maintain all aspects of equity in pay plan design, and to link compensation systems with the strategic management of the organization.

With increased ability to gather information electronically, e-compensation tools provide HR professionals greater access to knowledge management databases, best practices in internal and external and individual equity design, as well as to competitive information. Web-enabled tools also enhance HR professionals' ability to distribute this key information and compensation metrics to employees and managers, thus making critical compensation information more available to support decision making. Finally, they increase HR professionals' productivity through automating information access and distribution of transactional compensation administration responsibilities to line managers and employees.

As shown in Figure 6.1, web-enabled e-compensation systems also serve line managers, employees, and senior managers. Line managers benefit from e-compensation functionality by being able to access compensation information and analytic tools. These tools also provide them with the ability to access compensation data, compensation metrics such as average salary, market salary, and salary budgets, and to edit and update employees' compensation information online. HRIS and e-compensation tools provide employees with the ability, through self-service modules, to access their compensation and benefits information. They also provide them with tools to assist them in understanding their compensation and benefit packages. Finally, upper managers benefit from e-HRIS and e-compensation tools in that these systems provide them with tools and relevant compensation metrics to evaluate and integrate compensation information into their strategic management.

e-Compensation software and systems (as portrayed in Figure 6.1) provide HR professionals with the ability to manage their compensation systems in order to meet the traditional compensation objectives of internal equity, external competitiveness, individual equity, and administration. Most web-enabled HRIS programs, on their own, however, do not currently provide sufficient compensation system design or strategic administration functionality. Instead,

HR departments gain this crucial functionality through the use of web-enabled add-on software tools and stand-alone systems. As both hardware and software technologies advance, however, so will improvements in the technical integration of e-compensation add-on tools into HRIS systems themselves. It will be up to HR professionals to ensure that organizations adopt and integrate these capabilities organizationally to leverage their potential.

References

Adams, S. (1965). Inequity in social exchange. *Advances in Experimental Social Psychology, 2,* 267–299.

Advanced Personnel Systems. (2003). *Compensation administration software: A special report.* Roseville, AZ: Advanced Personnel Systems.

Barber, A., & Bretz, R. D. (2000). Compensation, attraction, and retention. In S. Rynes & B. Gerhart (Eds.), *Compensation in organizations* (pp. 32–60). San Francisco: Jossey-Bass.

Berger, D. R. (2000). Millennium compensation trends. In L. A. Berger & D. R. Berger (Eds.), *The handbook of compensation* (pp. 17–25). New York: McGraw-Hill.

Bergman, T. J., & Scarpello, V. G. (2002). *Compensation and decision making.* Cincinnati, OH: South-Western.

Brink, S., & McDonnell, S. (2003). IHRIM Go-TO-guides: e-compensation, *The e-merging technology series* (pp. 1–18). Burlington, MA: IHRIM.

Dulebohn, J. H. (1997). Social influence in organizational justice: Evaluations of processes and outcomes of human resources systems. In G. R. Ferris (Ed.), *Research in personnel and human resources management* (Vol. 15, pp. 241–291). Greenwich, CT: JAI Press.

Dulebohn, J. H. (2003). Work redesign and technology implementation: The need for compensation system congruency. In D. Stone (Ed.), *Advances in human performance and cognitive engineering research* (Vol. 3). Greenwich, CT: JAI Press.

Fitzgerald, L. (2000). Culture and compensation. In L. A. Berger & D. R. Berger (Eds.), *The handbook of compensation* (pp. 531–540). New York: McGraw-Hill.

Gerhart, B., Minkoff, H. B., & Olsen, R. N. (1995). Employee compensation: Theory, practice, and evidence. In G. R. Ferris, S. D. Rosen, & D. T. Barnum (Eds.), *Handbook of human resource management.* Oxford, England: Blackwell.

Gherson, D., & Jackson, A. P. (2001). Web-based compensation planning. In A. J. Walker (Ed.), *Web-based human resources* (pp. 83–95). New York: McGraw-Hill.

Henderson, R. (2000). *Compensation in a knowledge-based world* (8th ed.). Upper Saddle River, NJ: Prentice Hall.

Hull, T. (2002). *Job evaluation: Back for the dead?* www.link-hrsystems.com/downloads/Jobevaluation.pdf.

Martin, T. (2001). Leveraging technology to communicate total rewards. *The next frontier: Technology and total rewards* (pp. 13–17). Burlington, MA: IHRIM/World at Work.

Milkovich, G. T., & Newman, J. M. (2002). *Compensation.* (7th ed.). New York: McGraw-Hill/Irwin.

Nerheim, L., & North, R. (2001). Unprecedented access: Web-based tools emerge for communicating total rewards. *The next frontier: Technology and total rewards* (pp. 18–20). Burlington, MA: IHRIM/World at Work.

Rynes, S., & Gerhart, B. (2001). Bringing compensation into I/O psychology(and vice versa). In S. Rynes & B. Gerhart (Eds.), *Compensation in organizations: Current research and practice* (pp. 351–384). San Francisco: New Lexington Press.

Shair, D. (2001). *Descriptions now 5.0.* www.knowledgepoint.com/coinfo/press/hrmag_2001.htm.

Thompson, A., & Hull, T. (2003). *Using the HR intranet to transform job evaluation.* Philadelphia: Link HR Systems, Inc.

Weir, J. (2003). Compensation planning and management in financial services: A framework for success (white paper). Aurora, Ontario: HR.com Research.

CHAPTER 7

eHR
Trends in Delivery Methods
Hal G. Gueutal
Cecilia M. Falbe

The delivery of HR services is undergoing the most significant change in the history of our field. Traditionally, we provided services to employees through personal contact and paper forms. For more forward-thinking firms, delivery may have included IVR (voice response) systems. That was yesterday. Today and tomorrow will be a very different world for HR professionals, managers, and employees. Virtually all large, and most medium-sized companies, now deliver at least some HR services via the Internet. On the positive side, managers will have much easier access to information and be able to more rapidly and efficiently manage their staffs. Employees benefit by being able to obtain information at times convenient to them, to manage their careers, and to maintain skill sets that help them stay marketable in an increasingly competitive job market. On the negative side, eHR technology can serve to isolate HR professionals, as employees interact primarily with a website rather than a human being. Indeed, one outcome of eHR could be a further alienation of employees from employers.

The advent of web-based self-service is transforming the practice of HR. For HR professionals, new skills such as knowledge and content management will become important. Many activities formerly handled by HR staffs are rapidly being transferred to employees and line managers. One impact of this trend is a dramatic reduction in the number of HR professionals required by organizations. Often the reduction in HR staff is on the order of 33 to 50 percent following implementation of self-service technology. Evidence of the commitment of corporations to eHR technology may be seen in a recent study by Towers Perrin, which reported that, even in a relatively weak economy, only 3 percent of firms surveyed planned to reduce spending on HR technology (Towers Perrin, 2002b). The same study reported that 80 percent of the HR executives surveyed felt that web technology could lower HR costs, although only 40 percent reported that they had observed such savings to date in their firm. Other research by the Aberdeen Group anticipated that spending on self-service applications would exceed $12 billion in 2003 (Authoria, Inc., 2003). Indeed, in 2003 spending on HR technology increased 27 percent over figures for 2002, according to the Cedar Group (Cedar, 2003).

eHR implementations range from simply using email to communicate with employees to sophisticated systems that personalize information for each employee. Examples of the latter might allow employees to complete a diagnostic skill assessment and tailor a training plan to their individual needs. New terms such as "knowledge base," "employee self-service" (ESS), "managerial self-service" (MSS), "strategic application" (SA), and "HR portal" have become part of our vocabulary. As of 2002, more than 70 percent of larger organizations had implemented some form of employee self-service, and most of the ones who had not planned to do so (Cedar, 2002). Likewise, MSS is growing rapidly, as almost 80 percent of larger organizations either have implemented MSS or plan to in the near future (Cedar, 2002).

This chapter serves as a review of the literature regarding new delivery methods for HR products and services. It is intended to provide a primer on best practices in this emerging area. The first section reviews the terminology and techniques that enable eHR. Each major type of self-service application is reviewed, along with examples of how the technology is used to deliver services to employees. The next section reviews the business case for these systems. That is, what evidence is there that these expensive systems work? What return on investment (ROI) is expected—and achieved—with these systems? How cost-effective are they? Do users like them? The third section discusses best practices in implementing these systems and identifies common errors to avoid. The final section takes a look at key issues in the ongoing management of the HR portal.

Before beginning our review, it bears mention that much of the published research in this area comes from the practitioner literature and from vendor and consulting firms. Clearly, much of this research accentuates success stories and the positive aspects of this technology. This is not to suggest that the literature is intentionally biased, only that it must be viewed with a critical eye. Unfortunately, there is very little peer-reviewed literature in the area. This is surprising, given the scale of the potential impact of this technology on our profession. We hope academic researchers will come to better understand this technology and provide a more substantial research base in the future.

Terms and Technology

As with any new way of working, eHR has its own vocabulary. In this section we will review a few of the key terms and technological applications. Also discussed is how these technologies are changing HR practice.

HR Portals

HR portals provide a single site for employees to visit for HR services. These are sophisticated websites that are designed to communicate a range of HR information. More than a third (36 percent) of larger organizations participating in a recent survey reported they currently had a portal strategy, and this number is projected to double by 2006 (Cedar, 2003). Another study by Towers Perrin found that 42 percent of the organizations they surveyed had implemented a portal strategy by 2002. An additional 31 percent planned to move to a portal approach in 2003 (Towers Perrin, 2002a). HR portals range from very complex sites that include information personalized for each employee to basic sites that only provide static information or allow only simple data maintenance. More sophisticated portals allow the user to customize the portal to the individual preferences of the employee. For example, a customized portal might allow the user to show stock quotes or scroll a news ticker on a portion of the screen. The site might also be tied into an instant message system with other workers. Portals typically offer the user a "single sign-on" to simplify access to a variety of organizational resources. Increasingly, portals provide role-driven services to employees. That is, the services and information offered to the employee depend on their organizational "role" or position. For example, regional managers may be given access to information about employees that is not available to first-line supervisors. Shown in Figure 7.1 is a sample portal for managers.

The portal can be an important tool for creating the employee brand. Employment brands give prospective employees an image or impression of what it would be like to work for the firm. While "branding" has long been a part of the overall strategy for marketing products, it is a relatively new concept in HR. Companies

Figure 7.1. Managerial Self-Service Portal from PeopleSoft.

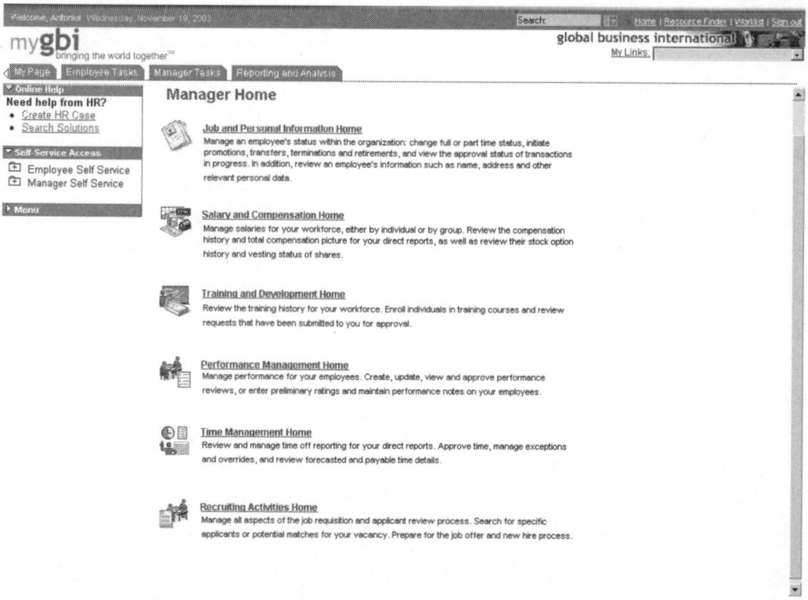

with a positive employment brand image can have a significant advantage in attracting the best applicants.

Today the portal is often the first stop in the employment process. Indeed, the first impression of the company for a prospective employee may be formed by the HR website. A poorly designed website filled with static and uninteresting content can cause high-quality applicants to look elsewhere. An attractive portal can also serve to entice applicants to apply and to collect résumés and data for initial screening. The portal has become HR's front door.

HR portals are seen as an important tool for HR executives who wish to assume a more strategic role in the organization. Having a sophisticated portal allows the HR group to showcase its products and services. It puts HR in front of the employees on a frequent, sometimes daily, basis. On an organizational level, the portal demonstrates that HR is technologically sophisticated and in tune with the move toward e-business.

Today, the trend is toward greater consolidation of HR functions and independent sites into a unified portal. Too often, organizations find that a large number of uncoordinated sites have developed to serve specific HR needs. This can be bewildering for both employees and HR managers alike. For example, the benefits group might have sites dealing with health insurance, retirement, open enrollments, and flex-spending accounts. The training group might offer sites dealing with online course offerings and maintain a training history for employees. The payroll group might post W-2 forms and pay stubs and handle sign-up for direct deposit. And the list continues. Consolidating sites into a portal offers the opportunity for significant cost savings and greater consistency in services to employees. A recent survey by Towers Perrin found that organizations delivering HR services via the Internet are quickly moving toward a unified site model. As of 2002, 58 percent of respondents in the Towers survey had "very unified" HR portals.

Portals are really a collection of HR services found at a single convenient location. These services can be grouped into three general categories of applications: employee self-service, managerial self-service, and strategic applications. These major types of applications are discussed in the following sections.

Employee Self-Service

Employee self-service applications are the single most popular form of eHR. They are typically the first eHR self-service application that an organization mounts. Published research disagrees on the penetration of ESS applications in organizations. Estimates range from near 100 percent penetration (Towers Perrin, 2002a) to about 50 percent penetration (Cedar, 2003). The difference in these figures may be somewhat accounted for by varying definitions of what constitutes an ESS application. However, there is general agreement that the trend in implementing these systems is continuing at a rapid pace.

What is ESS used for? Here's a partial list of the HR services that an employee may find on an ESS website.

- Input and edit personal information such as address, phone, emergency contact, and so on
- Model retirement options, varying key factors such as contribution rates and investment return
- Receive company communications and updates
- Review and change allocation of new and existing retirement investments (may be via a link to a vendor website; link may be transparent)
- View a current or past paycheck
- Change a W-4 form
- Enroll in benefits programs, including flex-benefits, health-care, childcare, and cafeteria plans
- Research various benefit options (for example, the site might link to various HMO vendors and allow employees to compare plan costs and services and review the credentials of physicians associated with the plan)
- Select benefits where choices are allowed (cafeteria plans)
- Enroll in training
- View internal job postings based on selection criteria established by the employee (for example, what jobs are available that meet these criteria: California location, electrical engineering, software engineering, managerial level 3, R&D division)

- Time entry, including recording time off
- Review and plan individual development activities
- Participate in 360-degree feedback programs
- Receive customized information relevant at the individual or job level (for example, at the individual level, workflow systems may route important "paperwork" to the individual automatically; at the job level, the system may deliver similar "paperwork" to all "team leaders")
- Access HR policy manuals and use natural language interfaces to ask HR questions (for example, "How many weeks of vacation do I get after four years of employment?")
- Complete employee surveys
- View the skill requirements of jobs and compare those skill requirements with the individual's skill profile
- Review personal performance appraisal records and schedules
- Order services and purchase company or other products
- Participate in training delivered via the web
- Link to other sites (for example, some firms allow employees to customize their ESS homepage with information from other sites, such as placing a stock ticker or his or her portfolio on the ESS homepage)
- Take diagnostic tests to identify training/development needs
- Submit and track expense reports

Inspection of this list gives a feeling for the range of HR services that can now be delivered to, and managed by, employees. Such services have been enabled by the near universal access to the Internet. Published studies suggest that between 78 and 90 percent of workers have either Internet or intranet access (Cedar, 2002; Towers Perrin, 2002a).

As noted earlier, ESS applications are the most popular area of HR technology.

In North America as of 2003, the most popular ESS applications were those shown in Table 7.1.

Other research (Towers Perrin, 2002b) provides more information in terms of the specific applications commonly in use. These results are shown in Table 7.2.

The move to ESS is driven by a variety of factors, not the least of which are the substantial cost savings possible via ESS service

Table 7.1. Percent of Organizations
with ESS Applications in Use or Planned.

ESS Application	In Use in 2003*	Planned*
Communications Information	79%	19%
Health and Welfare Benefits Management	57%	31%
Personal Data Management	50%	40%
Retirement Management	65%	11%
Time Management	38%	35%
Pay-Related Management	35%	46%

*Approximate percentages

Source: Cedar 2003 Human Resources Self-Service/Portal Survey.

Table 7.2. Percent of Organizations
with Specific ESS Tasks in Use or Planned.

ESS Application	Available in 2002	Planned for 2003	Planned for 2004	Total
View Job Posting	86%	7%	5%	98%
View HR Policies	83%	8%	9%	100%
Apply for Jobs (Internal)	71%	9%	8%	88%
Change Personal Data	52%	14%	23%	89%
View Pay Stub	43%	18%	21%	82%
Change Direct Deposit Information	32%	17%	19%	68%

delivery. While the business case and cost data will be discussed later in this chapter, a short discussion of the impact of ESS on HR practice is appropriate here.

Probably the greatest impact of ESS technology is to change the manner in which employees acquire information and interact with HR. Data is available to employees 24/7 and 365 days per year. Employees no longer have to wait until "regular business hours" to access information and services. Employee convenience is enhanced, at least for those with Internet access. On the downside, there is the risk that HR becomes more depersonalized and further isolated from our customers. In addition to changes in the manner of information acquisition, the nature of HR work is also changing. The Cedar 2002 Human Resources Self-Service/Portal Survey suggests a rather dramatic shift in the plans of organizations for delivering HR services. Today, the majority of HR services are still delivered by HR specialists, although for many HR service requests there are multiple information sources available to employees (for example, call center, IVR, ESS applications). However, a very different world is envisioned by senior HR executives. Investment is clearly slanted toward web-based applications, and few, if any, organizations plan to increase investment in HR specialists as a delivery method. Table 7.3 shows the results of the Cedar 2002 survey.

As can be seen from Table 7.3, executives do not plan to spend the time of HR specialists on many of the data retrieval and approval

Table 7.3. Percent of Organizations Using Various Delivery Methods.

Type of HR Service	Percent Using This Delivery Method Today	Percent Planning an Increase in Use of This Delivery Method
Simple Questions		
HR Specialists	98%	0%
Web-Based Self-Service	65%	33%
Call Center	45%	11%
Simple Data Change		
HR Specialists	80%	< 5%
Web-Based Self-Service	55%	42%
Call Center	25%	10%
Approval-Based Change		
HR Specialists	88%	8%
Web-Based Self-Service	25%	58%
Call Center	25%	8%

Note: Percentages are approximate.

tasks that are common today. Also clear is the plan to rely more heavily on ESS systems and to reduce the use of call centers. These data alone demonstrate the potential impact the ESS and web technology have, and will have, on the HR field. For example, International Paper changed its ratio of HR staff to employees from 1:80 to 1:126 by implementing new eHR technology (Roberts, 2002b).

Shown in Figure 7.2 is a sample ESS page from SAP. It illustrates many of the features that can be found on ESS systems today.

Managerial Self-Service

Managerial self-service (MSS) is the second major application area that underlies eHR. MSS applications allow managers to access a range of information about their staffs and electronically process much of the HR "paperwork" that typically flows through the hands of the manager. For example, a manager might go to her MSS website to complete a requisition to fill an open position. The

Figure 7.2. Employee Self-Service Portal from SAP.

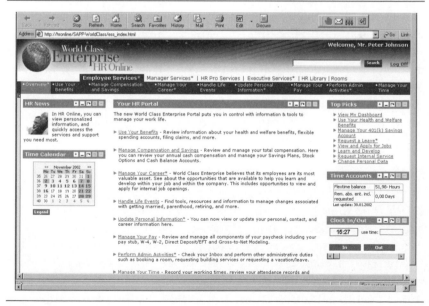

Copyright © SAP AG.

system would post the opening on the internal job posting site and even filter the responses based on selection criteria specified by the manager (for example, sales experience).

MSS systems provide several benefits to the organization. Cost savings is the most obvious, as managers can more quickly and efficiently handle HR tasks, freeing time for other managerial work. SAP estimates that organizations can save approximately $500 per year per manager in managerial time through the use of MSS (Kuppe, 2003). MSS systems also have the potential to increase consistency in HR practice by managers, as processes and information are delivered in a similar fashion to all employees. This can reduce the potential for litigation based on inappropriate actions by managers. MSS systems can also assist managers by reducing the cycle time for HR actions. For example, positions can be posted and filled in less time, thereby improving service to customers and enhancing the competitive position of the organization. HR managers also gain time by reducing the amount of coaching that line managers require, as they can get answers to HR questions, and increasingly advice, via the MSS website.

MSS systems typically go beyond HR management and often include tools to assist in budget review and reporting and mundane tasks such as expense reimbursements. MSS sites are often integrated into the ESS site relevant to the manager. That is, the web page delivered to the manager contains links that allow the manager to handle personal employee transactions (ESS), but also provides options for accomplishing managerial tasks. Often the specific managerial options delivered to the manager are based on his or her "role" in the organization. Indeed, role-based ESS/MSS delivery is a best practice today.

MSS applications are not as prevalent as ESS applications. In 2002, somewhere between 30 and 45 percent of larger organizations had implemented some form of MSS (Cedar, 2002; SAP-AG, 2001). The most frequently implemented categories of MSS applications as of 2003 were budget management (42 percent), reporting applications (46 percent), and staff management applications (41 percent; Cedar, 2003). In terms of specific uses, the 2003 Service Delivery Report (SAP-AG, 2001) shown in Table 7.4 highlights the MSS applications in place or planned for the near future.

Figure 7.3 shows a sample screen from the MSS website for SAP.

Table 7.4. Organizations with Various MSS Applications in Use or Planned.

MSS Application	Available in 2002	Planned for 2003	Planned for 2004	Total
View Résumés	45%	11%	27%	83%
Merit Reviews	45%	5%	22%	72%
Job Requisitions	44%	11%	18%	73%
View Salary History	37%	12%	22%	71%
View Performance History	33%	10%	21%	64%
View Training History	33%	9%	21%	63%

Figure 7.3. Managerial Self-Service Portal from SAP.

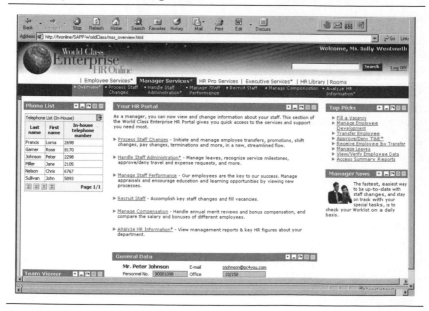

Copyright © SAP AG.

MSS implementations sometimes face resistance from managers who view the new technology as pushing "HR work" onto managers. The perception can be that MSS applications are a way of unloading onerous HR paperwork on the line manager. While little research exists to speak to this issue, what has been published suggests that experience with these systems serves to mitigate these perceptions. Two studies suggest that most commonly (47 percent), managers see no change in their workload after implementing MSS, and in more than a third of the cases (39 percent), managers reported that their workload actually decreased after MSS introduction (Towers Perrin, 2002a; SAP-AG, 2001). Results related to the ROI for MSS applications are generally positive and will be discussed later in this chapter.

Strategic Applications

Strategic applications (SA) represent the third component of web-based eHR applications. In 2003, almost half (47 percent) of the organizations participating in the Cedar survey reported they were currently using SA technology, and another 28 percent planned to deploy this technology in 2004 (Cedar, 2003). SA include tools and services that serve groups external to the organization as well as serve strategic HR objectives. Examples of strategic applications include online application systems that are part of virtually all company websites. These applications often include marketing material designed to reinforce the HR brand and attract qualified applicants. The application may collect applicant data, administer screening "tests," and send follow-up information to applicants. For example, Home Depot places kiosks in stores to screen job applicants. They report saving $4 per test administered and $135 per applicant in reduced administrative costs. Interestingly, they also found an 11 percent reduction in turnover among candidates screened through the kiosk application.

Another very popular area for strategic applications is in workforce development. For example, organizations have embraced various distance learning approaches to training. SA systems can assist users to identify personal training needs, enroll in training, monitor completion and user satisfaction with training, and update training history to assist the organization in compliance and intellectual capital management. Skills management is a growing area for eHR. Given today's environment of fewer workers and greater competitive pressures, maintaining a clear picture of the skill sets of employees has become paramount. Employees with critical job skills and competencies can be quickly identified, allowing the organization to respond to opportunities in the market. SA can help identify individual and organizational level development needs and allow senior HR managers to target development dollars. This has become a more critical concern, as one of the best predictors of turnover among highly skilled professionals is a perceived lack of developmental opportunities.

Strategic applications were some of the first web-based HR services. As soon as organizations created company websites, options were added to allow interested applicants to learn about job opportunities and submit résumés or applications. This trend is continuing. In 2002, over 50 percent of the firms participating in the Cedar HR Self Service/Portal Survey reported using web-based technology to attract talent, and another 34 percent planned to implement this technology in the future. Talent development and related applications still lag behind other areas of web-based HR, with only about 20 percent of participants in the Cedar survey reporting the current use of such systems. However, almost a third of the remaining organizations plan to implement these applications in the future. Strategic applications are now the fastest growing eHR application area.

Knowledge Bases

Knowledge bases provide the core content for MSS and ESS applications. That is, when an employee submits a question to the system, the answer comes from the knowledge base. For example, if an employee wants to know the organization's policy on banking sick days, the system will access the knowledge base to provide a response. The knowledge base in many ways contains the information that formerly resided in policy manuals, and more interestingly, in the heads of the HR staff. Cedar reports that more than 70 percent of the firms they surveyed either currently use a knowledge base or plan to use a knowledge base to support their web-based applications.

Knowledge bases have several advantages for organizations. First, developing or customizing a knowledge base can be a diagnostic activity for HR. That is, often the existing HR "knowledge base" exists in many locations, ranging from policy manuals to individual experts and the undocumented local practices of individual units. When a self-service application is implemented, these multiple sources of HR information must be unified and reconciled. The process of establishing this database can help identify inefficiencies and inconsistencies in HR processes. While this task can seem overwhelming, several vendors now supply "best practices" knowledge bases as part of the ERP system. These "best practice" applications can serve as the starting point for a customized, company-specific knowledge base. The process of developing the new knowledge base can drive the kind of HR transformation sought by senior management.

The term "knowledge base" is a generic term and may refer to a variety of different types of software. These range from very sophisticated vendor-supplied databases employing artificial intelligence to home-grown collections of relevant documents. Variations include call center support tools that customer service representatives use to respond to employee questions and lists of frequently asked questions available online. In ESS and MSS systems, the knowledge base is the engine that drives the application. Most systems employ standard web navigation techniques to allow users to access information. For example, a link might provide information about the dental plan in which the employee is currently enrolled. More sophisticated systems allow employees to input questions in text statements (for example, What dental plan am I enrolled in?). Rather than the employee having to call an HR representative, the system is able to "answer" the question. Knowledge bases also can help to avoid "answer shopping" by employees—that is, making multiple calls to a service center or HR representative in order to find an answer the employee likes. With a knowledge base, there is one consistent answer. Support for this approach can be found in the 2003 Cedar Survey, which reports that 65 percent of organizations "planned to use a structured repository of HR-oriented knowledge."

Several vendors provide "standard" knowledge bases of HR rules and practices customized for a particular country (for example, the United States, the UK, and Canada). Typically the organization has to engage in some degree of customization to reflect the specific HR policies of the company. Often, specific knowledge bases are included to support specific applications. For example, open enrollment might be supported by a benefits knowledge base with information on healthcare options, while a manager inquiring about hiring processes might be supported by a general HR knowledge base. Vendor-supplied knowledge bases are used by approximately 43 percent of organizations (Cedar, 2003). Indeed, knowledge base vendors and knowledge base services are one of the fastest growing segments of the eHR market.

The Business Case and Cost-Effectiveness

The Business Case

eHR technology represents a significant investment for organizations. Today, approximately 70 percent of organizations in North America require a business case be made for funding eHR systems (Cedar, 2002; PeopleSoft, 2002). This makes the question of ROI critical in making the business case for eHR systems. The starting point for this discussion is to examine the objectives that organizations set for such systems. Several studies have examined this issue. For example, PeopleSoft found that 75 percent of their users cited all five of the following objectives for their systems (People-Soft, 2002):

- To enable HR to be more strategic
- To improve service
- To reduce administrative costs
- To streamline services by reducing process steps, approvals
- To increase employee satisfaction

Similar results were reported by the Cedar group in their survey work (Cedar, 2002). Table 7.5 shows these findings.

In addition to the objectives cited in the PeopleSoft and Cedar surveys, another important rationale for new systems is the need to integrate multiple disparate systems. Most organizations have had various portions of their HR services automated to some extent. This may include applicant tracking systems, early HR applications, training databases, and multiple HR systems from different

Table 7.5. Rationale for Implementing eHR Technology.

eHR Objective	Percentage Endorsing Objective
Reduce administrative costs	98%
Improve service to employees and managers	98%
Increase information access	97%
Eliminate process steps/approval/forms	93%
Enable manager access for improved decision making	86%
Enable the HR function to serve more strategically	79%

vendors in different divisions. Often this has occurred through mergers, acquisitions, and decentralized approaches to HR management. For example, Seagate Technology implemented a new self-service approach to HR delivery in part because of the need to consolidate seventeen different HR management systems (Roberts, 2002a). General Motors consolidated some eighty-five separate websites containing various types of HR information into a single HR portal (Jossi, 2001). In some ways, having multiple systems can help make the case for new integrated systems. Often the financial, as well as managerial, cost of duplicated and incompatible systems far outweighs the cost of the new system. Vendors now often provide tools and templates to assist potential clients in making the case for new technology. Users should expect vendors to assist them in preparing the business case.

ROI Evidence

Over the past several years, a growing body of reports has surfaced that speaks to the ROI and cost-effectiveness of eHR technology. In this section we will review much of this research, but a word of caution is in order. Most of this research was conducted either by software vendors and/or consulting firms that implement these systems. Thus it is likely that there is a "bias" toward reporting the successes and not the failures—and there are failures. However, these reports do provide data on what can be achieved in terms of various measures of effectiveness.

Return on investment is the foundation of any business case. It has become an article of faith that HR technology reduces cost. Towers Perrin found that 80 percent of HR executives believed self-service technology could lower costs, but only 40 percent of those surveyed found that the promise had been realized (Towers Perrin, 2002a). In general, the typical payback period today is about thirty-six months, although there are examples of shorter as well as longer payback periods. The trend is toward longer payback periods. Over the last three years, the average payback period has grown from twelve months in 2000 to twenty-two months in 2003 (Cedar, 2002; Cedar, 2003). This is due in large part to the increase in sophistication of today's applications and user demand for systems to offer a broader range of services. It is very common for organizations that implement a "basic" ESS system with limited functionality to quickly be faced with users demanding more features. Remember, the comparison standard for users is not the old paper-based system, but rather the best of breed commercial websites such as Amazon or Yahoo. Vendors have responded to this trend and offer much greater functionality in "basic" applications when compared with offerings of a few years ago. As a result, payback periods are growing.

There is an increasing number of success stories. In terms of ROI and related success measures, several criteria can be considered. These include the payback period, cost savings, efficiency increases, and user satisfaction. A variety of case studies as well as survey data are available. The 2003 Cedar Survey provides data on a variety of ROI indicators. Table 7.6 presents these results.

Inspection of Table 7.6 suggests that new systems can have a significant impact on the organization. Probably the most striking finding was the reduction in inquiries to the service center. If these findings generalize to most organizations, we can expect call centers to decrease in popularity as an HR delivery method. Today, almost 50 percent of larger companies use call centers as a delivery method. Call centers allow HR expertise to be concentrated and shared throughout the organization. Until the advent of web-based applications, call centers were viewed as the most efficient method of delivering HR information to managers and employees. Today, however, new technology is rapidly changing the role of call centers, as the simple employee questions are answered by websites

Table 7.6. Cedar 2003 Survey ROI Results.

Success Metric	Result
Cost Per Transaction	Average 43% reduction
Cycle Time	Average 62% reduction
Headcount Changes	Average 37% reduction
Return on Investment	Average 40% reduction
Payback Period	Average 1.8 years
Employee Satisfaction	Up to 50% improvement
Inquiries to the Service Center	Average 50% reduction
Usage	Up to 100% increase

supported by knowledge bases. In the 2002 HR Service Delivery Survey Report, Towers Perrin highlighted some of these changes. They noted that almost a third of respondents report fewer inquiries to the call center after implementing ESS, but that the calls received were more complex. They also reported that the call center now had to handle questions about the ESS website.

Similar ROI results have also been reported by major vendors. PeopleSoft commissioned a survey of users of PeopleSoft 8. Based on a sample of sixty-eight users, the ROI period ranged from 1.5 to 3 years, with an average of a 33 percent reduction in HR administrative costs. Likewise, SAP provides case study evidence of the value of these systems (SAP-AG, 2003). As noted earlier, SAP argues that MSS applications can save organizations $500 per manager per year in managerial time (Kuppe, 2003).

Cost and Cost-Effectiveness

How much do these systems cost? How cost-effective are they? How do the costs break down? As with most systems, eHR systems tend to cost more than originally budgeted (Cedar, 2002). With that in mind, let's review the cost data. Overall, organizations spend an average of $1,300,000 annually to administer and maintain an HR portal/self-service application (Cedar, 2002), with actual cost running about 15 percent ahead of budget. As would be expected, budgets vary with organizational size. Smaller organizations (under 1,000 employees) budgeted an average of $337,000, while medium-sized organizations (5,000 to 10,000 employees) budgeted $751,923. The largest organizations (more than 50,000 employees) budgeted approximately $2,000,000. These numbers represent the ongoing cost of the systems. Initial costs for system purchase and implementation also vary widely depending on a variety of factors, including the existing hardware and software infrastructure, sophistication of application chosen, degree of integration with other IT systems, and hosting choice (in-house, vendor, ASP). Implementation often runs approximately 150 percent of the cost of the software. On the individual employee level, costs drop rapidly with economies of scale. For example, the cost for small organizations is quite high (around $2,400 per employee) and is as low as $35 per employee for the largest organizations.

Specific examples as well as cross-organizational summaries of cost savings support the cost-effectiveness of self-service applications. Typically, comparisons are made with traditional HR personal contact, IVR, and call centers. Authoria, a vendor of knowledge bases used to support self-service applications, reports that answering an employee inquiry via a call center costs between $5 and $30, while an IVR answer costs between $0.10 and $0.50, and a web-based self-service response is approximately $0.05 (Authoria, Inc., 2003). General Motors reports similar findings. For GM, calls to the employee service center cost between $1.50 and $2.00 per minute, while a web-based response was less than $0.05 per minute. Other research suggests that the cost of providing HR services to employees using traditional methods ranges from $1,000 to $2,000 per year, but that self-service applications can cut that cost anywhere from 20 to 66 percent (Bartholomew, 2002; Sorenson, 2002). PeopleSoft reports that a survey of its customers showed a 33 percent reduction in costs and a 20 percent reduction in HR headcount after implementing PeopleSoft 8 (Harlty & Matin, 2002).

Case studies and anecdotal evidence showcasing the success of self-service implementations are common in the literature. For example, shown in Table 7.7 is a summary of the experience of one organization.

American Airlines saved $3 million per year by offering employees just two self-service applications (Roberts, 2003). These

Table 7.7. Sample Cost Savings Using ESS Delivery.

Task	Manual Cost	ESS Cost	Percentage Saved
View Benefit Profile	$6.00	$0.50	92%
Access Policy Handbook	$4.00	$1.00	75%
Change Home Address	$10.00	$2.00	80%
Provide Current 401(k) Statement	$50.00	$0.60	99%
View Paycheck	$3.00	$0.50	83%
Post Job	$8.00	$0.50	94%
View Skill Profile	$1.50	$0.50	67%
Employee Change Action	$12.00	$4.00	67%

Source: The Cedar Group, 1999 Human Resources Self-Service Survey.

were employee travel reservations and open benefits enrollment. Microsoft saves over $1 million per year with ESS applications that allow employees to handle a variety of payroll tasks, such as viewing pay stubs and changing W-4 forms (Mecham, 2001). People-Soft provides case studies of several organizations in the financial services and insurance sector. These case studies show the impact of self-service in terms of cost, reductions in cycle time, employee time savings, and a variety of other factors. The results show consistent improvement on all criteria (PeopleSoft, 2002). Likewise, SAP provides an in-depth look at the experience of a Canadian utility. The utility, TransAlta, reported a payback period of 4.9 years and a ten-year cost savings of $31 million.

User Satisfaction

Most of the publicly available data suggests that employees, managers, and organizations are generally satisfied with their self-service implementations. Again, we are more likely to hear about the successes than the failures, but there does appear to be convergence in much of the published information. The Cedar 2002 Human Resources Self-Service/Portal Survey suggests that success rates are quite high overall, although ESS applications seem to be a bit more successful than MSS applications. Table 7.8 summarizes these results.

Another look at system success is provided by Towers Perrin in its 2003 Service Delivery Survey Report. Survey participants were asked whether their employee self-service applications improved service in three key areas: timeliness, accuracy, and HR workload. Positive results were found on all three criteria. Increased timeliness was reported by 80 percent of organizations, while 74 percent reported improved data accuracy and 60 percent reported a reduction in HR workload. Of those who did report a reduction in HR workload, more than half reported at least a 30 percent reduction.

On the negative side, many users (44 percent) still report that information is difficult to find, given the amount and complexity of information available (Towers Perrin, 2002a). The data with regard to actual reduction in HR workload is also mixed. One of the promises of self-service is that routine transactions will occur without HR intervention, thereby reducing the workload on HR staffs. While several studies cite reductions in HR workload, the data are inconsistent. For example, Towers Perrin reports that HR staffs are still involved in many HR transactions, even after implementing managerial self-service applications. Their survey results are summarized in Table 7.9.

Organizations must also keep in mind that self-service applications cannot handle all HR transactions. Systems are great for retrieving data and answering relatively simple questions; however, they cannot counsel employees and handle emotionally laden issues such as discrimination, serious health problems, or substance

Table 7.8. Success Rates for Self-Service Applications.

Application Type	Less Than Successful	Somewhat Successful	Successful
Employee Self-Service	6%	41%	54%
Managerial Self-Service	14%	41%	45%

Table 7.9. HR Involvement Post-MSS Implementation.

Transaction	Review Only	Involved Only for Exceptions	Approve All Transactions
Change Unpaid Leave Status	14%	38%	49%
Transfer Employee	13%	33%	53%
Change Work Status	12%	35%	54%

abuse problems. Indeed, many organizations run a serious risk in trying to divest too much to a website and knowledge base. Strategically, HR cannot afford to "outsource" too much HR support to self-service applications and risk losing internal HR capability. The objective of self-service is, after all, to improve service to employees, not to make the employer seem uncaring and impersonal.

Best Practices in Implementing Self-Service Applications and Common Errors

The biggest challenge faced by organizations moving to self-service is in implementing the new system and changing the HR culture of the organization. Whether it is a complete portal solution or basic ESS application, the new system represents an entirely new way of delivering services to employees. It will change HR roles, skill requirements for HR staff members, HR processes, and the perception of HR within the organization. A successful implementation is the first litmus test in transforming HR. Fortunately, given the widespread growth of self-service applications, we now have a good handle on what makes a project successful. Let's look at the experience of organizations that have implemented these systems.

General Trends

In order to expand on the published literature in researching this chapter, several senior executives were interviewed by the authors. These interviews included senior consultants at specialized implementation firms as well as executives at firms currently implementing large-scale eHR systems. These individuals identified a number of factors that facilitate eHR implementation.

The first factor relates to the key skills needed both by implementation consultants and by employees of the organization. These include listening skills and problem-solving ability. For the implementation partner, this means developing more than technical skills in the staff. Time and again, we heard that consultants who are skilled at listening to the needs of organizations and who approach implementation as a problem-solving process are most successful. Employees of the client firm need the same types of skills, not only to work effectively with the implementation partner, but also to be effective working with others in the organization impacted by the new system. Knowledge of the system and technical skills are commodities in today's market. Now it is equally important to understand the culture or personality of the organization and to be ready to adapt the system to the organization. In the past, expert consultants provided "the answer" to clients. Today, however, consultants must also be familiar with the organization and the client's business in order to be effective.

The second major factor impacting implementation success is the long-term commitment of sufficient financial resources and human capital to the process. One good practice is to develop realistic timelines from both vendors and organizations. Frequently, timelines are underestimated in an attempt to "control costs." Implementation always takes longer than anticipated. This occurs for a variety of reasons, including changes to the system specification, data quality issues, software changes, and the need for more customization than anticipated. Organizations need to be realistic about the time commitment that will be required of their employees. All too often, employees are asked to do double duty, adding implementation responsibilities to their already demanding jobs. The result is turnover, poorer service to employees, and invariably, implementation delays. In the short term, unrealistic timelines and fewer dedicated employees may appear to reduce costs, but in the long term this approach increases costs significantly. Our expert panel recommended adding at least 33 percent to initial time and cost estimates!

Several additional factors emerged from our discussions. These include the importance of promoting the vision of eHR and the need to convince people of the strategic implications of the new systems. Support from key decision makers in the organization is a critical success factor. One executive noted that lack of such support resulted in the rollout of a system with minimal functionality and resulted in a corresponding decrease in the contribution of eHR to achieving the company's strategic goals. The complexity and difficulty of implementing systems for global applications was also mentioned as a concern. Finally, it is clear to those interviewed that a successful implementation must include plans for maintenance and future upgrading of the system. This involves support for continuing cycles of learning and improvement, as well as developing robust systems to measure the contribution of eHR for achieving strategic goals.

The themes noted above are also consistent with published research. To identify common barriers to successful implementation, Cedar (2002) asked organizations to rate the severity of each of the following barriers to a successful implementation. A three-point scale was used, ranging from 1 = low severity to 3 = high severity. The results were as follows:

Cost of ownership/limited budget	2.1
Other HR initiatives take precedence	1.6
Security/privacy concerns	1.4
Technical infrastructure not in place	1.4
HRMS or other key application not in place	1.2
Unavailability of technical skills	1.0

Not surprisingly, system cost was the most significant barrier. On the other end of the continuum, technical skills were not considered a significant hindrance. This seems to suggest that HR executives are much more comfortable with technology and no longer see technical obstacles to implementing systems.

Many lists of "best practices" have been developed in recent years. While there is some variance in their exact content, common themes can be found. Following is a summary of best practices based on case studies, surveys, and opinions from firms specializing in system implementation.

Best Practices in Implementation

Budget Is Always the Number One Issue

Implementation costs are often difficult to forecast, and systems invariably cost more than anticipated. There are several reasons for this finding. Cost can increase as organizations begin to realize the amount of change that self-service involves. HR processes often need to be reexamined and redesigned. Upon close inspection, data in existing systems often prove unreliable or incomplete. The amount of customization required is usually more than planned. The hardware infrastructure may not be so strong as originally believed. Indeed, implementation costs often run 150 percent of the cost of the software, and costs often run about 15 percent over budget. It is important to be realistic in the budget estimates and to make sure the business case is strong enough so that, if costs are more than anticipated, the firm can still show a reasonable ROI.

Support from Senior Management

Senior management is a broad term and applies to those within and outside of HR. Clearly, it is critical to maintain support of top management, especially given competing demands for resources. For this group, ROI measures are likely the most critical. However, the greatest impact of the new system will likely be on the staffs of senior HR managers. For example, a benefits manager may lose significant staff with the advent of an open enrollment application and may resist the new system. Thus, as noted above, it is critical to maintain the support of key managers at all levels throughout the implementation process. Remember, the longer the implementation time, the greater the chance that senior management will change and new executives will need to be convinced of the value of the project.

Importance of Change Management

It is easy to underestimate the importance, time, and cost associated with the change management aspects of the implementation effort. Remember, a move to self-service will have dramatic effects on the HR staff and more limited impact on all employees. MSS will change the job of managers and their relationship with HR. A clearly articulated change management strategy including a communication plan and specific responsibilities for change management activities should be part of the implementation plan. Cedar found that change management costs averaged 12 percent of total implementation costs, and that this component was projected to increase in the future (Cedar, 2001). By 2003, the investment in change management as part of the implementation process had increased by 150 percent compared with 2002 (Cedar, 2003). It is critical to communicate to employees that the new system is not an effort to push HR work onto employees, but rather to give employees more control over their information and make access to HR information more convenient to them. The importance of frequent communication with all stakeholders is a very common theme in the published literature.

Cooperation Between HR and IT

A strong working relationship with IT is critical for a successful implementation. eHR systems clearly cut across traditional boundaries in the organization. In general, it is a good idea to have a degree of IT expertise in the HR function to serve a communication role between HR and IT. Also, it is critical to fully understand where the self-service application fits into IT's priorities. Issues of control and ownership should be addressed up-front and monitored throughout the implementation process.

Use an Implementation Partner

The road to eHR success is littered with companies that failed in their implementation efforts. A very common reason for implementation failure is the lack of internal expertise and capacity to put a very sophisticated system in place. Few organizations have successfully implemented eHR systems by relying solely on in-house resources. Internal staff still have day-to-day responsibilities, and few organizations have the slack to support a major systems implementation without external assistance. Implementation vendors offer the technical skills, but in addition can assist with the critical change management aspects of an implementation. Organizations are twice as likely to use an outside vendor to assist with implementation as to rely solely on internal resources (Cedar, 2003).

Best Practices in System Design

Clearly Identify the Vision for the System

Why are we implementing self-service? How will we judge its success? Where do we want to be in three years? Asking these questions early can help to guide the implementation process and focus the HR transformation roadmap.

Metrics Are Important

A variety of indices can be used to evaluate the system. It is important to identify the metrics that will be used to judge system success early in the process. Common metrics include:

- Reductions in cycle time
- Headcount savings
- User satisfaction
- Process improvement in terms of reduction in steps
- Reductions in calls to HR or the call center
- Website hits
- Utilization of web-based training
- Cost savings per transaction
- Increase in interest by applicants (for recruiting-oriented websites)

Reduce the Number of Points of Contact for Employees

This practice typically translates to actions such as unifying websites into a single portal, replacing onsite HR staff dedicated to transactions with web applications, and focusing the call center on the more complex questions that cannot be adequately addressed by the website.

Knowledge Bases Are Becoming a Key Component of the System

Knowledge bases provide the majority of the content for the site. They codify HR processes and are critical for both operational and legal reasons. In general, organizations should consider purchase of a vendor-supplied solution as a starting point for their knowledge base. Such systems can provide a good beginning, as they will contain the HR information that is common across organizations. For example, the legal requirements of the Family and Medical

Leave Act are common across organizations. However, users should anticipate the need for some degree of modification to reflect the organization's HR practices. How does your organization operationalize the FMLA? Who must be notified of a pending leave and what evidence does your organization require? How do sick and vacation time fit in?

When evaluating knowledge bases, consider the quality of the search function associated with the product. How effective is it at interpreting questions? How robust is the system in understanding the context of the questions and tailoring answers? How "smart" is the knowledge base? How often is it updated? Will the vendor be responsible for any litigation that arises from errors in the information provided to employees?

Plain Vanilla Is the Goal for the First Generation of the Self-Service Application

Many vendor systems supply their version of self-service "best practices," often customized for specific industries. Try to do the least customization possible. Require a strong justification for any customization. Customization increases costs dramatically, both immediately and down the road, as upgrades must also be customized. Remember, too, that this approach means buying into the vendor's view of HR and will likely mean a greater degree of change in your HR practices than originally anticipated.

User Demand Will Increase

Design the system both for the initial implementation and the follow-on services that employees will invariably demand. Employees will quickly request more services on the web, and the organization will need to add new functionality to meet that demand. Remember, new services typically mean greater employee convenience, more efficiency, and increased cost-effectiveness. The best-case scenario for self-service is a growing demand for services. For example, General Motors now receives between fifteen and twenty million hits per month on its HR portal, one year after its introduction. They implement a new release of the portal every six months in order to keep up with the demand for new and expanded employee services.

Consider the Content

What type of information will be most beneficial to the end user? What will hook them in and make them want to use the system? Aon Consulting suggests that portal content can be divided into five categories and has identified the content that might be associated with each area. Their view provides a useful way to look at HR web content (Folan & Mitchell, 2003). The Aon model is shown below, along with sample types of content for each category.

1. Safety and Security

- Building safety procedures and updates
- Security alerts
- Leadership communications and company information
- Personal financial tools for planning and risk-management

2. Rewards

- Benefit plan information
- Links to retirement plans, stock purchase plans, saving plans
- Reward or bonus statements
- Reports recognizing outstanding employee performance

3. Affiliation

- Notices of corporate events
- Communications about company success
- Chat rooms for employees in similar positions

4. Growth

- Postings of job openings and online applications
- Online training courses
- Career progression information and advice

5. Work/Life Harmony

- Information on daycare or family care options
- Stock and investment links and information
- Wellness and healthcare links
- Convenience links to products and services

Ease of Use Is Critical

User acceptance, whether it is in the form of ESS or MSS applications, is critical to long-term success. The web interface must be designed for ease of navigation and reflect best practices in website design. Users will compare your website to others with which they are familiar. If information is difficult to find or navigation is confusing, users will have negative early experiences and be less likely to go to the system for their HR services.

Initial Services Should Be Those That Users Access Often

Early experience with the ESS or MSS system will determine later success and use. Target the services that users will access most frequently for initial implementation. This will help them get used to going to the system for their HR services and make the transition to the self-reliant employee more successful. For example, American Airlines' initial self-service included employee travel reservations, a very important benefit to their employees. They termed this a "sticky" application, which helped employees get used to going to the web for employee services (Roberts, 2003). One firm related that their MSS site was less successful, partially because users did not have a need to use the site often. This resulted in low visibility for the site, poor user satisfaction, and a poor ROI for the investment.

Personalize the Content

Information is more valuable if it is customized to the user. Think about the last time you visited Amazon.com and how book selections there were tailored to your interests. eHR systems can function in much the same way by giving users targeted information based on their position, work history, and interests. Personalized content will increase use and positive regard for the system. Remember, organizations only save money when employees use the system.

Consider Security

Security is always an issue on the Internet, especially when personal information about employees is involved. Today, the trend is toward "single sign-on" systems that streamline access and provide a reasonable level of security. Consider also encryption protocols and do the maximum to protect the portal from hackers and other threats to the system.

Promote Collaboration

One of the principle objectives of most systems is to facilitate communication. Today, this may include instant messaging, chat rooms, bulletin boards, and calendaring programs. Design the portal to make it easy to contact others in the organization and to share information. Something as simple as building a phone/email directory into the website can have a large payoff.

Key Issues in Managing the HR Portal

Managing Content

A number of issues have been identified as important in the ongoing management of the website. Presented here are the top three. The toughest challenge is the *management of portal content*. Websites are valued by users for their content; thus, content management becomes a central concern for HR. This is a relatively new role for HR. We never really managed content before. Content resided primarily in the HR staff and was not systematically collected or "audited." We typically had numerous "knowledge bases" walking around the office. With a portal, we need to systematize this information and monitor it for accuracy and currency. This creates the need for new policies and procedures. For example, who "owns" various parts of the website? Who can change the information? Who is responsible for monitoring the environment for changes such as new policy, legislations, news items? How do we ensure the information is relevant and easy to locate? How do we manage the dynamic portion of our content? That is, portals often draw content from other sites, such as from health plan vendors. How do we ensure that the information being supplied to employees is accurate? What if an employee makes a decision based on information from an ESS that is wrong? Clearly, content management is probably the biggest challenge to the ongoing maintenance of the portal. Part of the design process should be explicit development of policy and procedure for content management.

Managing Employee Expectations

The second greatest challenge is *managing employee expectations*. That is, once employees become used to accessing the portal for HR services, they will expect to be able to conduct more and more of their personal HR business via the website. Remember, your HR website is being compared with commercial sites for utility, convenience, and ease of use. Expect the demand for new functionality to increase each year. This is especially true in the early years, as there is a range of services that can be added to the website. From a managerial point of view, this means a continual implementation process. Collection of various metrics to document the success of the system becomes important to ensure that the case for continued funding can be made.

Managing the Impact on the HR Function

The third challenge is *managing the impact on the HR function*. As mentioned previously, self-service offers the potential for significant reductions in HR staff. This is clearly threatening to staff members and can cause resistance. While it is comforting to suggest that HR staff will be reassigned to more strategic or value-added roles, the reality is that an HR portal can reduce the need for HR staff by 30 to 50 percent. The reductions fall most heavily on lower-level members of the HR staff, who previously spent most of their time in transaction processing and responding to employee questions. To most employees, these individuals are "HR." Often these staff members are fairly specialized, are the walking knowledge bases of the HR group, and are difficult to move into new roles. In order to be successful, the new system will have to incorporate their expertise and knowledge. Given that these individuals are most at risk in a future HR restructuring, it is often difficult to gain their support. Part of the implementation plan should consider how the impact on these individuals can be mitigated (for example, retraining, early retirement, and other means).

Call center employees are also likely to be heavily impacted as routine questions and transactions are handled via the web. The nature of call center work will increase in sophistication, and the level of knowledge demanded from call center workers will increase dramatically. Call center specialists will handle the exceptions to HR policy and complicated issues, and therefore will require more training and education and have a greater decision-making role in interpreting HR policy.

New skills are also likely to be required to manage the portal. New roles such as "Super Content Masters" (SCMs) will evolve to support web applications (Gueutal, 2003). These individuals will be responsible for content maintenance of the website and the knowledge base that supports the website and call center. They will be highly qualified experts in specific HR content areas. SCMs will work with knowledge base vendors to tailor "generic" knowledge bases to the culture and values of the organization. They will be the "last resort" for expertise within the HR organization.

"Organizational Effectiveness Generalists" (OEGs) will be the second major group of HR professionals. These individuals will be responsible for many of the traditional HR roles in fostering employee motivation, team building, and group effectiveness. They will be the onsite professionals working to implement and maintain HR policies and improve employee effectiveness. This suggests that OEG professionals will need to develop skill sets relevant to this new role. These include skills in team building and coaching, mentoring, individual training, change management, general business, project management, and program implementation. For employees, OEGs will be the new face of HR.

Senior HR managers must consider and plan for the impact of self-service applications on the HR staff. This challenge is made more difficult by the fact that the support of the HR staff is critical for a successful implementation. This may include the need to evaluate the currency of the skill sets of staff members, identify training needs for newly required skill sets and roles, and determine specific employees to target for long-term retention. Those unlikely to remain must be given a reason to participate fully in the implementation.

Conclusion

The delivery of HR information and services is undergoing a radical change. It is easy to underestimate the impact of the technology on our field. For years, we heard about the way information systems would change HR, but we saw little real change. With the advent of the web, many of the promises of technology can be delivered. We are now free of much of the day-to-day transaction processing that used to consume us. Systems can handle most of the routine questions. The challenge today is to make the transformation from a support role for HR to that of a true business partner. It is a time of opportunity for those willing to work in new ways, and a time of risk for those mired in the past.

References

Authoria, Inc. (2003). *Self-service to self-sufficiency: Employee communication through an HR portal; Regaining the personal touch with personalized HR knowledge.* Waltham, MA: Authoria, Inc.

Bartholomew, D. (2002). Let them serve themselves. *Industry Week 10*(3), 21. [Retrieved September 12, 2003, from ABI/INFORM Global database]

Cedar (2001). *Cedar human resource self-service/portal survey.* Baltimore: Cedar Enterprise Solutions, Inc.

Cedar. (2002). *Cedar 2002 human resources self-service/portal survey: Cedar's fifth annual survey and lessons learned from the early adopters of 1997.* Baltimore: Cedar Enterprise Solutions, Inc.

Cedar. (2003). *Cedar 2003 workforce technologies survey* (6th ed.) Baltimore: Cedar Enterprise Solutions, Inc.

Folan, L. J., & Mitchell, G. (2003). All work and no meaning: Will an HR portal keep your employees from jumping ship? *Communication World, 20*(2), 22. [Retrieved September 12, 2003, from ABI/INFORM Global database]

Gueutal, H. (2003, Spring) *Career security: Skill sets for the future.* Alexandria, VA: iLinX/Society for Human Resource Management.

Harlty, L., & Matin, A. (2002). *Human capital management: Its payback time, providing the value of IT investments.* Pleasanton, CA: PeopleSoft, Inc.

Jossi, F. (2001). Taking the eHR plunge: At General Motors, eHR is on the fast track. *HR Magazine, 46*(9), 1–5. [Retrieved September 18, 2003, from www.shrm.org/hrmagazine/articles/0901/0901jossi.asp]

Kuppe, M. (2003). *Make your line managers better cost accountants with manager self-service.* SAP-AG: www.FICOExpertOnline.com.

Mecham, K. (2001). How Microsoft built a cost-effective HR portal. *HR Focus, 78*(8), 4–5.

PeopleSoft. (2002). *Human capital management: Delivering on the promise of return on investment.* PeopleSoft White Paper Series. PeopleSoft, Inc. www.peoplesoft.com.

Roberts, B. (2002a). Content to order. *HR Magazine, 47*(7), 79–82. [Retrieved September 12, 2003, from ABI/INFORM Global database]

Roberts, B. (2002b). Processes first, technology second: For International Paper, successful HR transformation depends on getting the steps in the right order. *HR Magazine, 47*(6), 1–5. [Retrieved September 18, 2003, from www.shrm.org/hrmagazine/articles/0602/0602roberts.asp]

Roberts, B. (2003). Portal takes off. *HR Magazine, 48*(2), 95. [Retrieved September 12, 2003, from ABI/INFORM Global database]

SAP AG. (2001). *SAP customer success story: F-secure selects mySAP human resources employee self-service* (ESS). www.sap.com.

SAP AG. (2003). *A business value assessment: mySAP human resources at Transalta: SAP case study.* www.sap.com.

Sorenson, S. (2002). Portal can ease HR burden. *Credit Union Magazine, 68*(4), 22. [Retrieved September 12, 2003, from ABI/INFORM Global database]

Towers Perrin. (2002a). *HR on the web: New realities in service delivery: HR service delivery survey report.* www.towersperrin.com.

Towers Perrin. (2002b). *Use of the web for HR service delivery growing steadily.* www.towersperrin.com.

CHAPTER 8

The Effects of eHR System Characteristics and Culture on System Acceptance and Effectiveness

Eugene F. Stone-Romero

Electronic human resource (eHR) systems are being used by a large percentage of organizations in North America and Europe (Cedar, 2002; Gueutal, 2003). Illustrative of this, a study of 299 organizations showed that approximately 73 percent of North American firms and 90 percent of European companies used eHR systems for one or more human resource (HR) purposes (Cedar, 2002). Among the many goals associated with the adoption of such systems are enhancing the efficiency and effectiveness of HR-related activities through such strategies as (a) decreasing the need for HR staff; (b) reducing the costs of HR transactions; (c) increasing access to HR information; (d) improving service to employees; and (e) freeing HR staff from many routine tasks and, thus, allowing them to devote more time and attention to strategic HR planning activities (Cedar, 2001; Towers Perrin, 2001; Ulrich, 2001). Regrettably, there is very little research on the degree to which eHR systems actually facilitate the accomplishment of these and other goals (Cardy & Miller, 2003; Gueutal, 2003; Stone, Stone-Romero, & Lukaszewski, 2003). As a result, many of the recommendations for practice that appear in the HR literature rest on a fairly weak foundation. Moreover, there is very little research evidence on the relative effectiveness of eHR systems across cultures.

In view of the above, this chapter has two major purposes. First, it considers the functional and dysfunctional consequences that may arise from using eHR systems for such purposes as employee recruitment, personnel selection, and performance management. Second, it deals with cross-cultural differences in the acceptance and effectiveness of eHR systems. The latter purpose is especially important because most such systems are predicated on values (for example, individualism, meritocracy) that are rooted in the cultures of the United States and several western European nations. As a result, the same systems may not be so effective in nations that subscribe to different values (for example, collectivism, egalitarianism). Consequently, various aspects of "canned" systems may have to be modified to make them compatible with the values of individuals in specific cultural contexts. In addition, because the employees of many organizations are multicultural, the eHR system of any specific organization may have to be flexible enough to accommodate individuals from different cultures. This flexibility should serve to increase employee acceptance of the systems and, thus, enhance their overall effectiveness. In view of this chapter's focus on the impact of values on the acceptance and effectiveness of eHR systems, the next section considers cross-cultural differences in values (cultural orientations).

Values and the Acceptance and Effectiveness of eHR

Research by Bond (1988), Hofstede (1980, 1997), Erez and Earley (1993), and Trompenaars and Hampden-Turner (1998) has identified national differences in values. In this regard, a major premise of this chapter is that such differences will influence the degree to which eHR-related policies and practices have desired effects. Consistent with this premise, Figure 8.1 shows a model dealing with the moderating effect of cultural values on the relation between (a) eHR system characteristics and (b) the outcomes of eHR system use (for example, employee reactions or effectiveness of practices). Numerous examples of this moderating effect are detailed here.

Although there is a sound basis for hypothesizing the just-described moderating effect, many eHR systems have been designed in a standardized way, with virtually no concern for differences in the values of employees. More specifically, many such systems are based on values that are common to the United States and several Western European nations. This is unfortunate, because even though they may be well-intended, organizational practices often will have diminished effectiveness if they fail to consider differences in employees' values (Stone & Stone-Romero, 2004; Stone-Romero & Stone, 1998; Stone-Romero, Stone, & Salas, 2003; Trompenaars & Hampden-Turner, 1998). For example, HR practices that are based on Western European (that is, Anglo-Saxon) values have proven to be difficult to implement in organizational contexts where different values are prevalent (Stone-Romero & Stone, 1998; Trompenaars & Hampden-Turner, 1998).

Consistent with the just-noted arguments, available theory and research suggest that eHR systems will be more accepted and effective in cultures that share Western European values than those that do not. There are at least three reasons for this. First, a great deal of currently popular eHR software was developed in either the United States (for example, by PeopleSoft) or Germany (for example, by SAP). Organizational policies and practices in these countries are often predicated on models of organization that have their roots in bureaucracy theory (see, for example, Katz & Kahn, 1978; Stone-Romero & Stone, 1998; Weber, 1947). Such models emphasize (a) the standardization of policies and practices; (b) the use of objective data in decision making; (c) the uniform and impersonal treatment of job applicants and job incumbents; and (d) the separation of the job and the job holder. As a result, most eHR systems will be more acceptable to individuals who share the values associated with the bureaucratic model than to individuals who do not (Trompenaars & Hampden-Turner, 1998). For example, such systems may be less compatible with the cultures of countries in Asia, South America, and Africa than with the cultures of nations in North America and Northern Europe. Second, organizations that use eHR software often implement it as it originally was programmed, as opposed to customizing it to reflect local cultural values (Cedar, 2002). Thus, it is likely that the benefits that might stem from local adaptations of eHR software are unrealized. Third, and finally, eHR systems will be more accepted by employees in organizations that have well-developed (mature) HR practices (for example, organizations in the United States) than those that do not (for example, organizations in Brazil). In view of the above, it is critical that researchers and practitioners consider the influence that values may have on the acceptance and effectiveness of eHR in international or multicultural contexts.

In light of the hypothesis that values will moderate the relationship between (a) eHR system characteristics and (b) the outcomes of eHR system use, the following section considers several values that appear relevant. Immediately thereafter, the chapter turns to (a) the functional and dysfunctional consequences of using eHR to facilitate such processes as employee recruitment (referred to below as recruitment), personnel selection (referred to hereinafter as selection), and performance management, and (b) the way in which culture influences reactions to eHR system characteristics.

Dimensions of Culture

The literature on culture suggests a number of values (cultural orientations) that differ across national cultures (for example, Bond, 1988; Hofstede, 1980, 1997; Triandis, 1994; Trompenaars & Hampden-Turner, 1998). In the interest of brevity, the consideration of values is restricted to the following values or orientations: (a) achievement, (b) individualism, (c) long-term perspective, (d) masculinity, (e) power inequality, (f) predictability, (g) specificity, and (h) universalism.[1] In subsequent sections we consider the implications of these values for the acceptance and effectiveness of eHR systems.

Achievement Orientation

In achievement-oriented cultures, individuals are evaluated on the basis of their personal accomplishments, whereas in ascription-oriented cultures, they are often evaluated on the basis of such factors as their kinships, gender, age, or personal relationships with others (Trompenaars & Hampden-Turner, 1998). Research by Trompenaars and Hampden-Turner (1998) showed that respondents from English speaking and/or Northern European countries (including Australia, Canada, Denmark, Finland, Germany, Ireland, New Zealand, Nigeria, Norway, Sweden, and the United States) were likely to endorse the achievement value. However, respondents from other countries (including Argentina, Austria, Bahrain, Brazil, Cuba, Hong Kong, India, Kenya, Kuwait, Oman, the Philippines, Saudi Arabia, Serbia, and Thailand) were likely to endorse the ascription value.

Individualism Orientation

In individualistic cultures ties between individuals tend to be relatively "loose" or weak and each person is viewed as being responsible for his or her own welfare. In contrast, in collective cultures people believe that in-groups or other collectives should look out for their welfare. In exchange for this support, individuals manifest a high level of loyalty to the collective. Research by Hofstede (1980) showed that support for individualism is relatively (a) high in such nations as the United States, Australia, Great Britain, and Canada, and (b) low in such countries as Taiwan, Peru, Pakistan, Colombia, and Venezuela.

Long-Term Perspective

On the basis of work by Bond (1988), Hofstede (1997) described a value that he labeled "Confucian dynamism." Individuals who subscribe to this value tend to (a) have a long-term perspective, (b) view relationships between people in terms of status differentials, (c) regard the family as the prototype of social organization, (d) subscribe to the Confucian version of the Golden Rule, (e) manifest sensitivity in dealings with others, and (f) value education, tradition, patience, frugality, and perseverance. The aspect of Confucian dynamism that differs most from the other values described by Hofstede (1980) is a long-term perspective. Research by Hofstede (1997) showed that support for this orientation was relatively (a) strong in such countries as China, Hong Kong, Taiwan, Japan, and South Korea and (b) weak in such nations as Pakistan, Canada, Great Britain, and the United States.

Masculinity Orientation

The masculinity value detailed by Hofstede (1980, 1997) is some-what similar to the just-described achievement value. More specifically, in masculine (as opposed to feminine) cultures, emphasis is placed on such factors as achieving worldly success, accumulating money, and possessing material goods. Men are socialized to be assertive and tough, whereas women are socialized to be modest and tender. In addition, in masculine cultures there tends to be high worker involvement in their work roles, an acceptance of work organizations "interfering" in the non-work lives of employees, and a domination of desirable organizational jobs by males. Research by Hofstede (1980) showed that the masculinity orientation tends to be relatively (a) strong in such nations as Japan, Austria, Italy, Switzerland, and Mexico and (b) weak in such nations as Finland, Denmark, Norway, and Sweden.

Power Inequality Orientation

This is the same value that Hofstede (1980) labeled power distance. However, the label of power inequality is used here because it seems far more descriptive of the nature of this value. In cultures with a high power inequality orientation, people accept unequal distributions of power across individuals in social systems and expect such distributions. In addition, in high power inequality cultures, subordinates tend to have dependent relationships with superiors and to maintain considerable emotional distance from them. Research by Hofstede (1980) showed that power inequality tends to be (a) strongly valued in such nations as Mexico, Venezuela, India, and Singapore and (b) not strongly valued in such countries as Austria, Israel, Denmark, New Zealand, and Ireland.

Predictability Orientation

Hofstede (1980) called this value "uncertainty avoidance." However, the term predictability is used here because it is simpler. Predictability reflects an orientation on the part of individuals to prefer situations in which events are stable or predictable and to avoid situations in which there is ambiguity or uncertainty. In work organizations, predictability can be enhanced by (a) clear rules, regulations, and policies and (b) practices that ensure stability (for example, of work schedules and employment). Hofstede's (1980) research showed that predictability is (a) strongly valued in such nations as Greece, Portugal, Belgium, and Japan and (b) weakly valued in such nations as Singapore, Denmark, Sweden, and Hong Kong.

Specificity Orientation

In cultures with a specific orientation such as the United States, individuals' interactions with others tend to focus on specific areas of life (Trompenaars & Hampden-Turner, 1998). For example, a manager's work relationship with a subordinate would be separate from a personal relationship that he or she might have with the subordinate. Note that in many Western organizations there is often a clear separation between the job and the job-holder (Katz & Kahn, 1978; Stone & Stone-Romero, 2004; Stone-Romero & Stone, 1998; Weber, 1947). In contrast, in cultures that have a diffuse orientation (China or Japan, for example), individuals tend to involve others in multiple areas of their lives (Imai, 1986; Morishima, 1982; Trompenaars & Hampden-Turner, 1998). In addition, relative to cultures with a specific orientation (the United States, for example), in cultures with a diffuse orientation, organizations tend to be more involved with the families and personal lives of their employees. Interestingly, research by Trompenaars and Hampden-Turner (1998) showed that respondents from many European and North American countries (for example, Bulgaria, Canada, Czech Republic, Denmark, Finland, France, Hungary, the Netherlands, Sweden, Switzerland, and the United Kingdom) were likely to endorse specific values. In contrast, respondents from several other nations (for example, Bahrain, China, Egypt, Indonesia, Kenya, Kuwait, Nepal, Nigeria, Singapore, South Korea, and Venezuela) were prone to endorse diffuse values.

Universalism Orientation

Individuals who subscribe to universalism believe that each person in a culture should be treated in a uniform manner, whereas those who endorse the value of particularism believe that each individual should be treated in a differentiated manner (Trompenaars & Hampden-Turner, 1998). The greater the belief in universalism, the lesser the degree to which emphasis is placed on (a) the obligations associated with personal relationships and (b) the way in which unique circumstances influence dealings with others. Thus, for example, consistent with the precepts of bureaucracy theory, a manager who subscribes to universalism would be likely to have impersonal (as opposed to personal) relationships with each of his or her subordinates and to treat each one in a uniform manner (Imai, 1986; Morishima, 1982; Stone-Romero & Stone, 1998). Interestingly, the results of research by Trompenaars and Hampden-Turner (1998) revealed that, whereas respondents from North American and European nations (for example, Canada, Germany, Ireland, the Netherlands, Romania, Sweden, Switzerland, the United Kingdom, and the United States) were likely to endorse universalism, respondents from many other countries (for example, Bulgaria, China, Cuba, Greece, India, Indonesia, Mexico, Nepal, Russia, South Korea, and Venezuela) were likely to stress particularism.

Having described several values that appear relevant to eHR systems, we now turn to a number of HR processes that are thought to be facilitated by them. For each such process, attention is devoted to two sets of issues. First, the functional and dysfunctional consequences of eHR systems for organizations and individuals (for example, job seekers, job applicants, job incumbents) are considered. Second, examples are presented that illustrate the moderating effect of values on relations between (a) eHR system characteristics and (b) the outcomes of eHR system use (see Figure 8.1).

Recruitment and eHR

In order to maximize organizational efficiency and effectiveness, organizations use recruitment to attract highly talented job seekers and encourage them to apply for jobs. Interestingly, a recent study showed that 100 percent of large firms in the United States use eHR systems for recruitment (Cedar, 2002; Gueutal, 2003).

Recruitment also serves the interests of job seekers. More specifically, they can use information gained through recruitment efforts as a basis for assessing the likelihood of organizations providing them with jobs that will lead to such outcomes as satisfying

Figure 8.1. The Moderating Effect of Culture on the Relationship Between eHR System Policies and Practices and the Outcomes of eHR System Use.

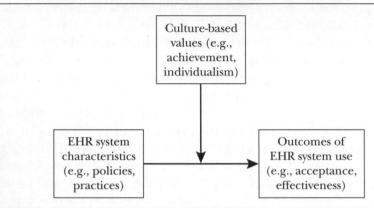

work, equitable pay, fringe benefits, job status, supportive social relationships, and developmental opportunities (Lofquist & Dawis, 1969; Porter, Lawler, & Hackman, 1975).

Appropriately designed eHR systems may prove beneficial to (functional for) both organizations and job seekers. However, as noted below, they also may lead to a number of dysfunctional, typically unintended, consequences.

Functional Consequences of Using eHR for Recruitment

The use of eHR for recruitment may lead to several functional consequences for job seekers and organizations. We consider these in turn.

Functional Consequences for Job Seekers
Well-designed eHR-based recruitment efforts may provide several benefits to job seekers. First, they can use organizational websites (referred to hereinafter as websites) to gather information about organizations around the world. This information can then be perused in as much detail as needed to assess the relative attrac-

tiveness of the same organizations. Second, websites may allow job seekers to assess the likelihood of being hired by any given organization. For instance, a job seeker may be able to determine the correspondence between his or her abilities and the ability requirements of any specific job. Third, information on websites may enable job seekers to assess the odds of being satisfied with a given job. This can be accomplished by comparing their needs with the reinforcers (for example, pay, fringe benefits) provided to job incumbents (Lofquist & Dawis, 1969). Fourth, to the degree that websites convey information about the values and goals of an organization, job seekers may be able to determine whether or not their own values coincide with those of the organization. Fifth, to the extent that websites provide information on the goals of organizations and the strategies used to pursue them, job seekers can use this information to manage positive impressions during the selection process. Sixth, websites can provide job seekers with a virtual preview of an organization (Johnson & Isenhour, 2003; Stone, Stone-Romero, & Lukaszewski, 2003). Seventh, and finally, websites can reduce the time needed for individuals to apply for jobs (Giesen & Frank, in press; Hesse, 2004; Johnson & Isenhour, 2003; Stone, Stone-Romero, & Lukaszewski, 2003).

Functional Consequences for Organizations

eHR-based recruiting may result in several functional consequences for organizations. First, it may allow for the cost-effective and timely communication of large amounts of information about an organization to a broad pool of job seekers. Second, it may enable organizations to reduce or eliminate the expenses associated with recruiting fairs. In fact, some large multinational firms (Ford Motor Company, for example) are replacing recruitment at college fairs with eHR-based recruiting. Third, to the extent that websites are attractive and engaging, they can attract and hold the attention of job seekers, enhancing the odds of them applying for jobs (Barber & Roehling, 1993). In support of this contention, recent research (for example, Anderson, 2003; Chapman & Webster, 2003; Scheu, Ryan, & Nona, 1999) has shown positive relations between the attractiveness of websites and applicants' reactions to organizations. For example, research by Higgs, Strong, and Light (2002) showed that eHR-based video clips about an organization enhanced applicants' liking for it. Fourth, to the extent that they are programmed to do so, eHR-based systems can reduce the time needed to scan the résumés of applicants and provide them with feedback on their suitability for jobs. Fifth, and finally, eHR systems can be used to evaluate the effectiveness of recruitment processes, including the degree to which such processes result in the attraction of well-qualified job applicants.

Dysfunctional Consequences of Using eHR for Recruitment

eHR-based recruitment may result in a number of unanticipated dysfunctional consequences. The following two subsections consider these with respect to job seekers and organizations.

Dysfunctional Consequences for Job Seekers

eHR-based recruiting may lead to several dysfunctional consequences for job seekers. For example, to the degree that they lack experience with computer use and/or lack access to computers, they may not be able to access and/or use websites. This is a very important issue because of the "digital divide problem." More specifically, relative to individuals in nations in which people have high levels of access to computers (for example, Canada, England, Germany, and the United States), large percentages of people in other countries (El Salvador, Somalia, and Vietnam, for example) lack such access. For example, recent research (Cedar, 2002) showed that among individuals employed by relatively large organizations, fewer people in Asian companies had access to the Internet than did people in either U.S. or European firms. In view of this, it seems likely that computer access was even lower for people who were either unemployed or were employed by relatively small firms. It is clear, therefore, that to the degree that individuals are unable to use computers or lack access to them, they will have diminished odds of benefiting from eHR-based recruiting.

It deserves adding that, even in countries where there are generally high levels of Internet access, such as the United States, members of several ethnic groups (for example, African Americans, Hispanic Americans, Native Americans) may have little or no access to computers. Thus, they will be unlikely to benefit from eHR-based recruiting. Similarly, because they lack computer experience, many older individuals will not benefit from such recruiting.

Interestingly recent research revealed that computer experience and computer self-efficacy are important determinants of computer use (Venkatesh & Davis, 2000). Thus, even if they are well-qualified for jobs, to the degree that job seekers lack experience and the self-efficacy that it brings, their chances of benefiting from eHR-based recruiting efforts will be diminished.

Dysfunctional Consequences for Organizations

Organizations that only use eHR-based recruiting may experience a number of dysfunctional consequences. First, to the degree that otherwise well-qualified job seekers lack access to websites, eHR-based recruiting will be less effective than traditional recruiting (such as job fairs or campus visits). Second, eHR-based recruiting may not provide organizations with as much information about job seekers as traditional types of recruitment do. For example, eHR-based recruiting may yield little or no information about the interpersonal skills of job seekers. Third, to the degree that eHR-based recruitment has an adverse impact on certain classes of job applicants (ethnic minorities in the United States, for example), it may lead to costly litigation in some countries (for example, the United States).

Cultural Influences on Reactions to eHR-Based Recruitment

As noted above, values may influence both the acceptance and effectiveness of eHR-based recruitment systems. In particular, many such systems were developed with the assumption that all job seekers have similar values and, for example, seek the same types of job-related outcomes. However, in view of the fact that there are important differences in values across various nations (Bond, 1988; Hofstede, 1980, 1997; Triandis, 1994), this assumption seems incorrect. Thus, eHR-based recruiting may be more effective in some cultures than in others. Illustrations of this are presented below.

Achievement Orientation

Recruiting systems based on eHR may be less acceptable to individuals from cultures that stress ascription than to individuals who value achievement. One reason for this is that people from ascription-oriented cultures (for example, those of many South American nations) are prone to use personal relationships or connections to gain access to jobs. Thus, they may react negatively to eHR systems that do not consider such relationships. Also, in nations with achievement-oriented cultures (for example, the United States) it is common for organizations to conduct job analyses and select job applicants who meet job requirements. In marked contrast, in organizations in several South American nations, individuals are hired and then allowed to write their own job descriptions (Trompenaars & Hampden-Turner, 1998).

Individualism Orientation

Although research on the issue is lacking, it seems safe to infer that individualists will respond more positively to eHR-based recruiting than will collectivists. One reason for this is that such methods are impersonal in nature and afford little or no opportunity for a person with collective values to pursue group interests. Thus, eHR-based recruiting should be viewed more positively in such nations as the United States and Great Britain than they are in such countries as Guatemala, Venezuela, and South Korea.

Long-Term Orientation

In view of the nature of the long-term orientation construct (Bond, 1988; Hofstede, 1997), it would appear that individuals who subscribe to this value will be more accepting of eHR-based recruiting than those who do not. There are at least two reasons for this. First, individuals with a long-term orientation will be accepting of such recruiting if they view it as adapting traditional ways to a modern context. Second, such individuals will value eHR-based recruiting to the degree that it is viewed as cost-effective. Regrettably, there is no research to support this speculation.

Masculinity Orientation

It seems safe to infer that eHR-based recruiting will be more acceptable to individuals in masculine cultures than to individuals in feminine cultures. Such recruiting should allow job seekers to find jobs that will allow them to achieve worldly success, and thereby accumulate resources. Research is needed to test this prediction.

Power Inequality Orientation

On the basis of what is known about the power inequality construct (Hofstede, 1980, 1997), it seems that individuals who are tolerant of high levels of power inequality will be more accepting of eHR-based recruiting than individuals who favor low levels of power inequality. The reason for this is that those who tolerate high levels will view such recruiting methods as the legitimate right of powerful organizations. Unfortunately, there is no research on this issue.

Predictability Orientation

On the one hand, to the degree that individuals value predictability and are accustomed to traditional recruiting practices, they may react negatively to eHR-based recruiting. This would be especially true if they had low levels of computer experience. On the other hand, eHR-based recruiting may lead to lower levels of stress among job seekers if it provides them with a sense of control over their activities. The same sense of control may be absent in face-to-face encounters with live recruiters. Research is needed on this issue.

Universalism Orientation

The acceptance and success of eHR-based recruiting is likely to vary across cultures that differ with respect of their standing on a universalism (for example, Germany, Sweden, the United Kingdom, and the United States) versus particularism (for example, China, Mexico, South Korea, and Venezuela) continuum. One reason for this is that eHR-based recruiting systems typically are designed by individuals from cultures with a universalist orientation. Thus, they are often highly standardized and impersonal in nature. For example, with such systems employment applications are processed by computer programs, as opposed to being reviewed by an HR professional. In addition, managers from universalist-oriented cultures are likely to value standardized processes, impersonal decision making, and the consistent treatment of job seekers or applicants. Because of this, eHR-based recruiting systems will be more likely to be accepted by individuals from universalist-oriented cultures than by people from particularist-oriented cultures (Trompenaars & Hampden-Turner, 1998).

Specificity Orientation

As noted above, research by Trompenaars and Hampden-Turner (1998) showed that people in some countries (for example, the United Kingdom and the United States) are likely to endorse specific values, whereas individuals in other countries (China, Singapore, and Venezuela, for example) are prone to subscribe to diffuse values. In addition, research by Lewin (cited in Trompenaars & Hampden-Turner, 1998) found that there are national differences in preferences for personal space. For instance, people in the United States stress public space more than private space, whereas individuals from Germany emphasize private space more than public space. Compared to people from the United States, people from Germany are more likely to have a smaller public space and guard access to their private space. However, once an individual from Germany allows friends to access his or her private space, they are granted access to a considerable amount of private information. The results of this research suggest that, compared to individuals from cultures with specific orientation, people from cultures with a diffuse orientation will be more concerned with protecting their privacy in organizational contexts. As a result, relative to individuals from cultures with a specific orientation, those from cultures with a diffuse orientation will (a) want more safeguards for information in eHR-based systems and (b) be more reluctant to divulge information during the recruitment process.

Selection and eHR

Research shows that selection practices differ across nations (Ryan, McFarland, Baron, & Page, 1999). However, in most organizations in the United States and other Western nations, selection involves the matching of the knowledge, skills, and abilities of job applicants with the requirements of jobs (Campbell, McCloy, Oppler, & Sager, 1993; Guion, 1976; Lofquist & Dawis, 1969). In order to achieve the matching, organizations often use a wide array of methods (for example, ability tests, personality inventories, interviews) to gather data about applicants.

eHR systems can be used to perform such tasks as (a) scanning applicants' résumés for key words found in statements of job requirements, (b) matching individuals' profiles with those of jobs (Pearlman & Barney, 2000), and (c) comparing the knowledge, skills, and abilities of internal candidates with the requirements of jobs (Stone, Stone-Romero, & Lukaszewski, 2003). In view of this, eHR-based selection may lead to functional and dysfunctional consequences for both job applicants and organizations, and these may vary across cultural contexts (Konradt & Hertel, in press).

Functional Consequences of Using eHR for Selection

eHR-based selection systems may lead to a number of functional consequences for job applicants and organizations. These are considered next with respect to each of these groups.

Functional Consequences for Job Applicants

Relative to traditional HR systems, eHR-based selection systems may result in a number of functional consequences. One is increasing the advancement opportunities of internal job candidates (that is, current employees) because of improvements in the availability of information about openings. A second advantage is convenience. With eHR systems, job seekers may be able to complete application forms and pre-employment tests online.

Functional Consequences for Organizations

eHR-based selection systems may result in several functional consequences for organizations. First, they may increase both the speed and the accuracy of the selection process, especially when there are large numbers of job applicants. Second, they may enable organizations to collect information about job applicants in a rapid and cost-effective manner. Third, they may allow for applicants to complete one or more predictor measures (for example, ability tests, personality inventories, self-assessments) online. Fourth, such systems may allow organizations to conduct background checks or reference checks on job applicants in a cost-effective manner. Fifth, the same systems may increase the amount of information available to decision makers. Sixth, eHR-based systems may help organizations assess the validity and utility of their selection practices. Seventh and finally, through appropriate placement activities, they may increase the organization's ability to utilize the skills and abilities of applicants who are hired.

Dysfunctional Consequences of Using eHR for Selection

eHR-based selection may lead to dysfunctional consequences for both job seekers and organizations. These are considered next.

Disadvantages for Job Seekers

Selection systems based on eHR may have one or more dysfunctional consequences for job seekers. First, once data are in an eHR-based system, applicants may not be able to ensure their accuracy (Barak & English, 2002; Bartram, 2000; Pearlman & Barney, 2000). This is not a trivial issue because of the inaccuracies found in databases. For example, research in the United States showed that 42 percent of the data in credit databases are inaccurate and may result in misclassification errors or a loss of job opportunities for individuals (Stone & Stone-Romero, 1998). Second, the standing of individuals on various dimensions (for example, skills, abilities, educational attainment, licenses) may change over time. However, data in eHR-based archives may fail to reflect such changes, and employees may not have the ability to update their records. Third, to the extent that eHR-based selection systems focus on limited types of data, they may not allow applicants to fully describe their job-related knowledge, skills (for example, interpersonal and team-related), and abilities. Fourth, such systems may be reductionist; that is, relatively complex information about job applicants (for example, their knowledge, skills, and abilities) may end up being represented by a simplistic, one-dimensional profile in a database (Cardy & Miller, 2003). Fifth, eHR-based selection systems may allow organizations to store data about job applicants and incumbents in large databases and disseminate it worldwide, even though the data subjects (for example, job applicants) may not be aware of such sharing or disapprove of it (Stone & Stone-Romero, 1998). This can be especially problematic when the information is inaccurate, leading to the stigmatization of data subjects (Stone & Stone, 1990; Stone, Stone-Romero, & Lukaszewski, 2003). Sixth, eHR-based selection systems may be perceived as invasive of privacy (Stone & Stone, 1990; Stone, Stone-Romero, & Lukaszewski, 2003). Not surprisingly, concerns about the widespread dissemination of information about data subjects prompted the European Union (EU) to enact privacy laws in 1998 that restrict the transmission of such information across national boundaries. Regrettably, there are no comparable laws in many other parts of the world (for example, the United States).

Disadvantages for Organizations

eHR-based selection systems may lead to a number of dysfunctional consequences for organizations. First, as noted earlier, they may provide an incomplete picture of the knowledge, skill, and ability levels of job applicants, resulting in increases in selection errors (that is, false positives and false negatives). For example, eHR-based selection systems may not provide information about the communication, interpersonal, or team-related skills of applicants. Second, if such systems allow applicants to complete various measures (for example, personality profiles, aptitude tests) online, there is no way of knowing whether they completed the measures on their own or were assisted by others.

Cultural Influences on Reactions to eHR-Based Selection

The available literature suggests that culture will influence individuals' reactions to eHR-based selection systems. Representative differences in reactions are considered in the following subsections.

Achievement Orientation

The extant literature suggests that eHR-based selection systems will be more effective in achievement-oriented cultures than in ascription-oriented cultures. An important reason for this is that in achievement-oriented cultures, individuals are judged on the basis of such factors as their measured abilities and accomplishments, rather than their personal relationships with personnel decision makers. Research is needed to test this prediction.

Specificity Orientation

The acceptance and effectiveness of eHR-based selection systems may differ between cultures with a specific orientation and those with a diffuse orientation. The basis for this prediction is that, relative to individuals from cultures with a specific orientation, people from cultures with a diffuse orientation will (a) be more concerned with protecting their privacy in the selection process and (b) react more negatively to eHR-based selection systems that collect large amounts of personal data about job applicants (for

example, through personality inventories and background checks).
Although some research has been conducted in the United States
on reactions to data collected for HR information systems (for
example, Eddy, Stone, & Stone-Romero, 1999; Stone, Lukaszewski,
& Stone-Romero, 2001) and applicant reactions to selection procedures (Stone-Romero, Stone, & Hyatt, 2003), we know of no
research that has examined cross-cultural reactions to eHR-based
selection systems. Thus, cross-cultural research is needed on reactions to eHR-based selection systems, including the extent to which
they are viewed as invasive privacy.

Universalism Orientation

eHR-based selection systems are often highly standardized, basing
selection decisions on specific types of data (for example, scores
on tests, personality inventories). They assume that the same data
are the most effective means of selecting individuals. However, this
assumption may be incongruent with cultures that have a particularist (as opposed to a universalist) orientation (Trompenaars &
Hampden-Turner, 1998). As noted above, individuals from particularist-oriented cultures are prone to attend to the obligations of
personal relationships and the merits of unique circumstances
(Trompenaars & Hampden-Turner, 1998). As a result, they may
not believe that selection decisions should be based on standardized or objective data and may resent the use of such data. As a
result, they may not be very accepting of eHR-based selection systems, reducing the overall effectiveness of such systems (Cober,
Brown, Levy, Cober, & Keeping, 2003; Wiechmann & Ryan, 2003).
In marked contrast, individuals from universalist-oriented cultures
may believe that the effectiveness and fairness of selection systems
is improved by the standardization of data and objectivity in decision making. Research is needed to validate these propositions.

Performance Management and eHR

In the interest of improving organizational efficiency and effectiveness, many Western organizations engage in such performance
management activities as (a) setting performance standards; (b) ap-
praising individual and work group performance; (c) giving employees and work groups performance feedback; (d) taking steps

to improve individual and work group performance; and (e) ensuring that employees are prepared to fill job openings that may arise (Porter, Lawler, & Hackman, 1975). Performance feedback is especially important in organizations that base rewards on performance.

Functional Consequences of Using eHR for Performance Management

The use of eHR systems for performance management may result in several functional consequences. These are considered next in terms of employees and organizations.

Functional Consequences for Employees

eHR-based performance management activities may lead to several functional consequences for employees. First, they can provide employees with information about the types and levels of behaviors that are desired by an organization (that is, role expectations), enabling the employees to better meet these expectations of their roles. Second, such activities may enable employees to obtain feedback about their performance on a timely basis, enhancing their chances of performing in such a way as to obtain rewards controlled by the organization. For instance, eHR systems may facilitate the use of 360-degree feedback, providing employees with performance feedback from their supervisors, co-workers, subordinates, and customers (Geister, Scherm, & Hertl, in press).

Functional Consequences for Organizations

eHR-based performance management systems may contribute to the attainment of several objectives, including (a) obtaining information about employee performance on a timely basis; (b) assisting managers with the provision of performance feedback to individuals and work groups; and (c) assessing the accuracy and effectiveness of performance appraisal (Stone, Salas, & Isenhour, in press). One of the ways in which they can contribute to the achievement of these objectives is by the use of management self-service systems to track, analyze, and organize data about individual and work group performance (Gueutal, 2003; Schaeffer-Kuels, in press). To the degree that such systems provide managers with timely data about employee performance, they can be instrumental in allowing managers to provide frequent performance feedback to individuals and work groups. This feedback can be on various aspects of behavior, including production quantity and quality, turnover, attendance, tardiness, and disciplinary problems.

Dysfunctional Consequences of Using eHR for Performance Management

A number of unanticipated dysfunctional consequences may result from the use of eHR for selection purposes. These are considered next with respect to employees and organizations.

Dysfunctional Consequences for Employees

The use of eHR systems for performance management may result in several dysfunctional consequences. First, it may depersonalize the feedback process, increasing the psychological distance between managers and their subordinates (Stone, Stone-Romero, & Lukaszewski, 2003). Second, it may decrease the level of social support experienced by employees. In accordance with this argument, research on the social impact of the Internet (for example, Kraut & Kiesler, 2003; Kraut, Kiesler, Boneva, Cummings, Helgeson, & Crawford, 2002) has shown that (a) online communication is viewed as less beneficial than face-to-face communication because it is less interactive and conveyed less contextual information and (b) relationships developed or maintained online are slower to develop and weaker than those developed by more traditional means. In addition, research by Ambrose, Adler, and Noel (1998) suggests that individuals may react negatively to electronic performance monitoring when there is no explicit justification for it. Overall, the use of eHR systems for monitoring individual performance may undermine relationships between managers and their subordinates, resulting in lesser trust and social support than traditional HR performance management systems (Hertel & Konradt, in press). Third, employees will view eHR systems negatively to the degree that they fail to consider all aspects of performance. Fourth, and finally, such systems may be viewed as invasive of privacy and employees may attempt to subvert them (Stone & Stone, 1990; Stone & Stone-Romero, 1998; Stone, Stone-Romero, & Lukaszewski, 2003).

Disadvantages for Organizations

eHR-based performance management systems may result in several dysfunctional consequences for organizations. First, managers may experience information overload problems as a result of the large amounts of data produced by them. Second, such systems may fail to provide information on such aspects of performance as interpersonal behavior and organizational citizenship behavior (Cardy & Miller, 2003). As a result, performance management activities may focus on only a subset of important criteria. Third, and finally, eHR systems may shift work that was previously performed by the HR department to line managers. Gutek (1995) calls this the "coproduction" problem and recommends that organizations avoid it.

Cultural Influences on Reactions to eHR-Based Performance Management

In view of the fact that many eHR-based performance management systems standardize the performance management process, base evaluations primarily on objective data, and depersonalize the feedback process, it seems likely that cultural orientations will influence reactions to them. Several moderating effects of culture are considered below.

Achievement Orientation

eHR-based performance management systems may be more effective in cultures that are achievement-oriented as opposed to ascription-oriented. One reason for this is that such systems often encourage decision making based on an individual's actual accomplishments. Such accomplishments are valued over ascription-based inferences about individuals.

Individualism Orientation

It would appear that eHR-based performance management systems will be more accepted and effective in cultures that value individualism than in those that stress collectivism. This is predicated on the assumption that individualists will view such systems positively because they offer the potential of establishing clear connections between performance data and valued outcomes.

Long-Term Orientation

It seems safe to predict that eHR-based performance management systems will be accepted more readily by individuals from cultures with a long-term orientation than in cultures with a short-term orientation. One reason for this is that people with a long-term orientation will value the efficiency associated with such systems and their potential to produce good outcomes in the long run.

Masculinity Orientation

eHR-based performance management systems will be better accepted in cultures that value masculinity than in cultures that stress femininity. This prediction rests on the assumption that individuals in masculine cultures will view organizational "intrusions" more favorably than will individuals in feminine cultures.

Power Inequality Orientation

Individuals from cultures that accept high levels of power inequality will be more accepting of eHR-based performance management systems than will individuals from cultures that have the opposite orientation. One reason for this is that individuals who are tolerant of power inequality will regard organizations as having the right to use such systems for controlling employee behavior.

Predictability Orientation

It seems that eHR-based performance management systems will be better tolerated in cultures that value high levels of predictability than in those that have considerable tolerance for uncertainty. The basis for this prediction is that the objectivity of such systems tends to eliminate rater-specific, idiosyncratic variability in performance evaluations (and the personnel actions that are based on them) that is common when performance evaluations stem from human judgments.

Specificity Orientation

Research shows that individuals from cultures with a diffuse orientation are more prone to guard their privacy than are people from cultures with a specific orientation. Thus, compared to individuals from cultures with a specific orientation, people from cultures with a diffuse orientation will be more likely to believe that eHR-based performance management systems are invasive of privacy, especially when performance data come from multiple sources. Research is needed on this issue.

Universalism Orientation

In view of the way in which most eHR-based performance management systems are designed, it seems that they will be more accepted in cultures that have a universalist orientation than in cultures with a particularistic orientation. One reason for this is that most such systems treat all data subjects (for example, employees) in a standardized manner, as opposed to being concerned with relationships and allowing for exceptions to rules. Thus, eHR-based performance management systems will be more effective in universalist-oriented cultures (that emphasize standardized policies and practices) than in particularist-oriented cultures.

Implications for Practice and Research

This section examines the implications of the material considered above for HR practice. In addition, it deals with some research-related issues.

Practice Issues

As a result of the proliferation of eHR-based systems, the role of HR professionals in many organizations is changing dramatically. More specifically, with eHR systems, HR professionals are increasingly faced with the need to develop and implement HR strategies, as opposed to performing relatively narrow HR tasks (such as administering employee benefit programs).

The overall effectiveness of HR professionals hinges on their ability to recruit, select, hire, and retain employees who have high levels of (a) motivation to perform and (b) job-related knowledge, skills, and abilities. To the degree that they are accepted by job seekers and job incumbents, eHR systems can lead to a number of functional consequences, including assisting HR professionals with the just-noted functions. Nevertheless, HR professionals must be aware of the potential dysfunctions stemming from the use of eHR systems. For example, the use of such systems will prove especially problematic in countries where the "digital divide" precludes large numbers of individuals from accessing and using them. In view of the fact that all individuals may not have access to eHR systems, for the next decade at least, it would appear prudent for most organizations to maintain a traditional HR system in parallel with an eHR system.

The effects of culture on the acceptance and effectiveness of eHR systems is an extremely important issue. In view of this, HR professionals must anticipate how the values of job seekers and/or job incumbents are likely to affect their reactions to such systems and take steps to mitigate unwanted outcomes. Thus, for example, in cultures with a particularist orientation, it may be prudent to limit eHR-based recruitment to the online submission of employment applications and the verification of information, with applicant screening handled by means that are culturally appropriate. In contrast, in cultures that have a universalistic orientation, HR professionals may use eHR systems for most recruitment and selection activities (for example, online applications, application screening).

A final practice-related issue concerns privacy. HR professionals must be sensitive to the way that eHR systems are likely to affect individuals' views about invasion of privacy and the effect that culture is likely to have on such views. Sensitivity to privacy issues is especially important in organizations that have international operations or operate in areas where employees come from a variety of cultures.

Research Issues

As noted above, there is very little research on factors that determine the acceptance and effectiveness of eHR systems. Thus, at present, there is not a firm foundation for many practice-related recommendations. In order to provide such a foundation, research must consider the degree to which eHR systems (a) are acceptable to job seekers and job incumbents; (b) lead to increased levels of individual, group, and organizational effectiveness; and (c) can be implemented successfully in cross-cultural contexts.

Conclusion

Clearly, eHR systems may produce both functional and dysfunctional consequences for individuals and organizations. In view of the rate at which such systems are being implemented in organizations, increased attention must be devoted to determining the outcomes stemming from their use. It is especially important to assess how culture affects various outcomes. eHR systems must meet the needs of both individuals and organizations. As such, HR practitioners and researchers can play a crucial role in determining whether eHR systems prove to be a blessing or a curse.

Note
1. In the interest of avoiding cumbersome labels, values are referenced by simple labels. For instance, masculinity is used in place of masculinity/femininity and individualism is used in place of individualism/collectivism.

References

Ambrose, M., Adler, S., & Noel, T. (1998). Electronic performance monitoring: A consideration of rights. In M. Schminke (Ed.), *Managerial ethics: Moral management of people and processes* (pp. 61–80). Mahwah, NJ: Lawrence Erlbaum.

Anderson, N. (2003). Applicant and recruiter reactions to new technology in selection: A critical review and agenda for future research. *International Journal of Selection and Assessment, 11,* 121–136.

Barak, A., & English, N. (2002). Prospects and limitations of psychological testing on the internet. *Journal of Technology in Human Services, 19,* 65–89.

Barber, A., & Roehling, M. (1993). Job posting and the decision to interview: A verbal protocol analysis. *Journal of Applied Psychology, 54,* 377–385.

Bartram, D. (2000). Internet recruitment and selection: Kissing frogs to find princes. *International Journal of Selection and Assessment, 8,* 261–274.

Bond, M. H. (1988). Finding universal dimensions of individual variation in multicultural studies of values: The Rokeach and Chinese value surveys. *Journal of Personality and Social Psychology, 55,* 1009–1015.

Campbell, J., McCloy, R., Oppler, S., & Sager, C. (1993). A theory of performance. In N. Schmitt & W. Borman (Eds.), *Personnel selection in organizations* (pp. 35–71). San Francisco: Jossey-Bass.

Cardy, D., & Miller, J. (2003). *Technology: Implications for HR.* In D. L. Stone (Ed.), *Advances in human performance and cognitive engineering research* (Vol. 3, pp. 99–118). Greenwich, CT: JAI.

Cedar. (2001). *Cedar 2001 human resources self-service/portal survey: Fourth annual survey.* Baltimore: Author.

Cedar. (2002). *Cedar 2002 human resources self-service/portal survey.* [Retrieved December 13, 2002, from www.peoplesoft.com/corp/en/products/line/hrms/exclusive/hcm_cedar thank_you.jsp]

Chapman, D., & Webster, J. (2003). The use of technologies in the recruiting, screening, and selection processes for job candidates. *International Journal of Selection and Assessment, 11,* 113–120.

Cober, R., Brown, D., Levy, P., Cober, A., & Keeping, L. (2003). Organizational websites: Website content and style as determinants of organizational attraction. *International Journal of Selection and Assessment, 11,* 158–169.

Eddy, E., Stone, D. L., & Stone-Romero, E. F. (1999). The effects of information management policies on reactions to human resource information systems: An integration of privacy and procedural justice perspectives. *Personnel Psychology, 52,* 335–358.

Erez, M., & Earley, P. (1993). *Culture, self-identity and work.* New York: Oxford University Press.

Geister, S., Scherm, M., & Hertel, G. (in press). Online-feedback systems: Regulation and HR development. In G. Hertel & U. Konradt (Eds.), *Electronic human resources management—Personnel work via Inter- and Intranet.* Gottingen, Germany: Hogrefe Publishers.

Giesen, B., & Frank, M. (in press). Recruitment of employees via internet. In G. Hertel & U. Konradt (Eds.), *Electronic human resources management—Personnel work via Inter- and Intranet.* Gottingen, Germany: Hogrefe Publishers.

Guion, R. (1976). Recruiting, selection and job placement. In M. Dunnette (Ed.), *Handbook of industrial and organizational psychology* (pp. 777–828). Chicago: Rand-McNally.

Gueutal, H. (2003). The brave new world of eHR. In D. L. Stone (Ed.), *Advances in human performance and cognitive engineering research* (Vol. 3, pp. 13–36). Greenwich, CT: JAI.

Gutek, B. (1995). *The dynamics of service: Reflections on the changing nature of customer/provider interactions.* San Francisco: Jossey-Bass.

Hertel, G., & Konradt, J. (in press). Electronic human resource management: Contents and definitions of central concepts. In G. Hertel & U. Konradt (Eds.), *Electronic human resources management—Personnel work via Inter- and Intranet.* Gottingen, Germany: Hogrefe Publishers.

Hesse, G. (2004). E-Cruiting bei Bertelsmann. In G. Hertel & U. Konradt (Eds.), *Electronic human resources management—Personnel work via Inter- and Intranet* (pp. 72–79). Gottingen, Germany: Hogrefe Publishers.

Higgs, E., Strong, D., & Light, A. (Eds.). (2002). *Technology and the good life.* Chicago: University of Chicago Press.

Hofstede, G. (1980). *Culture's consequences: International differences in work-related values.* Beverly Hills, CA: Sage.

Hofstede, G. (1997). *Cultures and organizations: Software of the mind.* New York: McGraw-Hill.

Imai, M. (1986). *Kaizen: The key to Japan's competitive success.* New York: Random House.

Johnson, R., & Isenhour, L. (2003). Changing the rules? Human resources in the 21st century virtual organization. In D. L. Stone (Ed.), *Advances in human performance and cognitive engineering research* (Vol. 3, pp. 119–152). Greenwich, CT: JAI.

Katz, D., & Kahn, R. (1978). *The social psychology of organizations* (2nd ed.). Hoboken, NJ: John Wiley & Sons.

Konradt, U., & Hertel, G. (in press). e-Assessment for selection and placement. In G. Hertel & U. Konradt (Eds.), *Electronic human resources management—Personnel work via Inter- and Intranet.* Gottingen, Germany: Hogrefe Publishers.

Kraut, R., & Kiesler, S. (2003). The social impact of internet use. *Psychological Science Agenda, 16,* 11–13.

Kraut, R., Kiesler, S., Boneva, B., Cummings, A., Helgeson, V., & Crawford, A. (2002). Internet paradox revisited. *Journal of Social Issues, 58,* 49–74.

Lofquist, L., & Dawis, R. (1969). *Adjustment to work.* New York: Appleton-Century-Crofts.

Morishima, M. (1982). *Why has Japan succeeded? Western technology and the Japanese ethos.* Bath, Great Britain: Cambridge University Press.

Pearlman, A., & Barney, M. (2000). Selection for a changing workplace. In J. Kehoe & E. Salas (Eds.), *Managing selection in changing organizations* (pp. 3–72). San Francisco: Jossey-Bass.

Porter, L. W., Lawler, E. E., & Hackman, J. R. (1975). *Behavior in organizations.* New York: McGraw-Hill.

Ryan, A. M., McFarland, L., Baron, H., & Page, R. (1999). An international look at selection practices: Nation and culture as explanations for variability in practice. *Personnel Psychology, 52,* 359–391.

Schaeffer-Kuels, B. (in press). Employee self-services. In G. Hertel & U. Konradt (Eds.), *Electronic human resources management—Personnel work via Inter- and Intranet.* Gottingen, Germany: Hogrefe Publishers.

Scheu, C., Ryan, A. M., & Nona, F. (1999). *Company web sites as a recruiting mechanism: What influences applicant impressions?* Paper presented at meeting of the Society for Industrial and Organizational Psychology, Atlanta, Georgia.

Stone, D. L., Lukaszewski, K., & Stone-Romero, E. F. (2001, April). *Privacy and HRIS.* Paper presented at the meeting of the Society of Industrial and Organizational Psychology, San Diego, California.

Stone, D., Salas, E., & Isenhour, L. (in press). Human resources management. In H. Bidgoli (Ed.), *The internet encyclopedia.* Hoboken, NJ: John Wiley & Sons.

Stone, E. F., & Stone, D. L. (1990). Privacy in organizations: Theoretical issues, research findings and protection mechanisms. In G. R. Ferris & K. Rowland (Eds.), *Research in personnel and human resources management* (Vol. 8, pp. 342–411). Greenwich, CT: JAI Press.

Stone, D. L., & Stone-Romero, E. F. (1998). A multiple stakeholder model of privacy in organizations. In M. Schminke (Ed.), *Managerial ethics: Moral management of people and processes* (pp. 35–59). Mahwah, NJ: Lawrence Erlbaum.

Stone, D. L., & Stone-Romero, E. F. (2004). The influence of culture on role-taking in culturally diverse organizations. In M. S. Stockdale & F. J. Crosby (Eds.), *The psychology and management of workplace diversity* (pp. 78–99). Malden, MA: Blackwell Publishing.

Stone, D. L., Stone-Romero, E. F., & Lukaszewski, K. (2003). The functional and dysfunctional consequences of using technology to achieve human resource system goals. In D. L. Stone (Ed.), *Research in human performance and cognitive engineering technology* (Vol. 3, pp. 37–68). Greenwich, CT: JAI.

Stone-Romero, E. F., & Stone, D. L. (1998). Religious and moral influences on work-related values and work quality. *Advances in the Management of Organizational Quality, 3,* 185–285.

Stone-Romero, E. F., Stone, D. L., & Hyatt, D. (2003). Personnel selection procedures and invasion of privacy. *Journal of Social Issues, 59,* 343–386.

Stone-Romero, E. F., Stone, D. L., & Salas, E. (2003). The influence of culture on role conceptions and role behavior in organizations. *Applied Psychology: An International Review, 52,* 328–362.

Towers Perrin. (2001). *Web-based self-service: Current state of the art.* HR survey. [Retrieved December 15, 2001, from www.towers.com/towers/webcache/towers/United_States/ publications/Reports/TP_Track_WebBasedSelfSer/TP_Track_WebBasedSelfSe.pdf]

Triandis, H. C. (1994). *Culture and social behavior.* New York: McGraw-Hill.

Trompenaars, F., & Hampden-Turner, C. (1998). *Riding the waves of culture: Understanding cultural diversity in global business.* New York: McGraw-Hill.

Ulrich, D. (2001). From e-business to eHR. *International Human Resources Information Management Journal, 5,* 90–97.

Venkatesh, V., & Davis, F. (2000). A theoretical extension of the technology acceptance model: Four longitudinal field studies. *Management Science, 46,* 186–204.

Weber, M. (1947). *The theory of social and economic organization.* In T. Parsons (Ed.), A. Henderson & T. Parsons (Trans.). New York: The Free Press.

Wiechmann, D., & Ryan, A. M. (2003). Reactions to computerized testing in selection contexts. *International Journal of Selection and Assessment, 11,* 230–236.

CHAPTER 9

The Next Decade of HR
Trends, Technologies, and Recommendations
Row Henson

Particularly with respect to technology, the saying "The only thing that is constant is change" requires this addendum: "and the speed of change is increasing." A critical part of the human resources (HR) business is to foresee rapid transformations in contributing factors such as demographics and technological innovation. Even more critical is HR's ability to strategically mobilize an organization to take timely advantage of opportunities to increase competitiveness.

No one can predict the future with accuracy. Yet, given past experience and current demographic and technological developments, we can gain insight into the future that becomes a valuable reference for the forward-thinking HR practitioner.

This chapter covers prospective changes over the next ten years in the workforce, technology, and global economic determinants as they impact human capital and the HR industry. Although we cannot separate the interdependencies of the workforce and technology, these two factors—the heartbeat and the toolset of the HR business today—appear in different but consecutive sections for clarity. This chapter also offers counsel to the HR professional of the future.

An Attitude of Adaptability

"It is not the strongest of the species that survive, nor the most intelligent, but the one most responsive to change."
—CHARLES DARWIN[1]

To succeed as an HR professional in the next ten years, awareness and adaptability will be mandatory. If change is not only certain but also increasing in velocity, only a mindset of resourcefulness and flexibility will keep HR above water.

Out of sheer necessity, HR will continuously revolutionize its thought leadership. Instead of being blindsided by change, the nimble HR organization will ride the waves of internal and external forces to capitalize on opportunities and minimize negative effects of the unavoidable.

The years leading up to 2015 will bring new solutions to old problems and new, unforeseen problems accompanied by the need for innovation to address them. Solving problems generated by change will increase the challenges inherent in the HR function. Dramatic shifts are ahead, resulting from combined, interdependent transformations in the workforce and technology, and compounded by the way these interact with global economics to transform businesses. These shifts will drive HR's adaptation for survival.

As we will see, the next ten years will run the gamut, from the readily predictable to bizarre futuristic technologies that impact the workforce, HR, human resources information systems (HRIS), and world economics. For example, instead of asking, "How do we become a better strategic influence?" HR professionals might be wondering how to categorize a worker whose brain, eyesight, and strength have been reinforced by biochips.

This will be the world in which HR must evolve and adapt.

The Changing Workforce

The makeup of the workforce is shifting in almost every aspect, and it will continue to do so. Significant alterations in the pool of available talent will occur both in measurable demographics and in the accompanying worker attitudes and preferences.

Demographics and the Diversification of Worker Groups

Three generations of completely diversified workers will make up the workforce over the next ten years: the baby boomers, Generation X-ers, and Generation Y-ers. Demographics—the statistical components of a given population—yield an objective worker profile going forward.

We can also form subjective conclusions based on trends. An understanding of the dynamics that have shaped each generation's perspectives will be a significant advantage for HR professionals. These generations represent the reservoir of talent upon which HR will draw: the workforce past, the workforce present, and the workforce future.

A decade-by-decade analysis reveals several age groups with distinct characteristics working together simultaneously. These groups were shaped long ago by historical influences, and both their concerns and their value to an organization evolve as they grow older. For HR to retain top performers and maximize worker productivity, each group will require different forms of management, compensation, training, and even technology. HR must also understand the needs of the new group emerging as those entering the workforce for the first time follow in the footsteps of employees currently in their twenties.

Those Born in 1950 and Earlier

These individuals, consisting of large numbers of baby boomers, grew up in a tough but stable post-war world.[2] They worked hard and expected their sacrifices to pay off in material and personal ways. Most employers of an older workforce benefit from this group's loyalty.

To enjoy the payoff from extensive overtime while they can, aging baby boomers often choose to retire early.[3] However, the next ten years will also herald the emergence of second careers. "Many see retirement as a chance to start a new career, doing work they find more exciting, interesting or stimulating than the work they have done most of their lives."[4]

Those born in 1950 and earlier will become HR's "workforce past" in the next decade. To take advantage of the long-standing base of knowledge, expertise, and experience these senior workers represent, HR must leverage its capabilities as an excellent, qualified source of contingent workers (part-timers, temporaries, contractors, and consultants). Even more importantly, HR should groom them as mentors and recruiters for younger generations. Rapid workforce change coupled with emerging new talent makes knowledge retention an issue. Long-term employees who have been storage vessels for company history and knowledge are extremely valuable for passing on their repository of information.

Those Born Between 1951 and 1960

Workers in this era are all baby boomers, representing an extensive resource. They entered the workforce with the knowledge that they were special and they had a voice. They believed that they could change the world and that hard work would lead them to the top.

The next decade will bring a maturation of the skills of these individuals. HR will do well to carefully groom them and then usher them into managerial roles. Upcoming worker shortages will create a demand for their experience in middle management and leadership positions. This is the primary age group that will shepherd tomorrow's workers. HR is responsible for thorough succession planning that develops this emerging segment as effective leaders.

Those Born Between 1961 and 1970

Upon entering the workforce, this group faced a world tumbling down. With the dissolution of the nuclear family, many workers had learned to face challenges alone. They lacked the foundation of a conventional home environment and possessed no real hero figures.

Because many of them resist strong ties to a given establishment, workers in this group will require compelling reasons for continuing to work for the same employer. Retention of top talent is crucial, and due to individualistic viewpoints of many in this age group, HR should build more flexibility and a larger array of choices into compensation and benefits programs. Work style and the structure of the work environment, along with learning and career planning opportunities, should also provide give-and-take.

Those Born in 1971 and Later

These workers seem to have found some stability, primarily based on self-reliance. Even more than those ten years ahead of them, they are tough-minded realists. Most of them are familiar with technology and open to the electronic economy of the future. Many belong to Generation Y, covered later in this section.

Conscientious career planning will benefit these individuals in the days ahead, and HR will do well to encourage their eagerness to gain knowledge and move forward. The task will be to direct their energy toward planning their careers along the lines of development and upward mobility within the organization. HR must leverage these young, talented workers by finding out what it is they want to do, then structuring a learning environment that retains them by helping them grow.

A Shifting Workforce Balance: What Demographics Indicate

The average age of the global workforce is increasing and will continue to do so over the next ten years. The baby boomers—by far the largest grouping—will, of course, age, some changing careers or remaining in the workforce later in life. Generation Y, representing a much larger group than Generation X, will provide a new wave of human capital. (See Figure 9.1.)

The rise in numbers of contingent workers has been and will continue to be overwhelming.[5] Training managers to evaluate and manage workers logging variable hours in unsupervised situations will become another challenging task for HR.

Telecommuting, where work is time-driven but no longer time-bound, is becoming more and more common. "By 2004, fully 30 percent of the workforce will telecommute. Powerful networks will keep work teams in touch around the clock. Because of shifting demographics, workers of the future will be younger and older than before. They will live in different countries and have unorthodox work arrangements. Highly mobile, they will not be wedded to one company or career as the New Economy puts a premium on the literate, the empowered, and the master of technology. It is this workforce that Human Resources must manage and satisfy."[6]

The number of women in the workforce is increasing at a faster rate than the number of men and will continue to do so until at least

**Figure 9.1. Shifts in the Numbers
and Average Age Range of Workers.**[7]

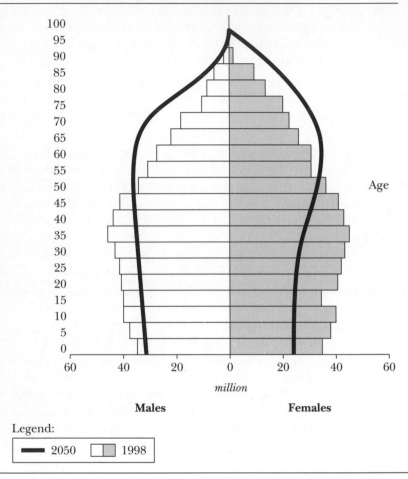

Legend:

━━━ 2050   ▢ 1998

2006, according to research by the Corporate Leadership Council. A related prediction is an increase in family-friendly benefits.[8]

With respect to cultural diversity, minorities are representing an increasing percentage of workers, Corporate Leadership Council research states.[9] It is reasonable to assume that eventually the term "minority" will disappear from the workforce. Cross-cultural communication will soon take on a life of its own.

We will see a noticeable shift to outsourcing in the next five years. As is already occurring with manufacturing, organizations will rapidly move intellectual jobs to the lowest-cost providers. Education improvements in countries like India, Poland, and China will make them low-cost producers. (We expand on this topic later in the section entitled "Impact of the Global Economy.")

Some predict that the dominant language by 2050 will be Chinese. Yet there is another language of a very different, futuristic kind vying for attention: the language of genomics. Genetic code will soon transform the economy and society.[10] We will address this topic later in this chapter in the discussion of the radical changes to be introduced by technology.

Numerous workers today have family for whom they are responsible, whether it be a spouse, children, parents, or grandparents. The number of children per family will decline, but there will be no decline in the divorce rate. There will continue to be large numbers of single people in the workforce.

For years HR has worked with the baby boomer "live-to-work" mentality. While the Generation X mindset has been "work to live," the primary emphasis of the soon-to-be workers of Generation Y will be work/life balance itself. Creating options for work/life balance will be pivotal to retaining an employer of choice in the next ten years.

According to the Corporate Leadership Council, "Maintaining an appropriate work/life balance is currently an integral element of being an employee of choice; of Fortune's '100 Best Companies to Work For' eighty-nine offer some sort of flexible working options." Trends indicate that "work-life balance initiatives will continue to grow although their emphasis may shift slightly for the future 'employer of choice'."[11]

Competition for a Diminishing Workforce

The rate at which the world population is growing is on the decline. (See Figure 9.2.) Workforce growth rates are likewise decreasing, and will do so from now until 2020.[12] "In Europe by 2010 older workers (55–64) will make up a greater percentage of the workforce than younger workers (20–29)."[13] Overall, we can foresee a drop in the number of workers, accompanied by a decline in the numbers of exemplary performers. Competition for top talent will therefore become more and more aggressive.[14]

Figure 9.2. World Population Growth Rate: 1950—2050.

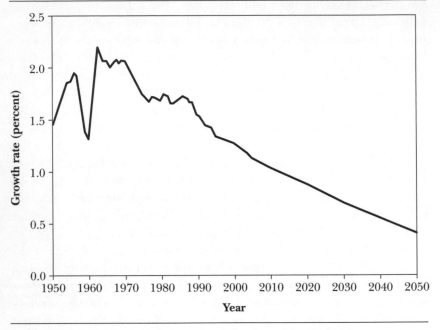

Source: U.S. Census Bureau, International Database, May 10, 2000.

Over the next decade, these older workers will be retiring or changing careers, thus moving out of the mainstream workforce. Baby boomers in particular will make an impact as they change careers for less responsibility-intensive occupations, lessen their involvement in their careers, or leave the workforce entirely. Technologically induced job creation exceeds, and will continue to exceed, workforce growth. By 2008, we'll face a shortage of ten million workers.[15]

It was only twenty-five years ago when workers would spend their entire careers with a single employer. In some industries and professions today, it is remarkable for an employer to retain an employee for two or more years. Moving from the Industrial Age to the Knowledge Age has altered the attributes HR looks for in the ideal worker and what workers want in their work environment.

Instead of seeking long-term careers with stable employers, college graduates now choose employers who will give them the most knowledge the quickest. These graduates also require flexible compensation, a fantastic work culture, and choices for work/life balance to suit their individual lifestyles.[16] "The movement of human capital around the world will be influenced by lifestyle and economic growth areas, regardless of borders, and that's a new phenomenon of the future."[17]

The HR practitioner needs to be a relentless, ever-vigilant competitor in the global war for talent. While job seekers will have increasing numbers of options, employers will struggle to design strategies to address the attraction and retention dilemma. "For every new member added to the workforce, 2.6 new jobs will be created between 2003 and 2010, Interbiznet predicts."[18]

The war for talent is clearly an ever-present battle.[19] It will become more and more ferocious in the knowledge economy, where the focus is shifted from tangible assets to intangibles such as patents and people. "We competed on quality in the 1970s, time in the 1980s, and information systems in the 1990s. In this decade we will take on the last critical dimension of competitive advantage: We will learn to compete through talent. Not just for talent— through talent."[20]

Global markets will increase the ferocity of the war for talent. For example, according to futurist James Canton, "For the first time in the United States, there's a brain drain of human capital going to Singapore and Europe for genomics research particularly around stem cells."[21] It is likely that the brain drain Canton referred to will impact all jobs and professions, not just genomics research. He also stated that "human capital will be attracted to fast-growth, high-tech centers that will be located in Africa, South America, and Asia, and not just Europe and the United States."[22]

The successful HR department of the future will leverage existing talent via succession planning and training. Proactively and aggressively securing the best people will also be important. Top performers and headcount in general will both be in high demand.

Strategies for Attracting and Retaining Employees of the Future

While HR policies and procedures will continue as grassroots HR functions, far more important will be the innovation and flexibility required to achieve and perpetuate employer-of-choice status. In light of the significant variations among generations and age groups, the HR practitioner will require know-how and insight when it comes to incentivizing, training, and creating customizable compensation packages. Making meaningful connections with each group will be critical for attraction, retention, and organizational productivity.

What will drive the employer selection process? In general, the diversified workforce of the next decade will come to work for you and stay working for you on the basis of a number of characteristics, described below.

Access to Knowledge and Technology in a Learning Environment

Top talent will not settle for working with antiquated technologies. As technology change gains momentum, an employer of choice must keep pace. The majority of desirable workers are upwardly mobile, seeking an environment of learning where they can enhance and develop their expertise, learn new skills, and take on additional responsibilities.

Such growth is also attractive because it increases the employee's earning power and future marketability. According to Walker Information, just 45 percent of employees believe that their companies care about developing people for long-term careers, while 31 percent believe they do not.[23]

People want access to knowledge. Be prepared—as you give them this access, they will want more. Workers across the globe, and Generation Y-ers in particular, are accustomed to finding close to anything they want at any time via the Internet.

Participatory Management

The worker of the future requires a voice. Organizational hierarchies have already begun to flatten and will continue to do so. Across the board, all workers of the future will desire to participate in company decision making and will prefer to be intensely involved in any form of organizational change.[24]

Total Compensation

The benefit plans of twenty-five years ago were stringent, uniform, and straightforward: everyone had the same health insurance and same retirement plan. The successful HR department of the future will further advance the existing flexible benefits environment to make customization available across all compensation, not just benefits.

Employees will work when and how they need to work, and a company will determine a worker's value according to a composite. Salaries will be defined in terms of compensation. For example, an organization might value a worker at $100,000 yearly. Payment of that amount will be discretionary, within the bounds of legality. Younger employees might include additional education in their compensation. A married employee might take some of it in childcare. Some might want parental care, deferred compensation, or early retirement. Employees will be able to take more vacation one year than another.

Flexibility in forms of compensation will be a big motivator for choosing an employer in the future. As a general rule, salaries won't necessarily be increasing, but will instead become more variable based on employee lifestyle. Just as we saw the evolution of flexible benefits in the 1970s and 1980s, that kind of flexibility will cover the entire spectrum of compensation in the years ahead.

An Attractive Corporate Culture

An organization attracts those who agree with the tenets of its culture. HR must carefully evaluate culture-related decisions as they pertain to an organization's talent requirements, as well as the needs and wants of available workers of the future. This is no small feat, as it includes baby boomers, Generation X-ers, and the up-and-coming workforce from Generation Y. All workers want to be influential in company decision making.[25]

The more clearly HR defines and propagates corporate culture across all mediums, the easier it will be to attract like-minded employees. Culture will also continue to be a key identifier for customers and suppliers. A successful organization builds a widely recognizable culture that values and treats people as primary assets and seeks employee input. As keepers of the corporate culture, HR professionals take responsibility for providing a sense of purpose, accommodating and celebrating diversity, and allowing active participation in company decisions by giving employees a voice. The extent to which an organization provides a learning environment also contributes to corporate culture, as does work/life balance.[26]

Addressing work/life balance will require flexibility in the years to come. Variations in marital status, family situations, and values among workers will demand increasing numbers of choices for adjusting this balance, because one size does not fit all.

HR has an important role to play in creating work practices for a diverse work population. Telecommuting, flextime, and part-time options, as well as PCs and entire home offices furnished by employers, are now all supported by technology that allows work to be done and decisions to be made from anywhere, any time. Therefore, HR practitioners should be creative when addressing work/life balance. Why not innovate by establishing a temporary or part-time environment in which the fifty-plus population will want to work? What about giving the new mom or dad opportunities to balance hours between work and home? Exhibit 9.1 sums up past and future characteristics of the worker, the employer, and HR practices.

A New Wave: Generation Y

When it comes to the talent shortage, will it be Generation Y to the rescue? This new wave of workers, born in 1978 and later and numbering approximately sixty million, will be entering the workforce in the next decade.

Some of them have already begun to work, following on the heels of Generation X, which is composed of those born between 1965 and 1977 and is less than one-third the size of Generation Y. Generation Y-ers are sometimes referred to as Echo Boomers or the Millennium Generation.[27] While Generation Y mainly represents the offspring of the seventy-two million baby boomers, their values and preferences are far different from their parents'. It will be HR's task to understand their perspective.

In the United States alone, one out of every four Generation Y-ers lives in a single-parent home, and 75 percent have working mothers. One-third of this diverse group is not Caucasian.[28]

Research indicates Generation Y-ers will write their own rules.[29] They anticipate having careers and plan for work/life balance and home ownership, some even while in their teens.[30] A suitable career is more important to Generation Y-ers than simply finding a job, and for an overwhelming majority of them, the rewards of job satisfaction take higher priority than monetary returns.[31]

Exhibit 9.1. The Transformation of Key HR Influences.

The Worker

Past Characteristics	Future Characteristics
Male	Female
Age 46	Age 36
Married, two children	Divorced
Baby boomer	Generation X/Generation Y
Career-oriented, loyal	Work/life balance–focused
Stable	Mobile
Ten years with one employer	Three years with one employer
Hierarchically organized	Organized by teams

The Employer

Past Characteristics	Future Characteristics
Local	Global
Office	Virtual
Stable	Nimble
Profitable	Competitive
Mechanized	Innovative
Hierarchical	Flat
Caretaker	ROI
Blue-collar compliance	Corporate governance

HR Practices

Past Characteristics	Future Characteristics
Local practices	Global practices
Hierarchical organizations	Flattened organizations
Jobs/positions	Self-directed teams
Points	Broadbands
Skills	Core competencies
Salary	Total compensation
Tactical	Strategic
Data/information	Knowledge/intelligence
Data collection/reporting	Reporting/forecasting

Source: PeopleSoft, Inc.

Familiarity with Technology and Rapid Change

HR will have Generation Y-ers entering the world of work who have never lived in a world without technology. Modern advancements such as instant messaging, DVDs, and cell phones are second nature to the majority within this group. Some were using computers in kindergarten and earlier.

Reinforcing familiarity with the electronic world is the active implementation of technology programs in schools. These initiatives give youth a running start with applying technology to the world of education and work.

"We've rapidly been exiting what could be described as a *linear culture*—a world where life, communication and education moved in streams, in sequence and in a structured order. That culture is being replaced by a *non-linear culture,* a faster-paced, more random and uncertain world where we work, live, love and learn."[32]

The Generation Y world is non-linear, running at a rapid pace and full of limitless stimuli. Generation Y-ers are accustomed to numerous concurrent sources of information. "Our culture has conditioned them to expect speed and change."[33]

Many Generation Y-ers seem to have it all as they prepare more effectively than any other generation that has to enter the workforce. Yet a number of them will lack skills HR has taken for granted in the talent pool.

A Need for Training

While Generation Y can help fill the job deficit, many will need training in specific competencies, ethics, and other work skills. While many Generation Y-ers grow up in technology-savvy environments, their comfort level with technology for academic and personal uses does not always translate smoothly to the world of work.

". . . Most high-school graduates simply lack the literacy and numeracy skills necessary to thrive in the technology-based knowledge society. The number of students pursuing and obtaining degrees in computer science and other information technology fields is plummeting. And not coincidentally, high-tech employers from Silicon Valley to NASA to government intelligence agencies are scrambling to find homegrown talent."[34]

Once they gain critical skills, the independent, individualistic, change-oriented Generation Y-ers should thrive in the world of mobile knowledge workers, role-based portals, personalization, and learning and travel opportunities.

"In an age of information and innovation, that means children must be grounded in timeless truths but prepared for constant change. Formal learning can no longer be confined to the first eighteen or twenty-one years of life. Instead, learning must become a part of life, as constant as change itself. Only those individuals, businesses, and nations capable of coping with this change and adapting to it will be able to flourish in the 21st century."[35]

Many workers today, age notwithstanding, share some Generation Y traits. In general, employees will become increasingly selective about where they work, what tasks they perform, and the kinds of compensation they receive. Generation Y challenges the status quo, and will also challenge HR in the areas of corporate culture, loyalty, recruitment, and retention.

Increasing Complexities in the Legal and Regulatory Arena

Legal and regulatory issues were related primarily to payroll, benefits, or diversity in the past. For many years HR has been involved in compliance around such regulations as the Occupational Safety and Health Act (OSHA), Employee Retirement Income Security Act (ERISA), and Health Insurance Portability and Accountability Act of 1996 (HIPAA). These are examples of regulations specific to the United States, and comparable laws extend throughout the world. Country-specific rules and regulations, Workers' Compensation issues, payroll tax filing and reporting, and more all represent responsibilities that will continue as basic HR functions.

However, the Enron debacle expanded HR's function to include responsibility for compliance in the executive ranks. There is a plethora of new rules focusing on corporate governance and accountability for upper management. The United States' Sarbanes-Oxley Act (SOX) is a case in point. While many consider SOX to be primarily financially oriented, HR must track reporting hierarchies, authority, roles, responsibilities, positions, and titles. Compliance with SOX also means tightened requirements and increased levels of detail and accuracy in upper management reports. HR must now work closely with upper management to conduct strict tracking and sign-off procedures.

Corporate malfeasance is a global phenomenon, and SOX is only one country's reaction. Most importantly, SOX and similar acts are not the end of regulation at the executive level. As the legal and regulatory police—both blue collar and corporate—HR can expect additional legislation along similar lines in the future.

The need for vigilance will also increase due to globalization, which multiplies the variety and number of compliance areas. Each country or region has different laws. As we will see in the next section on technology, the role-based nature of a portal is very effective for delineating laws and regulations that apply to a specific worker in any given region.

The Impact of Technological Innovation

Technological change has shaped HR dramatically over the years, and will continue to do so at increasing speeds. Possibilities we can hardly imagine today might well be commonplace by 2010.

Technology: Building Momentum

Like a jumbo airliner gathering speed as it takes off from the runway, technology has been changing faster and faster—and there's no end in sight. History tells part of the story, and developments waiting in the wings indicate a quickening of technological change with each generation. If for twenty-five years we used the mainframe and in the next ten years jumped to client/server architecture, only to find it replaced by Internet applications, what's next? Will every new technology have half the shelf life of the last one?

Developments came slowly at first. The mainframe era lasted close to twenty-five years before the introduction of dumb terminals and the mid-sized computer. These early systems were mainly batch-oriented, and HR leveraged them for certain financial functions such as payroll to help ease the burden of routine administration activities. The application software industry in itself was still in its infancy in the late 1960s, but as the personal computer (PC) gave rise to client/server architecture, HR soon began to realize the benefits of computerization. Networked systems and intranet/Internet applications yielded vast benefits in the form of self-service, analytics, and other collaborative functions.

HR processes readily evolved as technology ramped up, and innovative applications from the HRMS community appeared to fill HR's demand for specialized advancements in such areas as e-recruiting and e-performance applications. The goal: automating the end-to-end HR business process to drive productivity through HCM.

The visual portrayal of paradigm shifts in technology in Figure 9.3 shows how each leading technology is maximally useful for a short period before its peak drops off as another technology moves in to replace it.

The HR Technologist

During the host era, the primary user of HR and all other systems was the IT professional. Technology evolved, and the primary user during the client/server era became the departmental user—in HR's case, it became HR staff. As more and more organizations move to the Internet economy, for the first time HR technology is appearing on the desktop of every employee.

Technology is now an integral part of any business and will be increasingly indispensable over the next decade. The HR practitioner therefore must become a technologist to effectively leverage innovation and bring about measurable productivity improvements

Figure 9.3. Technology Marches Onward.[36]

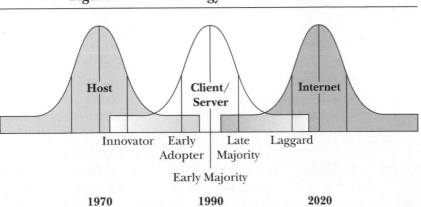

from it. Just as an engineer, CIO, or operations manager wields technology as a regular component of the job, to thrive in tomorrow's corporate world HR must regard technology as second nature, a tool of the trade. From becoming a formidable contender in the war for talent to leveraging analytics that help drive corporate strategy, HR professionals of the future must fully understand and actively exploit technological advancements to be competitive.

Rise of the Knowledge Worker

"Through 2007, progressive enterprises will formalize strategic planning, architecture, standardization, platforms, and support structures, resulting in a cohesive set of enterprise-wide application and infrastructure services. A critical subset of these infrastructure services will target knowledge workers and organizational productivity needs."[37] Architecture efforts around knowledge workers are predicted to mature through 2007.[38]

With the Internet as the foundational delivery mechanism for company information, HR systems will expand to embrace participation by every employee. Technology will enable employees to own larger and larger portions of the HR process as portals and related collaborative systems become integral to every HR infrastructure.

Technology is under continuous transformation, becoming smarter, cheaper, easier to use, and less structured. As this occurs, the working environment will also evolve to become more and more about the access of knowledge. We are moving into an information-intensive world where knowledge is accessible by all and continuous learning and knowledge retention are critical.

Studies by the Hudson Institute underscore the influence of the Knowledge Era on the workforce. "Consider how 20th-century conceptions of career and time have already begun to collapse. Yesterday, workers in industrial economies went to school from the age of 5 to 18, earned vocational certificates or degrees from 19 to 25, paid their dues from 25 to 35, rose through the ranks from 35 to 50, ascended to senior levels of management and business ownership from 50 to 65, and then retired. But in a knowledge-based society, workers will go to school throughout their careers, rise and fall within multiple organizations, work in virtual offices for virtual organizations, and be productive well beyond the age of 65."[39]

Highly structured data environments of the past have given workers only a small percentage of the knowledge that they actually need for optimization. The available knowledge has been segregated and scattered across written materials, data-storage systems, information accessible electronically, and third-party sources.

The Internet, coupled with supporting technologies such as sophisticated document management systems and telephony, now opens the door to accessing unstructured data. We're adding voice clips, text, and more to make information not only acceptable but easily digestible.

Designing portals that are increasingly intelligent will result in more advanced use of the Internet, thus boosting the agility of the knowledge worker. For example, the more often a user interacts online with Amazon.com, the more the site "knows" about that person. With every order, Amazon.com's system learns more about a person's style, tastes, and preferences, making correlations between past purchases and available merchandise. The system itself suggests new items to purchase and takes advantage of cross-selling opportunities without human intervention.

The same will be true of HR systems. The more people use online information via a portal, the more data portal systems will gather about how well various types of individuals digest that information. Portals that incorporate languages such as XML and intelligent self-service will identify for HR professionals whether a person is left- or right-brained, whether HR should deliver training interactively or establish a mentoring program, what kind of incentives are appropriate for workers in a given country and cultural environment, and so on.

Knowledge workers will have fingertip access to anything they need to do their jobs. Material will be customized and digestible for each individual in the form of better, cheaper, faster, and easier technology as HR pushes out role-based information in precisely the right way. Intelligent self-service and portals will provide just-in-time knowledge in a form that fits a given person's work style.

As we will see later in the chapter, future technologies resulting from cognitive science and studies of the human brain will bring enhancements to the workforce that reshape the way HR addresses training and learning for the knowledge worker.[40]

The Near Future in Technology

As we step into the technology of the future, our view encompasses what's just around the corner: more widespread use of collaborative technologies and the interchangeability of collaborative tools. Ubiquitous computing leads us to the edge of what we can currently grasp.

The Collaborative, Connected Enterprise

The technology of the future will be both collaborative and connected. We can see the first hints of this as greater numbers of companies implement pure-Internet systems that allow collaboration among employees, customers, and suppliers.

Increasingly widespread use of intelligent self-service is imminent. Also called smart self-service, this indispensable collaborative HR tool—best administered through a portal—integrates content and analytics and filters information based on a user's role. The result is secure access to material as well as improved decision making. The portal recognizes an individual's role, work styles, and preferences and supplies quick access to material required for task completion.

Intelligent self-service via an employee portal means just-in-time information delivery to the knowledge worker. Portal delivery will become increasingly personalized and customizable, furthering training initiatives via intuitive learning.

The near future will also bring increased use of HR scorecards that are coupled with workforce analytics and decision trees. A convergent business model will drive transaction processing, and we'll be seeing increases in process automation and the use of online analytical processing (OLAP) for processing raw data.

Collaborative systems turn data into organizational intelligence so many people can work together on a common task, problem, or issue. Collaboration integrates both internal and third-party content, transactions, and analytics with back-office applications. The entire collaborative enterprise is connected via an intranet or the Internet. HR applications specifically designed for collaboration are XML-based for Internet systems integration. Ideally, information is available company-wide through a portal that maintains data security by revealing only the material authorized by a user's role upon sign-on. To be effective, collaborative systems draw data from a single location: a data warehouse that provides timely, accurate information to all users.

The collaborative, connected enterprise of the future will provide the workforce with higher and higher percentages of all available knowledge in increasingly palatable, individualized forms. As a result, we will see better and more rapid decision making across those organizations whose HR departments are wielding collaborative technology effectively.

Interchangeability of Devices

The future will undoubtedly bring faster and cheaper access to accurate real-time HR information. Data access tools will be interchangeable for HR staff and the rest of the workforce. We can already see this happening as innovative enhancements to telephony, video, email, and fax are making collaboration easier and increasingly convenient. These and other communication tools are blending to the point where it is increasingly simple to convert one to the other.

For example, advancements in wireless technology will soon integrate phone, handhelds such as personal digital assistants (PDAs), and personal computers. The mobile communication world will encompass a wider and wider range of computing devices and capabilities. Voice activation and automated answers will be increasingly sophisticated to the point that they will be a more acceptable customer service offering.

Systems turn voice into text and convert text to knowledge that is made available across networks. Interactive media makes collaboration almost second nature.

The worker of the future will be able to work anywhere, any time—and on any device. This represents both good news and bad news for the HR professional. Employees interested in true work/life balance will have more options and more control. They'll be able to work where it's convenient for them to work, and strongly motivated employees can become maximally efficient. For example, a two-hour commute will translate into two hours spent working from home or at another convenient location, and if one happens to lack access to electricity or wired networks, satellite will be an easy alternative.

The bad news is that the workaholic will now have access to work twenty-four hours a day. There are always individuals who are not good at balancing work and day-to-day life. When people are able to work all the time, some workers will abuse the situation and suffer from burnout. Other bad news comes in the form of unexpected workloads for HR because employees can work at varying times. This means no quiet time for HR anymore.

As collaborative options meld, we will see the resulting ubiquitous access create great improvements in employee effectiveness and efficiency. Ubiquitous computing will blur the boundaries we now see as walls and lead the way toward startling developments in the future.

Bizarre But Likely: Radical Changes

In the past, people made things in a manufacturing-centric economy. Now people service things and other people in today's knowledge-centric economy.[41] As the dynamics of the Knowledge Age point toward increasing emphasis on human capital, we face the likelihood of technologically enhanced humans and biologically enhanced robotics—perhaps not in the coming decade, but likely before we're prepared. Unfortunately, people can only see technology as far out as they can touch it.

The ongoing challenge for HR will be balancing the use of technologies with the variability inherent in the human element.[42] As lines become blurred, HR must also distinguish between the two.

In *Technofutures: How Leading-Edge Technology Will Transform Business in the 21st Century,* Dr. James Canton combines research and little-known facts of the technologically feasible with imaginative exploration of future realities. Founder of the Institute of Global Futures,[43] Canton describes what he calls the four Power Tools that together will drive future change: computers, networks, biotech, and nanotech.[44]

Computers[45]

Computers of the future will become intelligent agents that make decisions and deliver information to workers on demand. Reduced in size, systems will be far more powerful, intuitive, and interactive.

Canton even sees the computer becoming a close model of the human brain.

Computers already dwarf the efficiencies of human-run processes. Onboard computers manage aircraft flights and recommend action in threatening conditions. Computerized data mining and analytic functions recommend online purchases and help make business decisions. The list goes on. Reliance on computers to manage and improve on functions customarily performed by humans will increase as computers provide valued extensions of human faculties and boost organizational productivity.

The computer-in-a-shoe and a mouse that reads emotions already exist. By 2015, some scientists predict that microchips will be embedded not only in appliances, but in clothes and human hearts and brains. It's possible that in many instances computers will think with and for people. The highly functional computers of the future—robots—will be able to see, hear, smell, taste, touch, and talk. Computers are beginning to embody the dream of artificial intelligence.[46]

Software is critical in and of itself. "Software may be the digital cognitive glue that makes this emerging intelligent infrastructure of commerce work. It means now that what I can do as a human, I can do so much more with the right software tied to the right infrastructure that's tied to the right on-demand global supply chain for products or services."[47]

Cognitive software can help maximize the capabilities and productivity of a workforce increasingly limited in numbers.[48] "The next generation of cognitive software will help us make decisions faster, make connections faster, and build networks and supply chains. The task will be to enable companies to build tools so human beings can multiply their capability set. That change will occur by 2020."[49] Transformations in cognitive software will bring an additional HR challenge: integrating the technology in a way that empowers, instead of threatens, workers.

Networks[50]

Earlier we mentioned the upcoming interchangeability of telephony, video, email, and fax. The convergence of the Internet, digital TV, and various wireless communication devices will incorporate communication technologies into a network of networks that will transform the way the world does business.

This vibrant network system is already in the making. Every ninety days, the size of the Internet doubles, and by 2005 more than one billion people will have online access. Wide ranges of consumers on the Internet will provide expanded opportunities for e-business. The highly efficient virtual supply chains of e-business will connect the manufacturing supply chain right to the customer or end user. As early as 2005, e-business might be generating in excess of $2 trillion in revenues around the globe.[51]

Human capital strategists must balance the corporation's struggle to compete in e-business with the basic human need for rest, coupled with computers' tireless capability of working nonstop.[52]

Biotech[53]

The revolutionary manipulation of DNA to redefine human life, health, and science, biotech uses the microchip to advance gene research. The biotechnology industry creates biochips, which resemble the integrated circuits of a PC but incorporate portions of DNA. Biochips placed in analytical instrumentation sharply reduce the time and costs involved in biochemical experimentation.

As scientists increase their understanding of the human genome, affordable analytic tools based on biochips will help physicians predict, diagnose, and custom-treat illnesses. The computer world will boost translation of human genetics to make people healthier and increase life expectancy. We will see smart drugs, implants and innovative medical devices, and bio-engineered food as better medical care becomes commonplace.[54]

The HR practitioner must be prepared for the possibilities of an artificially enhanced workforce. "Cognitive science and HR have not become friends, and part of the reason they haven't become friends is that we have not invested in this science and know very little about it," stated Canton in an interview. "Some people may be enhanced in the future by having actual devices at the nano scale embedded in their brains to give them advanced capabilities they need for their jobs." Such capabilities might include total recall memory or the ability to download and learn several spoken languages in an afternoon. However, given advanced future research surrounding cognitive science and the human brain, "We may be able to create new kinds of learning, human capital enhancement tools, and education to help people acquire the same types of capabilities without having to have invasive or synthetic augmentation."[55]

Nanotech[56]

The fourth of Canton's Power Tools, nanotechnology refers to extremely minute, atomic-level engineering. To grasp this radical, hardly imaginable phenomenon, consider television's *Star Trek*, in which the mechanical race called Borg powers and controls drones.

Industry leaders such as IBM, Lucent, and Sun, in company with scientists from well-respected institutions—MIT, Cal Tech, and NASA, for example—apply extensive resources toward nanotechnology. Their efforts to develop equipment one-thousandth of the diameter of a human hair might one day result in injecting machines into the bloodstream for such purposes as attacking cancer cells. These infinitesimal machines could also rearrange atoms to create food, energy, steel, and water.[57]

Is this science fiction? After all, it was only a little more than one hundred years ago when Henry Ford first introduced his horseless carriage to the world in 1896. In light of technology's quantum leaps in the last forty years, the ideas outlined from Canton's work—as well as numerous others' predictions—could easily become day-to-day reality.[58] Our focus on the next decade of HR points to awareness and preparedness, while at the same time we continue to deal effectively with concrete issues we face in the present.

Security Redefined

Technology is transforming and perfecting itself, taking on a life of its own. Paradoxically, as much as we desire to be connected, we're also creating an entire body of technology simply to help us remain separate. The Internet in particular has given rise to the concept of data privacy. Powerful steps are being taken in the security space to make sure people, organizations, and political entities only reach information they have the right to see. From an international standpoint, privacy is an extremely complex issue.[59]

Certainly security will continue to be an issue—for a while. By 2015, however, computing will be so ubiquitous that security will almost become a non-issue due to its impossibility. Implications for HR are again in the form of both good news and bad news. The good news is that, as an HR professional, you will have access to almost limitless information about everything. The bad news is that others will also have access to a lot of information about you and your company.

Impact of the Global Economy

Hudson Institute's book, *Workforce 2020*, emphasizes that growth in the economy hinges on "a vibrant workforce, and the vibrant workforce of the future would be shaped by new technologies, openness to immigration, training and education, and liberal trade policies."[60]

Globalization is propelling us to the point where the diverse workforce, worksite flexibility, and technology will make immaterial the actual location where work is accomplished. One direct result of this development is that e-business will move outsourcing to the forefront in the next ten years.[61] Organizations of all sizes will be global.

However, future trends in outsourcing herald something very different from just letting a specialized firm handle payroll. Outsourcing might involve processes, talent, content, development, manufacturing, or an entire department. Some might be competency-, time-, or finance-driven. Technology's speed of change will increase the attractiveness of outsourcing of all kinds because of the difficulty of keeping current with the latest innovations that boost competitive advantage.

From a technology standpoint, outsourcing will be transparent because all a worker requires is a browser and an Internet connection. Work will occur from anywhere, any time—and from anybody. HR will be responsible for the virtual mobile worker in a virtual global workplace full of telecommuters, contractors, contingent workers, and more.

The cultural aspects of globalization are the most difficult. HR professionals must be experts at bridging cultural diversity gaps and making sure worksites in each location do not become isolated. Active communication and collaboration should transcend distance and time zones.

The employee portal represents a critical tool for managing international worker populations. Role-based collaboration via a portal will become increasingly valuable as HR addresses workers of varying cultures and culture-based motivations. Portals will handle multilingual applications and translation issues on the fly.

When it comes to fluctuating worldwide economic conditions, HR will need to be aware and nimble. The growth of e-business and its powerful impact on both the global economy and the nature of competition is a case in point, forcing HR to either capitalize on opportunities or sink beneath them. As always, the forward-thinking HR practitioner must master the skill of leveraging analytics to maximize employee productivity in times of scarcity or plenty. We have seen how economic boom and bust—such as the rise and fall of the dot-com era—drives corporate decision making. The faster an HR department can arrive at intelligent business responses to external and internal variables, the healthier an organization will be as it rides the waves of change.

From Tangibles to Intangibles

Today, only 15 percent of our resources are tangible, represented by easily quantifiable equipment, products, and plants. A whopping 85 percent of our assets are intangible: knowledge capital and people.[62]

If we looked back fifty years, we'd find that statistic to be just about the opposite. However, throughout these years, we've seen no change in our accounting practices, which were developed for tangible asset accounting. HR must look for better ways to account for intangible assets, emphasizing the entire people side of the business.[63]

We categorize the difference between total market value and book value as intangible assets. Figure 9.4 shows the scope of those assets.

Intangible Assets

"Behind the tremendous productivity improvements enabled by information technology are the people who do all of the knowing, building, planning, collaborating, executing, supporting, and competing." While executives understand a cost focus, it does not

Figure 9.4. The Intellectual Capital Model.

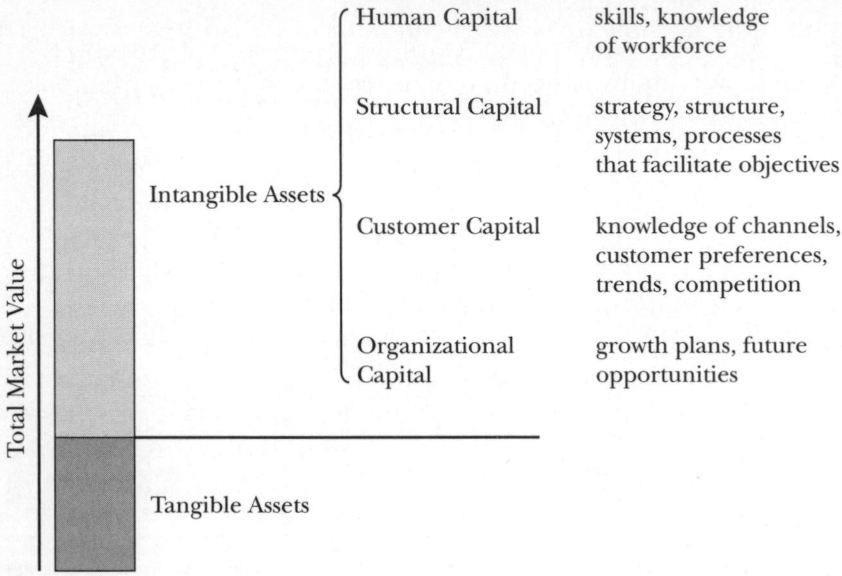

Human Capital — skills, knowledge of workforce

Structural Capital — strategy, structure, systems, processes that facilitate objectives

Customer Capital — knowledge of channels, customer preferences, trends, competition

Organizational Capital — growth plans, future opportunities

Intangible Assets

Tangible Assets

Total Market Value

Copyright © 2004 PeopleSoft.

account for the dynamics of people. Human capital is the key strategic factor that drives the return on all tangible capital investments.[64]

In the next decade, people will become the most critical part of an organization's intangible assets. HR therefore must adapt its financial practices to the unprecedented: accounting for intangibles.

Future employees will plan on staying with an employer for only about three years. Unless HR can retain a worker, that person becomes a very fleeting intangible asset. The successful HR practitioner will become extremely skilled at identifying true talent and increasing the amount of time those particular people want to stay with the company. This has extensive monetary implications due to the high cost of hiring or replacing top performers.[65] An updated financial system will clearly account for the fact that the practice of retaining the best workers and turning over non-performers does have bottom-line implications.

Technology and Intangibles: A Balance

We've looked at the tremendous power of technology to propel us forward. However advanced technology becomes, it is and will be limited in its ability to accommodate for the ambiguity inherent in organizations driven by the unpredictable: human beings. In his article "Hard Systems, Soft Systems: New Challenges for Twenty-First Century HR Systems, Stakeholders, and Vendors," Bob Stambaugh elaborates on this ambiguity and the importance of the quality of life as well as systems quality.[66]

Our good news/bad news predictions for the future underscore the necessity of embracing the realities of intangibles. The good news is that we have much better technology at our fingertips than we did twenty-five years ago. The bad news? Technology is changing so quickly that we have difficulty keeping up with it. HR must be smarter than technology when it comes to the variability of the intangible.

Stambaugh outlines eight criteria that distinguish between the requirements of what he appropriately calls the structured world (technologically supported and quantifiable processes) and the unstructured world of intangible assets, where quality of life is paramount. To summarize:

- Identifying distinct functions and addressing them with stakeholders in isolation detracts from effective holistic systems thinking.
- Variability promotes longevity, and too much specialization leaves organizations vulnerable to destruction. HR must standardize with caution because the greater the human component, the greater the need for flexibility.
- Human capital often means disorder of a necessary kind. HRIS should support structure in some key areas but keep an open space for questioning, creativity, and the overall nurturing of human capital.
- Because measurable goals can be meaningless by the time HR realizes them, HR must abandon rigid strategies in favor of strategizing, scenario planning, and incorporating flexible processes. Extrapolating from metrics mainly works with the tangible and stable.

- HR and HRIS must consciously but informally foster a culture of collaboration for the sharing of ideas in an arena meaningful to all employees, not only to management systems.
- Advanced HR reporting of the future will involve storytelling, a comprehensive, big-picture communication tool that frees executives from the distraction of detail and helps them combine their experience with intuition for decision making.
- Boundaries are still important when eliminating silos. To avoid the destruction of critical but perhaps hidden intangible assets, HR and HRIS must carefully assess the full impact of structural changes on all aspects of the workplace and preserve limits when necessary.
- In a healthy system, change will be evident everywhere. Too much stability indicates sickness, or at best, a lack of growth.[67]

The Practical Side of the Future: HR as an Anchor

HR functions have long been the backbone of every organization. This is true whether or not they have been acknowledged as such.

Changing Roles and Delegation

HR professionals are accustomed to wearing many hats—and this chapter has shown that the HR role is not becoming any simpler. Amidst workforce and technology changes, HR organizations will be extremely valuable as a consistent force that guides the adaptation to change, like quality shocks and good steering on an automobile. However, HR practitioners must be careful to manage their time and energy efficiently amidst the increasing complexities of their role.

HR also faces the organizational challenge caused by resistance to change. For example, certain managers can only manage what they can see, creating a backlash in the face of efforts to collaborate and innovate. HR must be prepared for this.

The often-discussed shift from record-keeper and administrator to strategic business partner will become a reality as long as it is a shift HR embraces. HR must change its own self-image. HR practitioners should begin seeing themselves as the main organizational infrastructure and view workers as valued intangible assets. HR will focus on building processes and HR practices that align managers and employees with the overall goals and objectives of the organization.

Becoming a true business partner is also about implementing best practices. These involve building an infrastructure that makes the right information available to the right people, building an employer-of-choice environment, creating compensation structures that are competitive and enticing, finding innovative ways to retain talent, and more. To the extent that it is possible, HR practitioners will become predictors of the future as they examine competencies the organization will require and conduct workforce planning and optimization. Measuring the impact of these activities will also continue to belong to HR.

Looking into a future fraught with upheaval, some have questioned whether HR will continue to exist. It certainly will—if HR attends to the responsibilities outlined here. The HR department that stays back-office operational will be the one that is outsourced.

Although HR might retain the connotation of being strictly a department, we're moving to a blended environment where everyone who has responsibility for a worker also has ownership of human capital. More and more, HR professionals will be delegating specific activities to line managers. It will be the line managers who perform many functions previously assigned only to HR, such as hiring, managing performance, and assigning access to knowledge.

Additional Recommendations for the HR Practitioner

Today, the access to technology is phenomenal. Things we never dreamed of twenty-five years ago we can now do quite easily. For example, we can bring together information from many sources into one cohesive portal that is acceptable by all employees. This is a massive shift, and it occurred just in the last ten years. Think of what the advantages of the next ten years can bring. (See Exhibit 9.2, a prediction from PeopleSoft.)

Can fallible human beings keep up with mercurial technological changes? HR must continually address the balance between technological structures and the human element. The practical, people side of business has never been an exact science. At the end of the day, HR will and must do what needs to be done, moving forward within the bounds of systems and people.

Exhibit 9.2. Workforce Technology in the Next Decade.

Based on information provided by HR data and driven by embedded knowledge and analytics, increasingly sophisticated portals will vastly improve the level of personalization by role and by individual. Available in multimedia from anywhere on any kind of device, the portal that we envision will recognize individual users and enable collaboration that makes business activities second-nature. These same portals will transport corporate culture to workers at their virtual locations across the globe.

Technology will drive increased worker autonomy, opening up new worlds of self-management for employees and contingent workers. The following types of changes will be in evidence:

- Portals will recognize an individual's role and preferences and supply quick access to material required for task completion.
- Self-service will be taken to the next generation: highly filtered, incredibly intuitive, and extremely easy to understand and use.
- Self-management will impact managerial and supervisory roles, changing the face of the job-role landscape as managers assume more HR responsibilities and HR takes on more business functions.
- A worker's portal will cater directly to the way that the individual likes to receive information and learning based on his or her work patterns, such as left-brained or right-brained learning styles and self-directed or mentored work styles.
- Multimedia will enable workers/managers to speak, touch, or type in questions and receive coaching, counseling, and knowledge tailored to their particular work styles.
- The personalized portal will provide only viable options and relevant material while suggesting choices in a manner similar to the way Amazon.com began doing when it set its e-business standard in the early Internet era.
- Content from external sources will be integrated with transactions. For example, benefits enrollment will link to relevant directories, training enrollment will link to relevant learning programs, jobs listings will link to relevant candidates, and so on.
- Training will be minimized, and most learning will occur while tasks are already in process via intuitive prompts driven by integrated content and analytics.

Exhibit 9.2. Workforce Technology in the Next Decade, Cont'd.

- Workers will use portal technology to help analyze their own degree of effectiveness and efficiency.
- Workers will be able to download just-in-time corporate, product, cultural, or language information as needed for specialized job functions.
- Robotics will handle a number of routine tasks, such as mail delivery and many blue-collar assembly-line jobs. Further dynamics will emerge as organizations introduce bionics into robotics.

Source: PeopleSoft.

HR will continue to adeptly interpret, cushion, and leverage powerful upcoming developments to effectively respond to change while advancing the productivity of human capital. In doing so, HR assumes the responsibility for being a backbone of stability that anchors the world of work.

"When things slow down a bit I'll get to this" is a common statement, but things are never going to slow down. We need to figure out how to get things done now—because the world of work will only change more quickly in the future.

HR practitioners must be better at understanding employees and delivering information to them. Here are a few more tips on the practical side:

- Learn how to measure the impact of people on the bottom line.
- Learn how to communicate the impact of your human capital to management.
- Develop practices that are in alignment with the overall goals and objectives of the organization.
- Be the owners of your corporate culture.
- Don't be afraid to delegate to line managers certain tactical tasks and responsibilities formerly associated only with HR.
- Don't be afraid to be strategic.

"The critical asset of the 21st century is knowledge. The critical skill is adapting quickly to change. The secret is learning—learning to adapt to a new digital economy will be the most strategic weapon of the next millennium. Adapting to the changing technology, the changing customers, the changing products and services, and the changing rules of the digital economy is *necessary*. Digital Darwinism means the end of companies stuck in the Industrial Age."[68]

This is the most exciting time in the history of HR and human capital because the world today is about knowledge. We have shifted into a knowledge economy where the primary asset in all organizations is human capital, HR's domain. Regardless of what organizations will call the HR department in the future, HR has the potential to be the owner of the intangible asset world, the owner of corporate culture as it relates to the human domain.

Organizations of the future will be human-capital-asset driven, and those that leverage best practices in the HR discipline will be leaders, not laggers. For HR professionals, the challenge is to step up to that leadership role.

Notes

1. Darwin, C. *The Origin of the Species.* New York: Macmillan, 1962. (Originally published 1859.)
2. Those of the baby boomer generation, 72 million strong, were born between 1946 and 1964.
3. In her article "2020: A Look at HR Technology in the Next 20 Years," PeopleSoft fellow Row Henson included a discussion of changes in the workforce. *IHRIM Journal,* June 2000, *IV*(2), pp. 8–12.
4. Moore, D. [www.dianemoore.com]. "Baby boomers redefining their 'golden years.'" *Toronto Star,* November 4, 2003.
5. Joseph H. Boyett of Boyett & Associates supports this assertion with respect to the United States in his discussion of workforce trends at www2.msstate.edu/~dd1/Boyett.htm.
6. Henson, R. "Human Resources in 2020: Managing the Bionic Workforce." *Benefits & Compensation Solutions,* 2001.
7. "Attracting and Retaining Your Human Assets: A Look at the Recruiting Dilemma." A PeopleSoft, Inc., white paper. Pleasanton, CA: PeopleSoft, November 2000, p. 5.
8. *Forecasting the U.S. Workforce and Workplace of the Future.* Corporate Leadership Council, Literature Review. Washington, DC: Corporate Executive Board, March 1999, p. 6.
9. Ibid., p. 5.
10. "Genomics will Transform Economy and Society." The Conference Board of Canada, news release, November 21, 2003. Juan Enriquez,

chairman and CEO of Biotechonomy and former director of the Life Sciences Project at Harvard Business School, emphasized that human capital is of primary importance in the knowledge economy. Genomics (the language of genetic code) will have a revolutionary impact on numerous industries. The biggest future challenge will be regulation.

11. *The Employer of Choice of the Future.* Corporate Leadership Council, Literature Review. Washington, DC: Corporate Executive Board, November 2000, p. 7.
12. Lange, M. "Human Capital Management: Strategies and Technology for Competitive Advantage." *Heads Count: An Anthology for the Competitive Enterprise.* Pleasanton, CA: PeopleSoft Inc., 2003, p. 337. The book, published by PeopleSoft with the assistance of printer/binder Edwards Brothers, Inc., combines articles from prominent thought leaders in HR disciplines. Mark Lange's article provides this and other related statistics from the U.S. Bureau of Labor Statistics (BLS) and The Towers Perrin Talent Report 2001.
13. *The Employer of Choice of the Future,* Corporate Leadership Council, p. 4.
14. Henson, R. "HR in the 21st Century: Challenges and Opportunities." *Heads Count: An Anthology for the Competitive Enterprise.* Pleasanton, CA: PeopleSoft, Inc., 2003, p. 257.
15. Lange, M. "Human Capital Management: Strategies and Technology for Competitive Advantage," p. 337. Sources: U.S. Bureau of Labor Statistics (BLS) and The Towers Perrin Talent Report 2001.
16. Henson, R. "2020: A Look at HR Technology in the Next 20 Years."
17. Futurist James Canton, Ph.D., as interviewed by PeopleSoft fellow Row Henson, January 21, 2004.
18. *Future Labor Market Trends.* Corporate Leadership Council, Literature Key Findings. Washington, DC: Corporate Executive Board, May 2003, p. 1.
19. Lange, M. "Human Capital Management: Strategies and Technology for Competitive Advantage," p. 337. Lange refers to a survey by McKinsey & Co. (*The War for Talent*).
20. Lange, M. "Human Capital Management: Strategies and Technology for Competitive Advantage," p. 355.
21. Futurist James Canton, Ph.D., as interviewed by PeopleSoft fellow Row Henson, January 21, 2004.
22. Ibid.
23. Walker Information. *The Walker Loyalty Report: Loyalty and Ethics in the Workplace.* September 2003. Statistic cited in M. Lange, "Human Capital Management: Strategies and Technology for Competitive Advantage," p. 339.
24. Henson, R. "HR in the 21st Century: Challenges and Opportunities," p. 253.

25. Ibid.

26. Ibid.

27. "Generation Y." *BusinessWeek Online, BusinessWeek* magazine cover story. www.businessweek.com/1999/99_07/b3616001.htm]. February 15, 1999.

28. Ibid.

29. Futurist James Canton, Ph.D., as interviewed by PeopleSoft fellow Row Henson, January 21, 2004.

30. Ibid.

31. Dunne, N. "The New Kid in Town." *Financial Times,* August 1, 2003.

32. Piotrowski, T. "Connect the Dots." Center for Parent/Youth Understanding (CPYU). [www.cpyu.org/pageview.asp?pageid=8121]

33. Ibid.

34. "About Hudson's Beyond Workforce 2020." Hudson Institute. [www.beyondworkforce2020.org/index.cfm?fuseaction=about_detail]

35. Ibid.

36. This illustration extrapolates from a drawing on p. 19 of *Inside the Tornado* by Geoffrey A. Moore (New York: HarperCollins, 1995). Mr. Moore's drawing shows the first two of the three bell-shaped curves.

37. Gotta, M. "Knowledge Worker Infrastructure: FAQs." Meta Group, *Delta 2681,* December 22, 2003.

38. Gotta, M. Meta Group, May 2004.

39. "About Hudson's Beyond Workforce 2020." [www.beyondworkforce 2020.org/index.cfm?fuseaction=about_detail]

40. Futurist James Canton, Ph.D., as interviewed by PeopleSoft fellow Row Henson, January 21, 2004.

41. Lev, B. "Intangibles: Management, Measurement, and Reporting." The Brookings Institution, June 30, 2001.

42. Stambaugh, B. "Hard Systems, Soft Systems: New Challenges for Twenty-First Century HR Systems, Stakeholders, and Vendors." *Heads Count: An Anthology for the Competitive Enterprise.* Pleasanton, CA: PeopleSoft, Inc., 2003, p. 108.

43. The Institute for Global Futures website is located at www.future guru.com.

44. Canton, J. *Technofutures: How Leading-Edge Technology Will Transform Business in the 21st Century.* Carlsbad, CA: Hay House, Inc., 1999, pp. 9–13. The Power Tools discussion also incorporates elements from Henson's article "2020: A Look at HR Technology in the Next 20 Years."

45. The material in this section is taken from Row Henson, "2020: A Look at HR Technology in the Next 20 Years," as well as Row Henson's book review "Technofutures: How Leading-Edge Technology Will Transform Business in the 21st Century, by James Canton, Ph.D."

(*IHRIM Link,* April/May 2000, pp. 62–63.) Canton covers this topic on p. 11 of *Technofutures.*

46. Ibid.
47. Futurist James Canton, Ph.D., as interviewed by PeopleSoft fellow Row Henson, January 21, 2004.
48. Ibid.
49. Ibid.
50. Henson addresses this material in "2020: A Look at HR Technology in the Next 20 Years" and the book review "Technofutures: How Leading-Edge Technology Will Transform Business in the 21st Century, by James Canton, Ph.D." Canton covers this topic on pp. 11–12 of *Technofutures.*
51. Ibid.
52. Henson also addresses this in "Human Resources in 2020: Managing the Bionic Workforce."
53. Henson addresses this material in "2020: A Look at HR Technology in the Next 20 Years" and the book review "Technofutures: How Leading-Edge Technology Will Transform Business in the 21st Century, by James Canton, Ph.D." Canton covers this topic on p. 12 of *Technofutures.*
54. Ibid.
55. Futurist James Canton, Ph.D., as interviewed by PeopleSoft fellow Row Henson, January 21, 2004.
56. Henson addresses this material in "2020: A Look at HR Technology in the Next 20 Years" and the book review "Technofutures: How Leading-Edge Technology Will Transform Business in the 21st Century, by James Canton, Ph.D." Canton covers this topic on p. 13 of *Technofutures.*
57. Ibid.
58. Recommended additional reading on the technology of the future: Joseph H. Boyett and Jimmie T. Boyett (contributor). *Beyond Workplace 2000: Essential Strategies for the New Corporation.* New York: Plume, 1996.
59. For more information, please see "Data Protection—A Global Challenge." A PeopleSoft, Inc., white paper. Pleasanton, CA: PeopleSoft, March 2001.
60. "About Hudson's Beyond Workforce 2020." Hudson Institute. [www.beyondworkforce2020.org/index.cfm?fuseaction=about_detail]
61. Henson, R. "Human Resources in 2020: Managing the Bionic Workforce."
62. Lev, B. "Intangibles: Management, Measurement, and Reporting."
63. Henson, R. "HR in the 21st Century: Challenges and Opportunities," p. 263.

64. Lange, M. "Human Capital Management: Strategies and Technology for Competitive Advantage," p. 335.
65. Henson substantiates this with a quote from Jac Fitzenz of The Saratoga Institute in "HR in the 21st Century: Challenges and Opportunities," p. 256.
66. Stambaugh, B. "Hard Systems, Soft Systems: New Challenges for Twenty-First Century HR Systems, Stakeholders, and Vendors," pp. 107–129.
67. Ibid., pp. 109–120.
68. Canton, J. *Technofutures: How Leading-Edge Technology Will Transform Business in the 21st Century,* p. 122.

Name Index

Subject Index